DATE DUE

TWENTIETH CENTURY VIEWS

The aim of this series is to present the best in
contemporary critical opinion on major authors,
providing a twentieth century perspective on
their changing status in an era of profound
revaluation.

Maynard Mack, Series Editor,
Yale University

FORSTER

A COLLECTION OF CRITICAL ESSAYS

Edited by
Malcolm Bradbury

Prentice-Hall, Inc. *Englewood Cliffs, N.J.*

A SPECTRUM BOOK

Current printing (last number):
10   9   8   7   6   5   4   3   2   1

To Arthur Smith

Contents

Introduction

by Malcolm Bradbury

I

The essays in this volume range from fairly early commentaries on Forster's work, written in the 1920's when Forster had a considerable cult reputation in England but was little known in the United States, to recent and on the whole more analytical essays, written in the confidence that Forster is a major English author of the twentieth century, a writer of great technical and intellectual significance whose work is sufficiently complicated and dense to deserve close study and analysis. Like the works of most English authors of the early twentieth century that are now accepted classics, Forster's novels came fairly slowly to critical attention and have received extensive criticism only since the war. This is largely true of Joyce, Lawrence, and Conrad, as well as Forster; yet Forster is, among these, something of a special case. The first three were often regarded as too difficult for comprehension, charged with being obscure and "technical"; Forster was apt to be regarded as old-fashioned, uncomplicated, much less modern and "advanced" than, for example, Virginia Woolf—with whom, because of their common concern with personal relationships, with the philosophy of *Principia Ethica,* and with the aesthetic and intellectual concerns of the Cambridge/Bloomsbury tradition, he has been frequently linked in critical discussion.[1]

Partly for these reasons, then, Forster tended until recently to be regarded by critics as an interesting novelist who was almost but not quite major, a writer of evident and distinctive merits whose work lacked that largeness of intention or of invention that would make him one of the great discoverers in modern fiction. His manner, tone, and literary procedure were often described as old-fashioned, directly inherited from the nineteenth century; his particular kind of mystical atheism invited us to place him intellectually with Butler, Meredith, "Mark Rutherford," Edward Carpenter—as a late Victorian somehow perpetuated into the tradtion of the twentieth century novel. Lionel Trilling has spoken of

[1] See, for instance, D.J. Enright's useful essay on Forster and Mrs. Woolf, "To the Lighthouse or to India?" in his *The Apothecary's Shop: Essays on Literature* (London: Secker and Warburg, 1957).

him as "sometimes irritating in his refusal to be great" [2]—as making a kind of ironic humility into his saving virtue. If, then, Forster's reputation was somewhat slow to emerge, it was not—as in the case of some of his contemporaries—that he was found too difficult for comprehension, but too easy; and thus even when the major writers, the great discoverers in twentieth century fiction were acclaimed, Forster was held to be not quite one of them. Walter Allen's judgment in his book *The English Novel* (1954) can be taken as a reasonably typical view:

> Yet though there are moments when one sees affinities between him and Mrs. Woolf in some respects, and Lawrence in others, he cannot be regarded as a pioneer, as a John the Baptist going before them. Technically he is a sport, a throwback; as far as his novels are concerned, neither James nor the French naturalists might have written; he is there, a man telling his story in his own voice, in the older English tradition which, beginning with Fielding, ends, we might normally assume, with Meredith.

Recent criticism of Forster has tended to take a different approach; in a variety of ways it has demonstrated that Forster's intellectual and technical character is a good deal more complex and more modern than the earlier view allows. What has been shown to us clearly over recent years is—among other things—the complexity and resource of Forster's fictional method, particularly in *Howards End* and *A Passage to India,* his last two novels. Forster himself has spoken of a wide range of literary indebtedness: "Samuel Butler influenced me a great deal. . . . He, Jane Austen, and Marcel Proust are the three authors who have helped me most over my writing, and he did more than the other two to help me look at life the way I do." [3] Some of these debts and connections have been well-explored in recent years; Leavis has made some useful connections with Jane Austen, Lee Elbert Holt (though much too schematically) with Butler.[4] Less has been made of the reference to Proust in a direct way, but perhaps the most important feature of this self-confessed debt is the part it has played in Forster's literary aesthetic, particularly as he expresses it in his *Aspects of the Novel* (1927). The importance of this book as a statement in modern aesthetics has been only fairly recently recognised;[5] and the application of the aesthetic principles it states or assumes to Forster's own fiction has shown how much more modern than we have cared to assume Forster's methods and literary intuitions actually are. Recently, special attention has been paid by critics to Forster's

[2] Lionel Trilling, *E.M. Forster* (New York: New Directions, 1943). The passage from which this comment is taken is contained in the excerpt from this book reprinted in this volume.

[3] Forster, "The Legacy of Samuel Butler," *The Listener,* June 12, 1952, 955.

[4] Lee Elbert Holt, "E.M. Forster and Samuel Butler," *PMLA,* LXI, September 1946, 804-19.

[5] Notably by E.K. Brown in his *Rhythm in the Novel* (Toronto: University of Toronto Press, 1950). An excerpt from the book appears in this volume.

use of "rhythm" and "symbol" (since these happen to be properties much in demand for the prosecution of modern criticism).[6] The technical use of these suggests a particular mode or aesthetic, and we have become much more aware that Forster writes in this mode. Frank Kermode's important short essay, reprinted in this volume, stresses the "symbolist" nature of Forster's aesthetic, and the point has been taken further in Barbara Hardy's study of the novel, *The Appropriate Form* (1964); here she shows how what Frank Kermode calls the search for a significant order leads Forster into creating characters who represent, symbolically, an aesthetic or ordering approach toward life, characters like Mrs. Wilcox and Mrs. Moore.[7] This view of Forster is now the familiar one in modern criticism, and to recognise that, aesthetically, there is a substantial kinship between the preoccupations of (say) Joyce and Virginia Woolf and Forster is, I think, to give a rather fairer stress to his quality as a novelist. On the other hand, the balance of criticism has now turned so far in favour of regarding Forster as a modern symbolist that we are sometimes in danger of forgetting the important fact about him that many earlier critics never got beyond—that he is a comic social novelist, a writer of comedy of manners, a man who manifests and is attentive to the social and historical context out of which he derives. This is not the whole Forster, but it is a Forster who never ceases to be present in all the novels, short stories, travel books, and essays.

There is another view of Forster—associated with the opinion that his fictional manner is Victorian—which has also tended to fade. This is the view that he is *intellectually* a Victorian, that he is visibly the child of English middle-class liberalism, a liberalism that has an evident historical location in the heyday of the advanced, but wealthy, intellectual bourgeoisie. To locate a writer like this is often an effective means of limiting him, a means of suggesting that his work has not transcended its determining situation, that it is not universal. Forster has been vulnerable to such criticism, often made from a Christian (frequently a Catholic) point of view, or from a Marxist one.[8] It has been said of Forster that he cannot reach beyond circumstances which he himself knows to be confining, and that the consequence of this is a vague aspiration toward religious feeling, or toward a new society, which never takes the form of an effective critique of his own situation. He may recognise and define the liberal dilemma, but he is also trapped within it, unable to follow out its logic and so to solve it. Certainly Forster does derive much from the Victorian intellectual tradition, particularly from such reforming phases of it as the Clapham Sect, with which his own family was linked. And this means that he

[6] See E.K. Brown, *op. cit.*, and the more extended attempt in James McConkey, *The Novels of E.M. Forster* (Ithaca, N.Y.: Cornell University Press, 1957).

[7] Barbara Hardy, *The Appropriate Form: An Essay on the Novel* (London: Athlone Press, 1964), pp. 73-82.

[8] Several such approaches are discussed in detail later in this essay.

derives substantially from the Romantic debate which continued through the nineteenth century and into the twentieth. Forster himself has made such debts quite plain; and he clearly does espouse many of the attitudes of nineteenth century romantic and political liberalism.[9] But he also confronts an essentially modern disquiet; the generous and positive optimism about the future that one finds in the nineteenth century is already uneasy in Forster before the First World War, which challenged that optimism so very radically. Forster, in *Howards End,* is one of the first novelists who portrayed in depth the struggle of the modern intelligentsia to define its alliances, who depicted both its disquiet about its independence and the principles that determine that independence. The view of Forster as the Edwardian liberal humanist is incomplete, not only because (as Lionel Trilling points out in his essay here reprinted) he has shown himself at odds with the liberal mind, while confessing to liberal atheism itself, not only because his scepticism and irony have turned against the pieties so often associated with him, but because he has pursued with a devastating moral rigour the twentieth century disquiet of the liberal humanist about himself and his position. His disinterested approach, his ironic detachment, is founded on a sense of the anarchy behind intellectual order. Like many important writers of the twentieth century (there is an interesting comparison to be made here with, say, Thomas Mann), he has recognised and met the challenge to humanist optimism, criticising Benthamite organization from the point of view of the need for diverse individualism, and criticising the indulgences of individualism with a deep commitment to the demands of the "unseen." Indeed, it is surely because (as I argue here in my essay on *Howards End)* he is not a novelist of solutions, because his fiction proposes incompleteness, that he seems to us modern. When we call him a liberal humanist, then, we must be aware of his impulse to mysticism, on the one hand, and his sense of the difficulties of liberalism and openness of view on the other. He is prepared to assert a reconciling, enlarging, invisible quality in the "unseen," and thus to challenge his classical rationalism; at the same time, his visions, though they may suggest an order or unity in the universe, are defined in terms of the anarchy that they must comprehend, and therefore they are never fully redemptive; there is always something they may not account for. In *A Passage to India,* for instance, the novel moves toward but never achieves a visionary resolution.[10]

[9] Thus in *Two Cheers for Democracy* (New York: Harcourt, Brace, and World, Inc., 1951), Forster comments: "I belong to the fag-end of Victorian liberalism, and can look back to an age whose challenges were moderate in their tone, and when the cloud on the horizon was no bigger than a man's hand." Forster's intellectual connections here are admirably explored in Trilling's study, and, in greater detail, by Frederick C. Crews, *E.M. Forster: The Perils of Humanism* (Princeton, N.J.: Princeton University Press, 1962). See also the article by H.A. Smith in this volume.

[10] Such would be my reading of it; but other critics would disagree. See McConkey's discussion of the novel (*The Novels of E.M. Forster,* pp. 132-60) for a supporting judgment.

Forster, I am suggesting, is much closer to Bloomsbury than to nineteenth century liberal optimism; but we cannot quite take him as fully representative of that group either. Bloomsbury—the group of writers, including Virginia Woolf, Lytton Strachey, Roger Fry, and others, who were closely related socially and who shared similar social, intellectual, and literary interests—was indeed a continuation of the close, family-linked, upper-middle-class intelligentsia of the late Victorian period, but its attitudes were radically formed by two things: a strong sense of participating in the revolution in philosophy that took place at Cambridge at the turn of the century, and in the revolution in aesthetics that took place among the post-impressionists in Paris and strongly affected English aesthetic thinking after about 1910. The philosophy led to a strong emphasis on the centrality and significance of personal relationships; the aesthetics, as expressed by Roger Fry, Clive Bell, and Virginia Woolf, has a strong emphasis on personal vision, on disentangling from the welter of multiple impressions the momentary organising core. Forster, undoubtedly, is of this ethos; his sense of culture and cultivation, his attachment to personal relationships, his concern with the developed heart, connect him in different ways with their interests, as does his sense of membership in an evangelising intelligentsia.[11] Forster's attachment to Bloomsbury was a critical one, however, and it is easily possible to overstress the community of opinion of the group. The important point here is that made in F.R. Leavis's essay (reprinted in this volume) which draws attention to Forster's Bloomsbury connection—"the weaknesses of Mr. Forster's work and of Bloomsbury are placed as such by standards implicit in what is best in that work." This is apt and enlightening, and once again it draws attention to Forster's capacity for self-scrutiny, for his power to be ironic and questioning in the face of a culture on which he draws and to which he is attached. That Forster is, in a positive way, a "representative" of a culture, or of several cultures, that he is a novelist much fed by his place and circumstances, is evident enough; what recent criticism has shown is the complexity of his position.

There still remains, however, the question of what stature Forster's critics can claim for him, the question, in fact, of how much another doubt about his work can be dissipated. For perhaps the most pressing and urgent critical statement that has been made about Forster is the charge, presented in a number of the essays here printed, that Forster's complexity and ambiguity lead him into difficulties of tone, into archness, into a damaging variety of intentions. On the whole, the argument about Forster's greatness has become centred more and more on the last two books, *Howards End* and *A Passage to India*, novels whose aims and scope are quite evidently greater than those of the first three novels and

---

[11] See J.K. Johnstone, *The Bloomsbury Group: A Study of E.M. Forster, Lytton Strachey, Virginia Woolf, and Their Circle* (London: Secker and Warburg, 1954), which provides much valuable material in this connection.

the short stories. The early books, though social comedies, lack the social dimension of the two last novels; they are also much more overtly comic, in the sense that the author's whimsy and his interest in the conduct of particular persons in particular situations of manners are more directly engaged. In all his novels, but particularly in the two last, one is aware of an urgent attempt to achieve some kind of reconciling and poetic vision, to approach through emotion, through the developed heart, those sensations of body and spirit that not only create a full life in the living but give a meaning to life, afford a visionary understanding of it. Forster's distinctive mixture of social comedy and "poetic" writing—his concern on the one hand with domestic comedy and quirks of character, and on the other with the unseen and the over-arching—make him a difficult writer to read and to define. The modern emphasis on Forster as a symbolist has, as noted earlier, caused critics to overlook some of his distinctive features. The emphasis upon technical experimentalism and symbolist procedure has tended to obscure both the presence and the value of an interesting balancing of traditional and modern elements within his work. By asking aesthetic and technical questions, critics have been able to define him as a deeply modern writer; but this means that some of his particular and distinctive excellencies are not always recognised in their quality and centrality—I mean, for instance, the way he has developed the English tradition of the socio-moral novel into a world of experience not usually found within its capacities; his positive sense of culture, and his awareness of its significance for the individual, and for individualism; his concern with the social dimension on a national or a world scale; and his sense of scrupulous integrity which drives him beyond any simple or conventional account of an event or experience toward scepticism and irony. Because these qualities do involve him in paradoxes and ambiguities, it is not surprising that much of the early criticism of Forster was concerned with trying to reconcile two apparently disparate elements —the novelist of society and manners, and the mystic. It is around this issue that much of the uncertainty about Forster's reputation and literary character has turned.

II

Thus to most of his early critics, Forster's work presented problems and difficulties. These were less (as with Joyce or even Lawrence) problems of technical complexity than problems deriving from an "oddity" in his vision and in his methods of presenting it. When Virginia Woolf, in the 1940's, published an essay on Forster, she spoke in it of "something baffling and evasive in the nature of his gifts"—finding him divided in his vision and inclined to be over-anxious in presenting it. Other critics of the 1920's and 1930's who wrote on his work—Katherine Mansfield, Edward Shanks, I.A. Richards, Peter Burra, Dorothy Hoare, Rose Macaulay, and F.R Leavis in England; E.K. Brown, Austin Warren and Morton D. Zabel in America—touch on the same point. Many of them found his work not only ambiguous and tentative, but also split in its intentions or in its effect.

By the outbreak of the First World War, Forster had published four of his novels and begun the fifth, which appeared, after further extensive work, in 1924. It was not, however, until 1927 (when, in fact, Forster had stopped publishing fiction) that the first important critical article appeared. This was I.A. Richards' "A Passage to Forster: Reflections on a Novelist" (reprinted in this volume), which appeared in an American journal, *The Forum*, and was designed to introduce to American readers an author with something of a cult reputation in England. Richards comments immediately on Forster's "oddness," which derives, he says, from an unusual outlook on life. In Richards' view, Forster's fiction has a mystical concern with survival or continuity—with the continuance of life from parent to child, with the quality of life in the sense of blood or race—and also a strong sociological emphasis, a concern with the separation within the society of the men of vision from the men of action; the split produces an "elusive weakness." Though most modern readers would probably find the two themes quite closely related, Richards did suggest something other critics were later to take up—that two modes and intentions, one concerned with the mystical, the other with manners, exist in his work, somewhat at odds with each other. In 1934 Forster was strongly attacked by Montgomery Belgion in T.S. Eliot's review, *The Criterion*, in a piece called "The Diabolism of E.M. Forster" (*The Criterion*, October 1934); he, like Richards, also speaks of the "mystery" of Forster's work—of his use of characters and events "peculiarly symbolical," yet hard to attach to any meaning. "Response" to these symbolic moments (the moments which, as Rickie says in *The Longest Journey*, stand "for some eternal principle") redeems characters for the author; the characters who do not respond are condemned; and thus a theory of predestination, a system of the saved and the damned, appears to operate, uncharitably, diabolically. In the same year, almost the opposite view was expressed in an article by Peter Burra, "The Novels of E.M. Forster," published in *The Nineteenth Century and After;* Forster himself approved the article and it was used as the introduction to the Everyman edition of A *Passage to India,* to which Forster contributed notes. Burra's essay, reprinted in this volume, argues that Forster has an aspiration to abstractness but at the same time possesses a serious concern with the political and economic questions of the outer world. The essay is particularly notable for its argument that Forster pays close attention to rhythm and pattern, to the creation of something "aesthetically compact," and that he exploits *leit-motif* (e.g., the wasp in *A Passage to India*); that he creates by using "elemental" characters (like Gino, Mrs. Wilcox, Mrs. Moore) who are "utterly percipient of the reality behind appearances"; and that the tendency of the books is toward the *reconciliation* of characters. By stressing the constructional method and applying *Aspects of the Novel* to Forster's own work, Burra contributes much value to Forster criticism.

In 1938, in a useful and sharp chapter in *Some Studies in the Modern Novel,* Dorothy M. Hoare argued, like Burra, that though Forster's novels contain dissonant elements—she calls them the "romantic" and the "ironic"—this produces a distinctive and original attitude. She stresses, too, the progression of Forster's work; Forster's early work shows a debt to Meredith, though his happy paganism may remind us more of D.H. Lawrence. The effect is "an extremely subtle and constant juxtaposition of opposing values," of a mood of detachment alternating with a sense of the religious which is unattached to any religion. In the earlier novels there is a clear virtue made out of a sense of harmony or rightness, a contact with the life of earth; but this is modified in the later books. The value of the free response is justified radiantly at the end of *A Room with a View,* soberly at the end of *The Longest Journey,* left wavering at the end of *Where Angels Fear to Tread;* by *Howards End* and particularly by *A Passage to India* the belief in pagan freedom has been modified, that in personal relationships sublimated, and a more complicated and tentative form of communication or vision is pursued.

Also in 1938 there appeared the first book-length study of Forster. This was Rose Macaulay's *The Writings of E.M. Forster,* containing some extremely valuable biographical information. Miss Macaulay sees Forster as a writer who, though a liberal, asserts a Vision of Reality, a way of life, with the urgency of a religion: "His humanist, liberal, classical mind welcomes religion as spirit but not as doctrine. . . ." She stresses the importance of his theme of human relationships, treating sex not with insistence, but "now casually, now with a gingerly aloofness, now with a welcome in which its peculiar incidence appears submerged or sublimated by reverence for it as a token coin of further and more important immensities." She suggests, in fact, a divided Forster, split by the difficulties of Edwardian liberalism—highly committed to personal relationships, yet revealing a sense of a transcendental realm in which human relations are finally unimportant. Her book provoked another important critical essay, F.R. Leavis's "E.M. Forster," originally a *Scrutiny* review of Miss Macaulay's study (it is reprinted in this volume). Leavis, too, picks up the charge of vagueness and weakness in Forster, and links these aspects with his poetic pretensions and his "spinsterish inadequacy" in confronting the life he values. Like Miss Macaulay, though with a rather different emphasis, he sees Forster's strength as lying in socio-moral comedy, and suggests its character—its sense of false living, its controlled ironic detachment, reminiscent of Jane Austen's. The article is important in that for the first time it offers close reading of the novels and makes distinctions among them. Leavis sees Forster's weaknesses as stemming not so much from twentieth century liberalism as from a lack of forceful intelligence that Leavis identified with Bloomsbury; Forster's strength is that he manifests the virtues of the liberal tradition against the weaknesses of Bloomsbury, and in this sense *A Passage to India* stands out as "a classic of the liberal spirit."

It is interesting to contrast with Leavis's view one from the heart of Bloomsbury itself; in Virginia Woolf's 1942 collection of essays, *The Death of the Moth and Other Essays,* in "The Novels of E.M. Forster," after praising Forster for his highly sensitive and creative intelligence she criticises him for failing to reconcile poetry and realism. The result is that in the moments of transcendence, when he shifts from realism to symbolism, "the object which has been so uncompromisingly solid becomes, or should become, luminously transparent," and then the conjunction of two different levels of reality casts doubt upon both of them. Mrs. Woolf's complaint seems essentially that one stratum of the novels is composed in a lower mode, a mode too attentive to ordinary reality, to the world of the day-to-day and the mean; it lacks in fact the luminosity which she herself pursued throughout her novels, and this discredits the transcendental moments which she valued most. She puts, in fact, the contrary point to Leavis's; and this in itself suggests the ambiguity it was possible to feel—and is still possible to feel—about Forster's work.

III

In America, where Forster's general reputation over this period was less high, the case for his work was argued, notably by E.K. Brown, Austin Warren, and Morton D. Zabel. Brown published extensively on Forster, beginning in 1934 ("E.M. Forster and the Contemplative Novel," *University of Toronto Quarterly,* April 1934), presenting first the case for Forster as a novelist of ideas, and then as a subtle user of "rhythm in the novel" (see his "The Revival of E.M. Forster," *Yale Review,* June 1944, which also provides a useful summary account of Forster's reputation in the United States; and his *Rhythm in the Novel* (1950), a chapter from which is included in this collection). Brown's argument that rhythm is a fundamental element of Forster's technical method—an argument begun by Burra—is important not only because it is in itself illuminating, but also because it is pursued with care and subtlety. The thesis has been developed by other critics, notably Reuben A. Brower and Richard R. Werry, but I have taken Brown as an example, because his approach is of historical significance in Forster criticism, and because it is part of an important *general* insight about the criticism of fiction. (Inevitably, most of the critics who have taken this approach to Forster have concentrated on *A Passage to India;* and a danger of this—in addition to that of being too schematic—is that it causes us to be disappointed by Forster's earlier fiction, which uses other methods of composition.)

In 1937, in *The American Review*, Austin Warren argued that Forster, though interested in the "inner life," rejects some of the literary implications of that interest, preferring to work in the social rather than the inward, psychological novel. He does so because the novel must, like life, have equilibrium, balancing the claims of existence, and essence, personalities and ideas. Thus technically, and humanly too, Forster is in search of the mean, of a full culture, a reconciliation of the inner and outer worlds. (Part of Warren's essay is reprinted here.)

In 1943, what is probably the most influential book-length study of Forster appeared—Lionel Trilling's *E.M. Forster*. Trilling, like Leavis, attends to the culture Forster manifests and explores; and his central point is that Forster, while a liberal, is in many ways at odds with the liberal mind, given to questioning its pieties with a rare moral realism. His literary manner is comic, but the comedy is the agent of a complex moral intention. Trilling's final point is that Forster asserts the moral and sceptical intelligence of art against panic and emptiness, and his evident partiality for Forster's interpretation of the cultural dilemma, for his mode of priorities, enables him to defend the cogency of Forster's mind in a way that no other critic has succeeded in doing. (Part of Trilling's argument is included in this volume.) This book played a decisive part in establishing Forster's reputation, and in the period after the Second World War his place as one of the important English writers of the twentieth century was generally granted.

IV

The sense that Forster proceeds simultaneously in two areas of the novel not normally brought together—the area of social observation and comedy, and the area of symbolic romance—has, I have suggested, been common enough among critics of Forster; and in most post-war criticism one or the other side of Forster has been stressed. Though many definitions of the novel tend to regard its primary means of imitation as that of social analysis, it can also be argued that a primary area of discovery in fiction is that of the inner life, which relates to mythic and symbolic fiction—the kind of fiction we might want to call the "romance." In post-war criticism of Forster, his main effort has been recognised, by different critics, as lying in both of these areas. Much English criticism has emphasized Forster's qualities as a *social* novelist, whereas American criticism has tended to emphasize his qualities as a *romance* novelist. This is perhaps revelatory of the fictional traditions, and the critical premises, of each country. In general, therefore, the exploration of Forster's mysticism, of its eclectic and even Whitmanesque scope, has been conducted in the United States, and Forster's reputation here has grown perhaps proportionately with the realisation that he has strong analogies with the interests and techniques of the American novel. Of the seven book-length studies to appear on Forster since the war, three have been by Americans; so, too, have many of the more important critical articles.

The first book-length study to appear in this period was James McConkey's useful and intelligent *The Novels of E.M. Forster* (1957), which applies to Forster's work the critical terminology—People; Fantasy and Prophecy; Rhythm—that Forster himself elaborates in his *Aspects of the Novel*. McConkey argues that the Fosterian hero is incomplete, "that incompleteness being the result of a dissociation between the character and his universe, between the individual in a seemingly chaotic, temporal world and the unifying, eternal reality." But Forster's voice is not that of a man who has pierced the heavens; he is not a mystic, and his intimations are made by symbols. Indeed, McConkey argues, we sense universality in Forster's writings "only when he implies man's inability to perceive his oneness with the universe." H.J. Oliver's slimmer, slighter *The Art of E.M. Forster,* published in 1960, affords a useful basic guide to the novels and the other writings, and it has a critical emphasis, distinguishing the "relatively immature" first three novels from the last two—on which Oliver bases his claim that Forster's work is "the most interesting product of the cultured mind in modern literature." In 1962 three books on Forster appeared, consolidating much of the earlier work and suggesting the new critical importance of the author. One, K.W. Gransden's *E.M. Forster,* is in a series of survey volumes and provides a balanced introduction to the author. The two other books represent a reversal of roles in the critical debate about Forster. The English study, J.B. Beer's *The Achievement of E.M. Forster,* is concerned with stressing Forster's romantic affiliations; Beer argues that "Forster is ultimately a romantic writer and that his work reflects some of the tensions and conflicts peculiar to romanticism." He picks out the way Forster employs the imagination to confirm the validity of passion, and the way he links the pursuit of moral seriousness with the good state of mind. Forster has a romantic existential commitment to the visionary moment, when truth comes like a blow—"in the moment of exaltation, reality is revealed," the reality by which other states of existence are to be judged as they sink into various forms of unreality. The American study, Frederick C. Crews' *E.M. Forster: The Perils of Humanism,* presents the other emphasis; though Forster's humanism has at its core a pessimistic awareness of the disparity between human meaning and supernatural truth, "a sense not only of the futility of other-worldiness, but of the instability of earthly value," his plots are habitually dialectical and seek a mean or balance. Crews analyzes valuably Forster's intellectual character and its essentially rationalist constituents; the world of Love and the Unseen are for him a dominating means of judging experience, and he does draw on a world of visionary insight conveyed by symbol and mythological reference; but his positions are modified, by scepticism, irony, and comedy. (Part of Crews' argument is reprinted here.)

By stressing Forster's use of symbolism, and his use of the rhythmic "method" which Forster himself elaborates, by musical analogy, in *Aspects of the Novel* (the function of rhythm being "not to be there all the time like a pattern, but by its lovely waxing and waning to fill us with surprise and freshness and hope"), modern criticism has brought us a greater awareness of the complexity both of Forster's structure and of his intellectual position. This in turn raises the question of the function of art itself in Forster's world-view. His liberal commitment to art as a humane activity, as a primary function of the human spirit, as a standard of the measurement of a society, has been noted by many critics; only lately, however, has its importance in Forster's general aesthetic been stressed in any detail. In Alan Wilde's book *Art and Order: A Study of E.M. Forster* (1964), the author argues that Forster finds in the harmony of art itself the best that man has done and may do in the face of the increasing disintegration of the world. His argument is close to that of Frank Kermode, who, in a short and concentrated essay reprinted here, presents Forster as a writer who declares for "the autonomy of the work of art," undertaking to discover and present an idea of order in his work, an essential line of significance. Hence recent general criticism on Forster has tended to see in him an inheritor of the experiences and the assumptions of romanticism, a seeker for vision and for a revelatory order discoverable through what he calls the "combustion" of the creative process; yet also to see him as one who modifies those assumptions (as most of his contemporaries did), and who does this very much in the spirit of the neo-symbolist aesthetics that characterise the modern movement in art.

Such views help us to recognise the essentially unified nature of Forster's varied modes. The present collection is designed to show the development of this argument through Forster criticism—and thus, to an extent, to reveal the changing emphases and assumptions of modern literary criticism itself. At the same time, of course, there have been numerous particular essays on single novels—the larger number of these being on *Howards End* and *A Passage to India,* which have more and more been taken by critics as Forster's two best books. Much of this textual analysis has taken place in the United States, and at times it has shared too much in the current mechanical fashion of symbol-hunting. Often, too, it has offered a simple exploration of the interconnection of elements within the single work, paying little attention to the life the work refers to, the life invigorated and interpreted in it. I have included a few of the best of the analyses of single novels, notably John Harvey's fine essay on *The Longest Journey.*[12]

[12] See the Selected Bibliography for fuller details of articles referred to in this section. Among the most important of these are Gertrude M. White, *"A Passage to India:* Analysis and Revaluation," in *PMLA,* LXVIII, September 1953, which presents that novel as a Hegelian dialectic and sees it as reaching an optimistic, reconciling conclusion; and Glen O. Allen, "Structure, Symbol, and Theme in E.M. Forster's *A Passage to India,"*

Also important to note is that there are many critics who have still found it difficult to reconcile the two main elements of Forster's work—that concerned with the standard of the unseen, with spontaneous passion and the heart's affection, and that concerned with the golden mean, with connecting the prose and the passion, with rational and moral liberal dilemmas. Such critiques have, as I have said, often come from Catholic or Marxist viewpoints, and I have chosen one of the best of them, D.S. Savage's Marxist analysis of Forster, as representative.[13] It is, I think, hard to accept the view that liberalism of Forster's kind is necessarily and inherently a barrier to the production of major literature, and indeed if we are to say that any writer whose sense of disorder and anarchy in the world prevents him from offering a total and unequivocal interpretation of experience has failed in some sense, then we must debar from excellence almost all the modern writers we call great. Yet we should observe that many of the critics of Forster have had a sense of disquiet about his work. Trilling's statement that Forster is "irritating in his refusal to be great" suggests the point of ambiguity, the way in which he is apt to be humble or ambiguous when we expect him to be confident and sure. The point is, I think, that though Forster must be recognised as a major novelist, we must accept that his difficulties are often due to ambiguities within himself. Modern criticism has now given him the kind of attention he deserves, and has shown us his complexity and difficulty. Nobody has yet resolved even the divergent accounts available of the meaning of *A Passage to India*. Is it—the case may be simply put—a novel which,

---

PMLA, LXX, December 1955, which presents the counter-argument. On *Howards End*, three essays are particularly worthy of note: the pieces by Frederick P.W. McDowall, Cyrus Hoy, and Thomas Churchill referred to in the article on *Howards End* in this volume.

[13] Savage's argument is usefully countered in another Marxist critique, Arnold Kettle's analysis of *A Passage to India* in his *An Introduction to the English Novel*, Volume Two (London: Hutchinson University Library, 1953). Three well-argued Catholic critiques come to conclusions similar to those of Savage. Alexander Boyle, in "The Novels of E.M. Forster," *The Irish Monthly*, LXXVIII, September 1950, argues that Forster's problem is scepticism; intelligent and exploratory as he is, he is not finally convincing, because an artist needs intellectual certainty. Ernest Beaumont, in "Mr. E.M. Forster's Strange Mystics," *The Dublin Review*, 453, Third Quarter, 1951, is a closer analysis of the way Forster exploits a pervasive extra-human quality in some of his characters, so that they have characteristics usually associated with sainthood. The argument is sharply put, and Beaumont concludes by suggesting that the mixture we have in Forster of a kind of classical pantheism with intimations of religious transcendence is both inconsistent and disconcerting. Dennis Hickley, in "Ou-Boum and Verbum," *The Downside Review*, LXXII, Spring 1954, argues that Forster seems to know only a Christianity of comfort, and the despair of his characters, which is presented as a loss of faith, is in fact the first religious experience. In his general study of liberalism in the modern novel, *The Free Spirit* (London: Oxford University Press, 1963), C.B. Cox argues that Forster's liberalism is in some ways evasive: he tends to withdraw into an idealised past, to overstate beyond the limits of intellectual integrity the claims of individuals, and thus to approve withdrawal into dangerously secure and limited areas of human experience, to pursue escape.

after attempting to reconcile the differences between races, religions, social creeds, nature and man, asserts failure?—or is it a novel which, reaching beyond accepted faiths and accepted interpretations of the mysterious, the unseen, asserts a positive vision of unity? Is Forster in his last two—best two—books a spiritual and social optimist; or are his conclusions those of pessimism and defeat? It is, perhaps, because of the difficulty of estimating these last two books that Forster's reputation is less fully achieved, even now, than those of some of the early twentieth century novelists. Yet his work is widely taught, in schools and universities in many countries; he has reached classic status; the body of criticism on him grows. If there remains something ambiguous about his work, there is no doubt of its increasingly wide impact. *Howards End* (as I argue in my essay later in this volume) is a remarkable and complex work; and *A Passage to India* is surely a major novel by any measure.

A Passage to Forster:

Reflections on a Novelist

by I.A. Richards

Turning over the leaves of a Public Library copy of *Where Angels Fear to Tread* I find, neatly scribbled on the margin of the seventeenth page, *"What is it all about?"* This seems an early page for such a query. Later on it might appear less surprising; but in any case Mr. E.M. Forster is not a writer whom we should naturally suspect of obscurity. In his ultimate intention, his philosophical goal, yes, perhaps; but not in his preliminaries, his superficial lay-out, the ordinary page by page texture of his writing. His prose seems, on the contrary, the clearest and simplest possible. And yet, like a mote in the eye, this scribbler's query has made me uneasily conscious of things that we ordinarily take for granted. There *is* something odd about Mr. Forster's methods as a novelist, and this oddness, if we can track it down, may help us to seize those other peculiarities which make him on the whole the most puzzling figure in contemporary English letters.

The oddness has to do with the special system of assumptions he tacitly adopts from the very first page in each of his books. Every writer, perhaps, starts with assumptions which he leaves the reader to discover. They make up his intellectual individuality and differentiate his angle of vision from that of the next man. The moment in our perusal when we first pick up these assumptions and feel our minds fit in, or fail to fit in, with his is the moment when we begin to judge him as an author, to decide whether we like his book or not. But in Mr. Forster's case the assumptions are less obviously aside from the conventional centre than in most cases, and for this reason they are the harder to pin down in words. Yet they influence his handling of every scene. Where another writer possessed of an unusual outlook on life would be careful to introduce it, gradually preparing the way by views from more ordinary standpoints, Mr. Forster does nothing of the kind. This very sentence tacitly assumes that the personal point of view is already occupied by the reader, who is

"A Passage to Forster: Reflections on a Novelist." From *The Forum*, LXXVIII, No. 6 (December 1927), 914-20. Reprinted by permission of the editors of *Current History* and the author.

left to orient himself as he can. This may lead to lamentable misunder-
standings. For example, once we have picked up the author's position we
see that the characters in his early books, Mrs. Herriton, Harriet, Gino,
Mr. Eager, Old Mr. Emerson, are less to be regarded as social studies than
as embodiments of moral forces. Hence the ease with which Miss Abbott,
for example, turns momentarily into a goddess. *Where Angels Fear to
Tread* is indeed far nearer in spirit to a mystery play than to a comedy of
manners. This in spite of the astonishingly penetrating flashes of observation by which these figures are sometimes depicted. But to understand
why, with all his equipment as an observer, Mr. Forster sometimes so
wantonly disregards vivisimilitude we have to find his viewpoint and
take up toward them the attitude of their creator. For some readers the
task is easy. A mute conspiracy becomes at once established. This is why,
although there is no Forster Society, and although no little handbooks
have yet been written expounding a Forster philosophy, something very
like a cult early grew up around his books. When with *A Passage to
India* he burst into public notice, many of his admirers undoubtedly felt
an obscure grievance. Unconsciously they had allowed their admiration to
take on a snobbish tinge. But they may have felt, also, and rightly, that
a great number of his new admirers were scarcely aware of their author's
presuppositions as these show themselves in his earlier books, and that if
they had understood them better they might have felt less in sympathy.

For the underlying bias in Mr. Forster's work is not one which a
reader as sincere as Mr. Forster would wish his readers to be will find easy
to accept or to adopt. Mr. Forster never formulates his criticism of life
in one of those principles which we can adhere to or discuss. He leaves
it in the painful, concrete realm of practice, presenting it always and only
in terms of actuality and never in the abstract. In other words, he has no
doctrine but only an attitude, differing in this from such exponents of
current tendencies as Mr. Shaw or Mr. Wells. He resembles an Ibsen
rather than a Ruskin—to name two authors with whose viewpoint Mr.
Forster's has some analogies.

It is a commonplace that English readers like pinpricks, but they like
them in the form of direct accusations or in the tickling form of satire.
They take to Mr. Shaw or to Samuel Butler as to an agreeable stimulant.
They are much less ready to listen to criticism when it comes from the
more wounding hands of an artist. For this reason Mr. Forster's novels
are unlikely ever to become a vogue. And even the small cult which I
have mentioned may be noticed perhaps to have a very large proportion
of deserters, and to contain not a few adherents whose motives are open
to suspicion. For Mr. Forster is a peculiarly uncomfortable author for
[those] who are not content merely to enjoy the surface graces of his writing and the delicacies of his wit, but make themselves sufficiently familiar
with his temper to see life to some degree with his eyes. His real audience
is youth, caught at that stage when rebellion against the comfortable con-

ventions is easy because the cost of abandoning them has not been fully counted. So as time passes Mr. Forster's admirers tend to forget him or to see him in quite another guise from that in which he first appeared to them. We become less enthusiastic for the light of truth as we realize how high a maintenance rate even a modest installation entails. The divine beam comes to seem merely hurtful to the eyes.

These may seem strange terms in which to discuss so suave and polished a writer. It is Mr. Forster's peculiarity that he offers his discomforting vision with so urbane a manner. He is no "holy howl-storm upon the mountains." He has no thunders, no hoots, no grimaces, nor any of the airs of the denunciating prophet, yet at the heart of his work there is less satisfaction with human existence as he sees it than in the work of any other living writer I can call to mind. The earliest of his books, *The Longest Journey,* is perhaps an exception to what has just been remarked about his manner. It has the rawness and crudeness and violence we should expect in the work of a very young writer. Those who have not realized the intensity of the dissatisfaction behind Mr. Forster's work would do well to read it. There is much there, of course, which time has mellowed. But the essential standards, the primary demands from life, which still make unacceptable to him so much that ordinary people find sufficient, have not altered.

Mr. Forster's peculiar quality as a novelist is his fiercely critical sense of values. What was, in the days of *Longest Journey,* a revolt, has changed to a saddened and almost weary pessimism. He has, in his later writings, in *Pharos and Pharillon* and in *A Passage to India,* consoled himself to some degree by a cultivation of the less militant and more humorous forms of irony. He has stepped back to the position of the observer from which in his *Where Angels Fear to Tread* he was at such pains to eject his Philip. But his sense of values remains the same. He has the same terribly acute discernment of and the old insuperable distaste for what he once called "the canned variety of the milk of human kindness" and for all the other substitute products that in civilized communities so interfere between us and our fellows. Most people after a while develop a tolerance, if not even a liking, for these social conveniences. Officialdom, overt or disguised, ceases to offend them. The impersonality of the doctor, for example, his lack of any but a professional interest in their case, comes to strike them as natural and even desirable. The artificial, inculcated brand of bonhomie and comradeship, to take another example, upon which in certain American universities social life is deliberately built, is for them a satisfactory *modus vivendi.* And the patriotism which springs from the suggestive power of a slogan is counted as better than nothing. These things appear to them the inevitable consequences of large communities, and life is not to be vitiated because such substitutes enter into it. But to Mr. Forster life does seem constantly vitiated by automatism, by official action, by insincerity, by organization when it touches charity, or any of the modes of human intercourse which once were governed, in small communities, by natural human feeling alone. That nothing itself would, after all, be better than the only life which now seems possible for millions, appears to be his final position. I am curious to know what Mr. Forster's Ansell, if he had outgrown his Hegelianism, would have thought of it.

We can trace to this horror of automatisms in human affairs, to this detestation of the non-spontaneous, very much that might seem unconnected and accidental in his books. The passion for the Italian character which animates *Where Angels Fear to Tread* and *A Room with a View,* the unfairness to the medical profession which crops up so markedly from time to time, as in *Howards End,* the exaggeration which mars his depiction of schoolmasters apart from Fielding, clergymen, and others in authority, his sentimentalization of Old England, and his peculiarly lively flair for social coercion in all its forms—all these spring from the same source. And I believe that the theme which more than any other haunts his work and most puzzles his attentive readers has the same origin.

A special preoccupation, almost an obsession, with the continuance of life, from parent to child, with the quality of life in the sense of blood or race, with the preservation of certain strains and the disappearance of others, such is the nearest description of this theme which I can contrive. In itself it eludes abstract presentation. Mr. Forster himself refrains from formulating it. He handles it in the concrete only, or through a symbol such as the house, *Howards End.* (Mrs. Wilcox, the most mysterious of his creations, was a Howard, it will be recalled.) This preoccupation is extremely far removed from that of the Eugenic Society—which would be, precisely, the canned variety; the speculations and calculations of the geneticist do not bear upon it, for it is to Mr. Forster plainly a more than half mystical affair, a vision of the ultimate drift or struggle of the universe and the refuge into which an original strong tendency to mysticism has retreated. The supreme importance to him of this idea appears again and again in his books and it is when automatisms such as social pressures and insincerities threaten to intervene here that he grows most concerned—witness *A Room with a View.* In *Longest Journey,* Rickie's mother appears to him in one of the most dreadful dreams in fiction. "Let them die out! Let them die out!" she says. His son has just been born a hopeless cripple. Gino in *Where Angels Fear to Tread* stands "with one foot resting on the little body, suddenly musing, filled with the desire that his son should be like him and should have sons like him to people the earth. It is the strongest desire that comes to a man—if it comes to him at all—stronger even than love or desire for personal immortality. . . . It is the exception who comprehends that physical and spiritual life may stream out of him for ever." Compare also the strange importance in *A Passage to India* of the fact that Mrs. Moore's children are Mrs. Moore's.

But the most fascinating example of the handling of this theme is in *Howards End,* the book that still best represents the several sides of Mr. Forster's worth, and in which its virtues and its occasional defects can best be studied. Two different aims are combined in *Howards End;* they have their interconnections, and the means by which they are severally pursued are very skilfully woven together; but it is true, I think, that the episodes which serve a double purpose are those which are usually regarded as the weakest in the book. One of these aims is the development of the half mystical, and inevitably vague, survival theme which we have been considering. The other is the presentation of a sociological thesis, a quite definite piece of observation of great interest and importance concerning the relations of certain prominent classes in Modern England. For that matter, they can be found without trouble in every present day community. To this second aim more than half the main figures of the book belong. A certain conflict between these aims is, I suggest, the source of that elusive weakness which, however, high and distinguished a place we may find for *Howards End,* disqualifies it as one of the world's greatest novels.

It will be convenient to begin with an instance of this weakness, a passage where the two aims come together and where there is a curious forcing of the emotional pitch of a kind which, were there no other explanation, we should be inclined to describe as sentimentality. Margaret Schlegel has just told her sister Helen of her engagement to Mr. Wilcox. The scene is a slope of the Purbeck Hills. "Helen broke right away and wandered distractedly upwards, stretching her hands towards the view and crying." This is a passage which, I am afraid, has gone home to many hearts and bosoms, yet if we consider it carefully, weighing especially the exact effort of that "somehow seen her" and the results of the sudden appearance of the adjective "brave," can we help but regard it as affected? It is a mild but a clear case of that literary imposture known colloquially as "putting it over." Mr. Forster has always had a peculiar gift for charging his sentences with a mysterious nervous shiver. The scene of the idiot messenger in *Where Angels Fear to Tread* is a notable example. So, too, is the wych-elm scene towards the close of *Howards End.* In these instances and, indeed, in all but a few places, nothing could be more admirable. But his admirers have not been without a fear that this gift might tempt Mr. Forster to overwork it, a fear which some of the Mrs. Moore scenes in *A Passage to India* have not lessened.

But, to return to *Howards End,* the few passages which awaken this discomfort in the reader are, I believe, all consequences of the mixing of the two aims of the book, the half mystical preoccupation with survival overforcing the emotion in scenes which have apparently only to do with the sociological thesis. It is time to expound this thesis more fully. It concerns the two kinds of people mentioned in the passage I have quoted—the able, competent, practical, effectual Wilcoxes, and the speculative, contemplative, critical, and imaginative Schlegels. It concerns the relations of these two sorts to one another in the community, the separation and antagonism of people of vision and people of action. The situation is illustrated by their reactions toward a third sort of person, one which is the result, ultimately, of their separation and antagonism—Leonard Bast, who is both crude as compared with the Schlegels and feeble as compared with the Wilcoxes, but a victim and horribly alive. The presentation of Leonard Bast, in its economy and completeness and its adequacy to the context, would be enough by itself to give any novelist a claim to enduring memory. Consider only Chapter VI, the description of Leonard and his "wife" Jacky in their semi-basement flat. It is only ten pages long, but what other novelist, though taking a whole volume, has said as much on this theme or said it so clearly?

While Leonard remains what he is here, the tragically revealing instance of Mr. Forster's thesis, no admiration is too much. But something happens, he becomes needed for another purpose. The other aim of the book, Mr. Forster's peculiar personal preoccupation with the continuance of life, claims him. A string of incidents is developed in which he becomes no more than a dummy. His collision—it is little more—with Helen, his last brief appearance when he is killed by Charles Wilcox, these do not match with the rest. There is a disaccord, and in a minor degree the same thing happens with the other figures in the book, with Helen and Margaret and Mr. Wilcox. They are used for a double purpose, and the two aims do not quite agree. Only Mrs. Wilcox and Charles Wilcox are free from the subtle inner disharmony, because each is claimed only by one purpose—Charles only by the thesis and Mrs. Wilcox only by Mr. Forster's incommunicable idea, his glimpse of the mystical significance of life. With this incommunicable idea, *Howards End* closes. It is purely, I think, to let Leonard live on, that he is so wilfully given a child. There is something in Leonard which Mr. Forster will not let die. Leonard himself being worthless is killed violently, and flung aside, but he lives on in Helen's child. This event is Mr. Forster's confession of faith.

The Novels of E.M. Forster

by Peter Burra

Perhaps it is chance, more than any peculiar devotion, that determines a man in his choice of medium, when he finds himself possessed by the obscure impulse towards creation. The distinction between the functions of one art and another is not clear; they have a tendency to overlap, to merge, even to identify themselves, in a manner which prevents definition. They have one common subject for discussion—the life that is lived and known by men; and since it is not at once apparent why men who are intimately involved in living that life should desire to contemplate so immediate an experience in any remoter way, another activity (criticism), as old as themselves, has attended upon the arts from their beginning, which has constantly and variedly, but never quite satisfactorily, attempted to explain the reasons for their being. In the advanced state of everything—of life, that is, and our ideas about life—that we have achieved to-day, people, including Mr. Forster, have set themselves to define the difference between the real life which we live and the life which the arts present to us. That such a difference exists is in itself sufficient indication of how advanced we are. Various processes have led to the existence of these conditions, and the most important is the artist's practice of "selection." "Most of life," says Mr. Forster, for example, "is so dull that there is nothing to be said about it"; and even if you disagree with that—Mrs. Virginia Woolf, for her part, seems to suggest that the whole of life is so significant that not one fleeting impression should be missed—the fact remains that the real life is chaotic and formless, and the artist is faced with the problem of confining his impressions of that life into a space which is infinitely smaller than itself and with at least one of the dimensions removed. He has no other alternative, there-

"The Novels of E.M. Forster." From *The Nineteenth Century and After,* CXVI (November 1934), 581-94. Reprinted as "Introduction" to *A Passage to India* (Everyman Library edition, No. 972, 1942). Copyright © 1934 by Simon Nowell-Smith, and reprinted with his permission.

NOTE: When this article appeared in the Everyman edition of *A Passage to India,* it was introduced by E.M. Forster, who praised Burra's sensitivity as a critic, and commented: "I have re-read it with pleasure and pride, for Burra saw exactly what I was trying to do; it is a great privilege for an author to be analysed so penetratingly, and a rare one."

fore, than to select what seem to him its most significant parts, and to arrange the chaos into some sort of an order. Inevitably the life he presents is something much neater and tidier than the diffuse reality. It is probable that most people take the impressions afforded by art—especially the novel—so much for granted that they sincerely believe life itself to be quite a neat and tidy event and suffer from shock or melancholy if something occurs to disturb their belief. Paradoxically, the more actually "like" life a work of art is, the more nonsensical it appears to them. One of the most interesting aims of modern writers and artists has been the attempt to dispel this illusion of life's tidiness.

How far this selection may be carried, and upon what judgment the selected items depend, are questions which have been insufficiently considered, seeing that from the exercise of them the finished work of art results. Selection is in itself an increasing tendency—that is to say, the artist tends to cut away more and more of the matter of immediate life, until he achieves the logical conclusion of the tendency, which is Abstraction. He is urged on to this by his passion to come at the very core of all truth, to perceive the vital spirit of very life, and he can only convey this spirit by cutting away as much as possible, in Mrs. Woolf's phrase, of the "alien and external."

Now of all art forms the novel is the least abstract, the one which has depended more than any other on the dress and decoration of life, and the one which has pretended most of all that life is a neat, well-patterned affair. This is the form in which Mr. E.M. Forster has chosen to put the thoughts of his rich mind into the world, but though he has shown both in theory and practice a marvellous understanding of it, yet it has constantly called from him expressions of dissatisfaction and irritation. "Yes —oh dear yes," he confesses with the greatest reluctance and distaste, "the novel tells a story . . . and I wish that it was not so, that it could be something different—melody, or perception of the truth, not this low atavistic form." All we can do is to echo his regret, and with still greater reluctance; for the *Aspects of the Novel* was written in 1927, and now it is 1934, and it seems—oh dear yes—as if the novel will tell a story till the end of time. Why, then, did Mr. Forster, who has felt so oppressively the attractions of abstract presentation, ever adopt the novel at all?

In the first place, he did attempt a compromise. Contemporary with his pre-war novels he wrote a number of short stories, some of which were collected, in 1911, in *The Celestial Omnibus*; others not till 1928 in *The Eternal Moment*. With the exception of the name-story in the second volume, these are all symbolic fantasies or fables. Most of them appear to be the sort of stories which Rickie was writing, or trying to write, in *The Longest Journey* (1907), Forster's second novel; and incidentally a peculiarly personal sympathy seems to have gone to the making of this character. Rickie's comments on his stories are perhaps Mr. Forster's own. "What nonsense! Where real things are so wonderful, what is the point of pretending?" But fantasy could never be more than half a solution. There is still too much the semblance of story about it. Rickie, like Mr. Forster, envied the musician. "Music has wings. . . . I can't soar; I can only indicate." Why did he not think of progressing from symbolic fantasy to pure fantasy, abstraction, music?

It is that he has ideas which need a more distinct articulation than music or abstraction can make. He is an artist on the fringe of social reform. He is interested in causes. He has never cut himself off, as most artists sooner or later do, from the political and economic questions of the outer world. "Some closing of the gates is inevitable after thirty," he writes, "if the mind itself is to become a creative power." Mr. Forster has never quite closed the gates. While he has never deliberately written, like Dickens, a novel with a "purpose"—an irrelevancy to the dangers of which this art form is particularly exposed—the fact nevertheless remains that *A Passage to India* (1924) is "a book which no student of the Indian question can disregard." His less-read works include *A History and Guide of Alexandria,* and some *Notes on the State of Egypt* published in 1921 with Recommendations by a Committee of the International Section of the Labour Research Department. Probably the writing of novels has not been the most important element in his life. We are constantly given the impression that there are better things in the world to do. Nevertheless, if, in passing, we may allow the aesthetic side of us to predominate, we must lament the extraordinary fact that between *Howards End* (1910) and the present day, *A Passage to India,* ten years ago, is the only novel that has appeared.

With some reluctance, then, he acknowledged that the novel tells a story, and decided, while wishing it were music instead, on the use of "this low atavistic form." Now one might reasonably suppose that a writer who had shown this distaste for it would try to reduce to a minimum its function in his work, would eliminate all complication of plot and put as little stress as possible on so disturbing a factor as incident. In point of fact, the exact opposite is true. We must quote in full a paragraph from *A Passage to India* to which we have already referred:

> Most of life is so dull that there is nothing to be said about it and the books and talk that would describe it as interesting are obliged to exaggerate, in the hope of justifying their own existence. Inside its cocoon of work or social obligation, the human spirit slumbers for the most part, registering the distinction between pleasure and pain, but not nearly as alert as we pretend. There are periods in the most thrilling day during which nothing happens, and though we continue to exclaim: "I do enjoy myself," or, "I am horrified," we are insincere. "As far as I feel anything, it is enjoyment, horror"—it's no more than that really, and a perfectly adjusted organism would be silent.

The most profound phrase there is the last one, and it bears on an important aspect of Mr. Forster's philosophy, but it is the paragraph as a whole which concerns us now, seeming, as it does, to stress incident, at the expense of that ceaselessly experiencing sensibility which for Mrs. Woolf is the proper stuff of fiction. And that, indeed, is what happens. Mr. Forster's novels tell stories. But what stories! What monstrous improbabilities they are! What fearful, sensational things they are made of! Manslaughter, bribery, and blackmail, slander and false witness, violent sex episodes, illegitimate offspring, village idiocy, public school intrigue, far-fetched coincidence, a mysterious housekeeper who has stepped straight from the pages of Gothic romance, death in carriage accidents, at level crossings, by drowning, on the football field. Inevitably one's first impression of his books is concerned with the violence of the plots. When we are least prepared we receive an electric shock. It is the author's deliberate plan; the writing is gradually keyed down to its gentlest mood, and suddenly a plain, terrible fact explodes. "Gerald died that afternoon. He was broken up in the football match." "By the time they arrived Robert had been drowned." In these and countless other cases—the deaths of Mrs. Wilcox, Leonard Bast, Rickie, and the arrest of Dr. Aziz—the critical event is so entirely unexpected that we read on, wondering for the moment whether it is not intended as metaphorical speech. Eventually we grow used to the trick. Often on a second reading we find that the shock has been prepared for, or its probability justified by slight indications, but so slight are they that we cannot be blamed for having failed to note their significance at the time. Nothing of the story in the four early novels can be believed in; little of it even seems to claim credibility. Yet this apparent artlessness must be more than a fine disregard for a "low atavistic form" only put up with as a convenient framework for his ideas about people. It is rather a planned violence, an assault on our sobriety, to incapacitate us from making untimely criticisms, to "bounce us" (in his own phrase), by fair means or foul, into accepting what he says. And it succeeds. It carries the sort of declamatory conviction that good opera carries. His stories are, in relation to themselves, true enough; the incidents, inside the books in which they occur, are relevant parts of a whole. And for the aesthetic compactness of a work of art, that is all that matters. It is only when we consider the possibility of such events in relation to ourselves that we feel doubtful. There is that scene, for example, in which Ansell, Rickie's undergraduate friend, denounces him—he is an under-housemaster—in front of all the boys at lunch, and passionately makes known, while the loyal prefects prepare to do battle, that their teacher has an illegitimate brother whom he refuses to acknowledge. What house, what school possessing such a house, would survive such a scene? Such things simply do not happen to ourselves. They are not true.

Yet in the book even that scene is true. It is written with such intensity that it carries a ringing conviction with it. It possesses that operatic truth.[1] Apart from which, its actual probability is almost prepared for in the previous exposition of Ansell's character. The scene is shocking, intentionally, but it is not surprising. It is consistent with everybody and with everything that has happened. One might still feel inclined to blame an author who chooses to mix together such characters and such incidents which develop into such a scene, but the feeling would be an irrelevant one. The fact is that, though the materials out of which they are made seem to belong more properly to sensational fiction, Mr. Forster's stories are the most distinguished pieces of craftsmanship. In his *Aspects of the Novel* he has analysed with great insight the novel's component factors, and the various sacrifices which one factor may have to make to another —character to plot, or vice versa. Mr. Forster contrives his plot only for the purpose of developing his characters, and makes it serve them, at whatever cost to probability. (We refer to the four early novels. In *A Passage to India* he has achieved as absolute a co-ordination of the component parts as has ever been made.)

And yet his books are beautiful; they are eminently works of art, the reason lying in the close attention he has given to the qualities which he describes as Pattern and Rhythm. By that he means the various devices by which the different parts of the novel can be linked up with one another. Their effectiveness depends, he points out, on the memory of the reader, and his power to recognize the significance of incidental detail; and

> the final sense (if the plot has been a fine one) will not be of clues and chains, but of something aesthetically compact, something which might have been shown by the novelist straight away, only if he had shown it straight away it would never have become beautiful.

Mr. Forster has developed the art of clues and chains to an unusual extent. In its simplest form it consists of throwing in hints that are a preparation for events that follow probably much later. They are generally so casually introduced that we hardly observe them; hence a full appreciation of his novels depends absolutely on a second reading. For example, the deaths of Mrs. Wilcox, Leonard Bast, and Mrs. Moore appear when we come upon them to be too sudden for credibility—the author had finished with them, so they died. In point of fact, they are quite deliberately prepared for by earlier remarks on the state of their healths which at the time were too commonplace for us to see their significance. Another good instance occurs in *Where Angels Fear to Tread*. Philip is asking Caroline about her conversation with Gino. "And of what did you talk?" "The weather—there will be rain, he says, by tomorrow evening . . ." etc. The torrential storm which results in the

---

[1] Other examples of this are the fight between Gino and Philip at the end of *Where Angels Fear to Tread*, and the death of Leonard Bast in *Howards End*.

carriage accident in which Gino's child dies is thus prepared for seventy pages before it occurs.

This simple ruse, whose purpose is to give tightness to the plot itself, develops into another ruse which Mr. Forster rather curiously calls rhythm, but which might more aptly be termed *leit-motif*. The example which he gives is the little tune of Vinteuil in Proust, and its significant reappearances. The *leit-motif* need not in itself be peculiarly significant, but by association with its previous appearance accumulates meaning each time it recurs. In *The Longest Journey* there are several examples —the star Orion is one of them, and recurs somewhat like Violets in *A Room with a View*. A more structural *motif* in the former book is the level crossing near Cadover. When Rickie and Agnes arrive at Mrs. Failing's, Stephen tells them accusingly that their train ran over a child at the crossing. There follows some futile badinage as to what has happened to the child's soul, which Stephen cannot endure. " 'There wants a bridge,' he exploded. 'A bridge instead of all this rotten talk and the level crossing.' " It appears later that a second child had been rescued by Stephen himself. The crossing is passed and repassed by Rickie later in the book, each time with the memory of death. At the end he is killed there himself, wearily saving Stephen, whom he finds drunk across the line. And in the concluding chapter we learn in a casual remark from Stephen that the railway has been bridged. A train is heard passing across the final darkness. The sense of completion is extraordinary.[2] The images which are used as *leit-motifs* fall very little short of becoming symbols. Mr. Forster nowhere uses symbols as Mrs. Woolf does, translating an inarticulate idea into an image; but he constantly uses images to suggest, by association, more than they themselves signify.

In *A Passage to India,* one of the most "aesthetically compact" books ever written, whose thought, like music's, cannot be fixed, nor its meaning defined, there is an extreme instance of one passage calling back to another. Mrs. Moore returns home to bed at the end of the first day in the book. She is alone.

> Going to hang up her cloak, she found that the tip of the peg was occupied by a small wasp. . . . "Pretty dear," said Mrs. Moore to the wasp. He did not wake, but her voice floated out, to swell the night's uneasiness.

The scene is simply a beautiful detail, and connects, apparently, on to nothing. But pages and years later, after her death, old Professor Godbole, who had once sung to her at a tea party, hits on an image in his wandering thoughts which, with extraordinary suggestiveness, calls us back to that scene.

[2] One is reminded of *Anna Karenina*. But there the accident at her first entrance *suggests* to her mind the way of her suicide at the end. Here it is a purely chance circumstance—an aesthetic irony such as Hardy delighted in.

Covered with grease and dust, Professor Godbole had once more developed the life of his spirit. He had, with increasing vividness, again seen Mrs. Moore, and round her faintly clinging forms of trouble. He was a Brahman, she Christian, but it made no difference, it made no difference whether she was a trick of his memory or a telepathic appeal. It was his duty, as it was his desire, to place himself in the position of the God and to love her, and to place himself in her position and to say to the God: "Come, come, come, come." This was all he could do. How inadequate! But each according to his own capacities, and he knew that his own were small. "One old Englishwoman and one little, little wasp," he thought, as he stepped out of the temple into the grey of a pouring wet morning. "It does not seem much, still it is more than I am myself."

Such beauty is not to be reckoned.

Most important of all, he uses buildings and places and the names of places—such places as can be appropriately associated with a recurring idea, and thus take on significance as symbols—to be the framework of his books. The Room with a View and Howards End represent thoughts which stamp their pattern on the story. *The Longest Journey* and *A Passage to India,* with their three parts—"Cambridge, Sawston, Wiltshire"; "Mosque, Caves, Temple"—are planned like symphonies in three movements that are given their shape and their interconnections by related and contrasted localities. In the later book the "Marabar caves" are the basis of a *tour de force* in literary planning. They are the keynote in the symphony to which the strange melody always returns. During the first half of the book constant reference to them directs attention forward to the catastrophe. After this, every reference to them directs our attention back to the centre, to the mystery which is never solved. The three structures, Mosque, Caves, Temple, are outward shapes of a man's spiritual adventures, but only by actual association in the story; pure symbolism would involve an unwanted unreality.

This, then, is what gives to the raw material of his stories such distinction—the quality which he comprehensively calls Rhythm, which means the use of *leit-motif* phrases and images to link up separated parts, with the additional function of dramatic irony and symbolism. This it is which gives pattern to the most diffuse of all forms. This device—of *motifs,* irony, and symbols—is, in fact, the modern equivalent of the classical unities, an invention of the greatest value, having all the classical advantages and none of their so severe limitations.

Mr. Forster, we said, was a musician who chose the novel because he had ideas to utter which needed a more distinct articulation than music could make. He is interested passionately in human beings; not only in the idea of them—which is presumably what most novelists mean when they lay claim to that passion—but in their actual living selves. His observation is so close, his power to describe so exact, that although we can see into their secret lives—which, as he says, it is the novelist's unique privilege to discover—his characters are as elusive, as incompletely realized, as our own living friends. He describes with extraordinary insight personal experience in relation to social; the social setting is for him an item which cannot be omitted in the analysis of a whole man. Hence the novel of social comedy, instead of a purer, more musical form.

"A proper mixture of characters," he tells us, is one of the most important ingredients of the novel. As a vehicle for conveying ideas everything depends on that. It is the nature of the mixture that distinguishes Mr. Forster's work; which is built invariably round the—generally violent—clash of opposites. In *Where Angels Fear to Tread* the clash is between the world of conventional morality and a world more akin to Nature. To heighten the contrast the conflicting elements are vested in England and Italy. "More than personalities were engaged; . . . the struggle was national." It is a fight between North and South, between Culture and the Beast. Culture and the Beast are again the conflicting opposites in *The Longest Journey*. Here the clash is between Rickie and Stephen, who eventually find that they are children of one mother—the one educated at Cambridge, the other brought up among shepherds in the Wiltshire downs. In both these books the violence of the plots, which we have already noticed, derives directly from the violence of this clash of opposites. In the next, *A Room with a View*, the clash is more quietly, more subtly presented, and the plot is at the same time a subtle one. Again a contrast is made between England and Italy; but, except in so far as the carriage-driver "Phaethon" and his lover "Persephone" bear on the story, the countries do not coincide with the opposites. The conflict is less externalized and takes place inside Lucy, in her struggle to choose between Cecil Vyse and George Emerson, between the "medieval" self-conscious life of culture and emancipated athletic honesty; between pretended feelings and true feelings.

Howards End is as violent as the earlier books. It is an extremely complicated piece of work, but (to state the conflict for the moment as simply as possible) it can be described as the clash between the business life and the cultured life; between "Wilcoxes" and "Schlegels" (the names come to be used almost as symbols of the two ways of living); between "the outer life of telegrams and anger" and the life of "personal relations." Again the author adds a deliberate detail for the sake of heightening the contrast—the Wilcoxes are English to the backbone, the Schlegels are of German origin.

In *A Passage to India*, which did not appear till fourteen years later, the clash seems at first sight to be a purely racial one. The distinction between types is less prominent, the political passion that describes the disastrous anomaly of the British in India is more obvious. The propagandist element in the book is undeniable, but one can hardly conclude that it was written with that for its final purpose. For one thing, in the last part of the book—"Temple"—the problem is a different one. "For here the cleavage was between Brahman and non-Brahman; Moslems and English were quite out of the running, and sometimes not mentioned for days." The intrusion of the English at Mau is incidental and designed only to reintroduce what is the real theme of the book—the friendship of Fielding and Dr. Aziz. The rocks that rise between them on their last ride together, the horses that swerve apart—they symbolize Indian differences, it is true, but differences that are not more great, only more particular, than the differences that exist between any two men, between Philip and Gino, Rickie and Stephen, Schlegels and Wilcoxes. Once again, therefore, the author's interest is in the clash of human beings, the struggle which any one individual must endure if he is to achieve intimacy with any one other. The fundamental personal difference is again deliberately heightened by an external circumstance—the difference of race.

Before we proceed to reject these analyses as being too bare to convey even a half-true impression, another aspect of the clash, which is common to them all, must be referred to. Mr. Forster introduces into each of these five books what one can only describe as an elemental character; one who sees straight through perplexities and complications, who is utterly percipient of the reality behind appearances, both in matters of general truth and of incidents in the story. Their greater wisdom, their particular knowledge, put into ironic contrast the errors and illusions of the rest. They are Gino, Stephen, George (together with his father), Mrs. Wilcox, and Mrs. Moore. In the case of the men the stress is laid on the athletic, of the women on the intuitive. The latter, Mrs. Wilcox and Mrs. Moore, play a distinctly minor part in their stories. It is curious to find vested in middle-aged women the elemental quality which is more obviously associated with the athletic, but we find it also in some of Shakespeare's heroines. Both discover on particular complicated occasions an unquestioning certainty about the truth of an event. Of Helen Schlegel's secret love of Paul "Mrs. Wilcox knew . . . though we neither of us told her a word, and had known all along." So of Dr. Aziz, "Of course he is innocent," says Mrs. Moore. Very few words are spoken by either of them. They both seem to have withdrawn from a world whose little stupidities and illusions have ceased to affect them except as they distract their inner life. They are both curiously mysterious, their personalities conveying with an astonishing force far more than there is actual evidence for. Mrs. Wilcox

> was not intellectual, not even alert, and it was odd that, all the same, she should give the idea of greatness. Margaret, zig-zagging with her friends over Thought and Art, was conscious of a personality that transcended their own and dwarfed their activities.

One rather strange accident attaches to both of them: they belong to the enemy's camp—that is to say, to the side of the clash with which we are least likely to sympathize. In fact, Mrs. Moore's Anglo-Indian setting does not call for our sympathy at all. They thus prepare the way for the merge of opposites to which we return later. Some of the mystery attaches as well to the three men. They are strange because in the middle of a social comedy they prefer to dispense with the disguises which the rest wear. As the Rev. Arthur Beebe remarks: "It is so difficult—at least I find it difficult—to understand people who speak the truth."

By the very nature of the conflict which he arranges it is clear how much store Mr. Forster sets by the athletic. The one chance which puts the deformed Rickie in the way of salvation is that "he had escaped the sin of despising the physically strong—a sin against which the physically weak must guard." In the person of Stephen physical strength is exalted into the most exciting beauty and the whole novel reminds one constantly of the work which Lawrence produced a few years later. When he makes his first appearance, a third of the way through the book, the writing is lifted up like music to herald his approach. He is the product of an intensely passionate imagination working upon closely recorded detail of behaviour and conduct. He is life, at the centre and at the circumference—he is the world's essential simplicity, transformed by the author's vision. His significance is clear to the reader at once; no other character —except Mrs. Failing when the mood is on her—perceives it, until Ansell, the articulate philosopher, sums him up:

> A silence, akin to Poetry, invaded Ansell. Was it only a pose to like this man, or was he really wonderful? He was not romantic, for Romance is a figure with outstretched hands, yearning for the unattainable. Certain figures of the Greeks, to whom we continually return, suggested him a little. One expected nothing of him—no purity of phrase nor swift-edged thought. Yet the conviction grew that he had been back somewhere—back to some table of the gods, spread in a field where there is no noise, and that he belonged for ever to the guests with whom he had eaten.

Gino and George Emerson are very different people, but they represent the same athletic honesty. Gino was "majestic; he was a part of nature." "Centuries of aspiration and culture" were defenceless against the impulses he aroused. The quality in George is contrasted with its absence in Cecil, whom Lucy is engaged to marry. At the beginning of the book it is latent but undeveloped in George, but each of his rare meetings with Lucy draws it out. Lucy comes to connect Cecil with a drawing-room that has no view, George is associated with a room with a view that looks out over life. Lucy and George meet from time to time, but always appear to be looking at each other "across something"—across "the rubbish that cumbers the world," across the little bundles of clothes which they strip for bathing, and which break into speech (the fancy reminds one of Daudet) "proclaiming: 'No. We are what matters. Without us shall no enterprise begin. To us shall all flesh turn in the end.'" And George, to whom physical nakedness has given a new certainty, greets her "with the shout of the morning star"; and eventually beseeches her to turn from the pretence of Cecil to his own manhood. Lucy cannot admit to herself that he is right, till a few minutes later Cecil is asked to make up a four at tennis.

> Cecil's voice came: "My dear Freddy, I am no athlete. As you well remarked this very morning, 'There are some chaps who are no good for anything but books'; I plead guilty to being such a chap, and will not inflict myself on you."
> The scales fell from Lucy's eyes. How had she stood Cecil for a moment? He was absolutely intolerable, and the same evening she broke her engagement off.

The athletic fitness of Gino, Stephen, and George is stressed in another significant way. Each realizes—exceptionally, we are given to understand —"that physical and spiritual life may stream out of him for ever." Stephen "would have children: he, not Rickie, would contribute to the stream; he, through his remote posterity, might be mingled with the unknown sea." "Ah, but how beautiful he is!" says Gino, bathing his baby. "And he is mine; mine for ever. Even if he hates me he will be mine. He cannot help it; he is made out of me; I am his father." And the story of George and Lucy ends: "Youth enwrapped them; the song of Phaethon announced passion requited, love attained. But they were conscious of a love more mysterious than this. The song died away; they heard the river, bearing down the snows of winter into the Mediterranean."

Gino, Stephen, George—these are heroes. They represent the same elemental quality as Mrs. Woolf's Percival in *The Waves*. But whereas Percival is presented as an adored, desired opposite, a symbol of the unattainable, Mr. Forster brings in these characters to make a clash, to conflict with the other side. Mr. Forster describes the clash of opposites, but not only the clash; he describes the merge as well. He realizes that, having regard to their common humanity, no two types, however much opposed, can be considered as absolutely distinct. Hence his point of view is constantly shifting—each side is alternately presented for sympathy, first impressions are contradicted, confirmed, contradicted again, so that a close attention and memory are required to add up the final sum. We cannot doubt that what is urged upon us in *The Longest Journey* is the return to Nature—what is emphasized is the value of the earth. Yet the tragedy does arise from Rickie's faith in her, learnt through Stephen, from his magnificent refusal to heed his aunt's warning "Beware of the Earth." When it comes to "warnings," Mrs. Herriton, Mrs. Failing, Mrs. Wilcox, the Anglo-Indians, people whom imagination has never visited, are always—right. It is in *Howards End* that our impressions are likely to become most confused. "Wilcoxes" and "Schlegels" are presented with as exact a balance of sympathy as is possible—much as Shakespeare presents Richard II and Bolingbroke, for example, or the royalists and the rebels, in *Henry IV*, Part I. So that it almost depends on the personal feeling of the reader to incline the scale finally either way.

In *Howards End* the two opposing points of view are woven across each other so closely that it is hardly possible to detach the threads. Two families, the Schlegels and the Wilcoxes, come into contact with each other as a result of a chance meeting. "Schlegels" consist of two sisters and a brother—Margaret, Helen, and the youthfully aesthetic Tibby. Their spiritual home is Queen's Hall, and they hold vaguely advanced opinions. "Wilcoxes" make money; "they are keen on all games," and they "think charm in a man is rather rot." The trouble begins when Helen and Paul think they are in love with one another—an illusion which does not last more than a few hours.

> "To think that because you and a young man meet for a moment, there must be all these telegrams and anger," supplied Margaret.
> Helen nodded.
> "I've often thought about it, Helen. It's one of the most interesting things in the world. The truth is that there is a great outer life that you and I have never touched—a life in which telegrams and anger count. Personal relations that we think supreme, are not supreme there. There love means marriage settlements, death, death duties. So far I'm clear. But here's my difficulty. This outer life, though obviously horrid, often seems the real one—there's grit in it. It does breed character. Do personal relations lead to sloppiness in the end?"
> "Oh, Meg, that's what I felt, only not so clearly, when the Wilcoxes were so competent, and seemed to have their hands on all the ropes."

"The world would be a grey bloodless place," comments the author, "were it entirely composed of Miss Schlegels. But the world being what it is, perhaps they shine out of it like stars." Such is his detachment. The two elements continue to play upon each other, and the greatness and limitations of each are revealed with an astonishing clearness. Helen withdraws further into the "personal life," but for Margaret the "outer life" gradually becomes a "real force," something that she could not attain to. She sees that it represents a "spirit without which life might never have moved out of protoplasm." Finally she becomes Mr. Wilcox's second wife. Then when the crisis of the book is reached and a catastrophe occurs, Wilcoxes are seen in all their weaknesses—they fail because they have never known the "personal life." It seems for the moment as if the author is going to separate them, suggesting that it is impossible to reconcile such opposites, and that "those who stray outside their nature invite disaster." But life returns to the normal. Margaret still accepts Mr. Wilcox. And at the very end, as tragedy goes off into the past, and much pain has been suffered and many wrongs have been revealed—"Nothing has been done wrong," she says to him with the final wisdom of acceptance.

For love, she sees, is a greater thing than opinions. What a folly it were to ruin the rare possibility of intimacy with any man, for so imaginary a cause as one's personal beliefs. The man himself is the important element, and not the way he thinks, nor the work he does. "I can't bother over results," she once remarked regarding the British Empire, "they are too difficult for me. I can only look at the men. An empire bores me, so far, but I can appreciate the heroism that builds it up." Again: "She hated war and liked soldiers—it was one of her amiable inconsistencies." It is possible that in that inconsistency Mr. Forster is enunciating his philosophy as definitely as he has done anywhere. You may be a convinced rebel—but do not pretend that you can resist empire builders. You may be a pacifist—but you are laying a false emphasis on consistency if you allow that to affect your appreciation of soldiers. What a man thinks and the way of life he goes will inevitably clash with other thoughts and different ways. But the man himself is more than his opinions or the accidents that attach to him. It is possible for Schlegels to accept Wilcoxes, it is possible for Englishmen to ride with Indians. And the final wisdom is to grant that "nothing has been done wrong."

The words have—to use a phrase of Mrs. Woolf's—the weight of the whole book behind them. They ring with that prophetic "tone of voice" which sounds right through his masterpiece *A Passage to India*—the tone in which the great writers of tragedy have spoken their last words of reconciliation. They rise up—as he says of great poetry—from that anonymous part of a man which "cannot be labelled with his name. It has something in common with all other deeper personalities, and the mystic will assert that the common quality is God."

So that in the end it will be more true to say that, after all, if Mr. Forster's novels "tell a story" as they do, they are these more desirable things as well—"melody" and "perception of the truth." No words can describe them; the melody cannot be heard through any medium but its own. All I have attempted here is some indication of the shape and the mode. Much that is most remarkable in his writing has scarcely been commented upon: his dazzling humour, acute and delicate satire that never misses its mark, his vivid characterization, whether in the "flat" or the "round"; his faultless sense of the style appropriate to individuals, especially in regard to their tricks of speech—these and other arts give the actual texture of his work its distinction. But these are stamped with his name. It is the Anonymous Prophecy that will remain with us, the transcendent beauty of the Mosque and Temple, and the athletic body of Stephen. It would be perhaps merely stupid to ask, in conclusion, for more. It is possible that the mind which saw so visionarily the significance of Stephen, and which could tell the Wilcoxes that "nothing has been done wrong," has acheived their own wisdom; that the organism, being perfectly adjusted, is silent.

E.M. Forster

by F.R. Leavis

The problem with which E.M. Forster immediately confronts criticism is that of the oddly limited and uncertain quality of his distinction —his real and very fine distinction. It is a problem that Miss Macaulay, in *The Writings of E.M. Forster,* doesn't raise. In fact, she doesn't offer a critique; her book is rather a guide, simply and chattily descriptive, to the not very large corpus of Mr. Forster's work. Nor does she provide the biographical information that, however impertinently in one sense of the adverb, we should like to have, and that we might have been led by the publisher's imprint to hope for, however faintly. We should like to have it because it would, there is good reason for supposing, be very pertinent to the problem facing the critic. Still we do, after all, without extra-critical pryings or impartings, know quite a lot about the particular milieu and the phase of English culture with which Mr. Forster's work is associated; enough, perhaps, to discuss with some profit the extent to which, highly individual as it is, it is also, in its virtues and its limitations, representative.

The inequality in the early novels—the contrast between maturity and immaturity, the fine and the crude—is extreme; so extreme that a simple formula proposes itself. In his comedy, one might carelessly say, he shows himself the born novelist; but he aims also at making a poetic communication about life, and here he is, by contrast, almost unbelievably crude and weak. Yet, though his strength in these novels, it is true, comes out in an art that suggests comparisons with Jane Austen, while it is in the element, the intention, relating them most obviously to *The Celestial Omnibus* that he incurs disaster, the formula is too simple. For one thing, to lump the four pre-war novels together is clumsy; a distinction has to be made. There is no disastrous weakness in the first of them, *Where Angels Fear to Tread,* or in *A Room with a View* (which, in order of publication, comes third). And the distinction here isn't one of "comedy" as against "poetry" or "comedy-cum-poetry." For though the art of

"E.M. Forster." From *The Common Pursuit* by F.R. Leavis. Copyright © 1952 by F.R. Leavis. First published in *Scrutiny,* VII, No. 2 (September 1938), as an essay-review of Rose Macaulay's *The Writings of E.M. Forster.* Reprinted by permission of Chatto & Windus, Ltd., and New York University Press.

the "born novelist" has, in these two novels, a characteristic spinsterly touch, that novelist is at the same time very perceptibly the author of *The Celestial Omnibus,* the tales in which suggest, in their poetic ambition—they may fairly be said to specialize in "poetry"—no one less than Jane Austen. Italy, in those novels, represents the same bent of interest as Pan and the other symbols do in the tales, and it is a bent that plays an essential part in the novelist's peculiar distinction. Pre-eminently a novelist of civilized personal relations, he has at the same time a radical dissatisfaction with civilization—with the finest civilization of personal intercourse that he knows; a radical dissatisfaction that prompts references to D.H. Lawrence rather than to Jane Austen.

In his treatment of personal relations the bent manifests itself in the manner and accent of his preoccupation with sincerity—a term that takes on, indeed, a different value from that which it would have if we used it in discussing Jane Austen. His preoccupation with emotional vitality, with the problem of living truly and freshly from a centre, leads him, at any rate in intention, outside the limits of consciousness that his comedy, in so far as we can separate it off, might seem to involve—the limits, roughly, that it is Jane Austen's distinction to have kept. The intention is most obvious in his way of bringing in, in association, love and sudden death; as, for instance, in Chapter IV of *A Room with a View.* It is still more strikingly manifested in *Where Angels Fear to Tread.* There Italy figures much more substantially and disturbingly as the critical challenge to the "civilization" of Mr. Forster's cultivated English people, and what may be called for the moment the Lawrencian bent is more pronounced. There is the scene (Ch. VII) in which passionate paternal love, a kind of elemental hunger for continuance, is enacted in the devotion of the caddish and mercenary Italian husband to the baby; and the baby it is that, in this book, suffers the violent death. There follows the episode in which the Italian tortures Philip Herriton by wrenching his broken arm. Yet none of Mr. Forster's books is more notable for his characteristic comedy, with its light, sedate and rather spinsterly poise. And there is, nevertheless, no discrepancy or clash of modes or tones: *Where Angels Fear to Tread* is decidedly a success. It seems to me the most successful of the pre-war novels.

A Room with a View is far from being a failure, but, though the themes here might seem to be much less dangerous, there are certain weaknesses to be noted. There is, as Miss Macaulay points out, a curious spinsterish inadequacy in the immediate presentation of love (in *Where Angels Fear to Tread,* significantly, serious love between the sexes doesn't come in, at any rate immediately). And old Mr. Emerson, though not a disaster, does lead one to question the substantiality of the wisdom that he seems intended to represent. Nevertheless *A Room with a View* is a charming and very original book—extremely original and personal. Yet decidedly it provokes a comparison with Meredith, for to *The Egoist* it obviously owes its inspiration. *The Egoist* tries only to do something simple (as we are bound to feel if we think of *The Portrait of a Lady*), but, apart from faults of over-writing, over-thronging and prolixity, *The Egoist* is entirely successful. The Lucy-Cecil Vyse-George Emerson trio who replace and imitate Clara Middleton, Sir Willoughby and Vernon Whitford are quite perfunctorily handled and but feebly animated—they are not realized, their emotions are stated but not convincingly conveyed, and the borrowed theme, losing its substance and force, loses also its symbolic strength. Being no longer a parable (though the fashionable term "myth" could be for once justifiably invoked for *The Egoist*) the Forster version achieves the status only of minor comedy; it is essentially trivial. And if we were unkind enough to bring out the story *Other Kingdom* from *The Celestial Omnibus* volume for similar comparison with its source, which is again *The Egoist*, we should have to make an even more saddening report in which the charge of "whimsy" would appear.

The reference above to D.H. Lawrence was, of course, an over-emphasis, but as a way of calling attention to Mr. Forster's peculiar distinction among Edwardian novelists it can perhaps be justified. The critic who deals so damagingly with Meredith in *Aspects of the Novel* is potentially there in the genuineness of the element in Mr. Forster's early novels that sets them apart by themselves in the period of Arnold Bennett, Wells, and Galsworthy. But having credited him with that distinction, one has to admit that in comparison with the *major* contemporary practitioners he appears very differently. Even leaving Conrad out as not inviting comparison, there are the two to whom he owes so much—Henry James and Meredith. His relation to Meredith we have discussed. And where the other is in question, Forster's art has to be recognized as only too unmistakably minor. Take even the slightest of James's stories which is fairly comparable: *The Marriages* is, we might say, at first glance entirely a "Forster" story, with just such characters, plot and setting as Forster chooses. Then we recognize, in its complex ironic pattern and its really startling psychological insight, the art of a master whose depiction of human behaviour is not marginal and whose knowledge of passion is profound.

But Mr. Forster's "poetic" intention is genuine and radical, even if in expression it may manifest itself as a surprising immaturity; and actually, in *Where Angels Fear to Tread* and *A Room with a View*, it for the most part commands a touch that is hardly to be distinguished from that of the comedy. Or perhaps it would have been better to say "is commanded by"; for when, coming to the other two pre-war novels, *The Longest Journey* and *Howards End,* we ask how it is that they should be so much less successful, we notice at once how the contrast brings out the sure easy poise, in *Where Angels Fear to Tread* and *A Room with a View,* of the artist's—the "born novelist's"—control. The art of the comedy is a distancing art, and it is a tribute to the novelist's skill that we should have no disturbing sense of a change in mode and convention when we pass to effects quite other than those of comedy. That is, the whole action is framed and distanced. Lilia, Gino's silly tragic victim in *Where Angels Fear to Tread,* Philip Herriton, commissioned to retrieve the baby, Miss Abbott and the rest, are all simplified figures, seen from the outside; it is only in a very qualified way that they engage us (though they engage enough for a measure of poignancy). The complexity of the situation we see as such: though we are interested and sympathetic, we are hardly worried. The critical scenes and episodes towards the end are, of course, not undisturbing; yet we are not immersed in them—the detachment, though modified, still holds. In this effect the Italian setting, exotic and quaint—its people seen as another kind from us, has its part; it lends itself beautifully to the reconciliation of the "comedy" with the "poetry" and of tragic intensity with detachment.

The other two novels are much less the artist's: in them the imposing or seeking of any such conditions of a detached and happily poised art has been precluded by the author's essential interest. *The Longest Journey,* perhaps one may without impertinence observe, has plainly a good deal of the autobiographical about it, and it offers, in the presentment of its themes, a fulness and intimacy of realization. True, we find there too the characteristic comedy (notably in all that concerns Mr. Herbert Pembroke), but we can no longer say the success of this carries with it a general success. In fact, there are discrepancies, disharmonies and disturbing shifts that go a long way towards justifying the formula thrown out and withdrawn in the second paragraph of this note. The poised success of the comedy in its own mode serves to emphasize the immaturity, the unsureness and sometimes the crudity of the other elements, with which it wouldn't have been easily congruent even if they had in themselves justified the intention they represent.

Passionate love and, close upon it, sudden death, come early in this book:

> He had forgotten his sandwiches, and went back to get them. Gerald and Agnes were locked in each other's arms. He only looked for a moment, but the sight burnt into his brain. The man's grip was the stronger. He had drawn the woman on to his knee, was pressing her, with all his strength, against him. Already her hands slipped off him, and she whispered, "Don't —you hurt—" Her face had no expression. It stared at the intruder and never saw him. Then her lover kissed it, and immediately it shone with mysterious beauty, like some star.

Gerald is a brutal and caddish minor-Public-School Apollo and Agnes a suburban snob, but this glimpse is for Rickie the hero, a revelation:

> He thought, "Do such things actually happen?" and he seemed to be looking down coloured valleys. Brighter they glowed, till gods of pure flame were born in them, and then he was looking at pinnacles of virgin snow.

While Mr. Pembroke talked, the riot of fair images increased. They invaded his being and lit lamps at unsuspected shrines. Their orchestra commenced in that suburban house, where he had to stand aside for the maid to carry in the luncheon. Music flowed past him like a river. He stood at the springs of creation and heard the primeval monotony. Then an obscure instrument gave out a little phrase. The river continued unheeding. The phrase was repeated, and a listener might know it was a fragment of the Tune of tunes. . . . In full unison was Love born, flame of the flame, flushing the dark river beneath him and the virgin snows above. His wings were infinite, his youth eternal. . . .

Then, a dozen pages later . . . :

Gerald died that afternoon. He was broken up in the football match. Rickie and Mr. Pembroke were on the ground when the accident took place.

It is a key-experience for Rickie. Its significance is made explicit—perhaps rather too explicit. This memory of pure uncalculating passion as a kind of ultimate, invested by death with an awful finality and something like a religious sanction, becomes for Rickie a criterion or touch for the real, a kind of test for radical sincerity, in his questing among the automatisms, acquiescences, blurs, and blunted indifferences of everyday living:

He has no knowledge of the world. . . . He believes in women because he has loved his mother. And his friends are as young and ignorant as himself. They are full of the wine of life. But they have not tasted the cup—let us call it the teacup—of experience, which has made men of Mr. Pembroke's type what they are. Oh, that teacup!

The theme of *The Longest Journey* is Rickie's struggle to live by the truth of the wine while being immersed in knowledge of the world.

Rickie writes stories like Mr. Forster's in *The Celestial Omnibus*. There is a note of ironic indulgence in the references to them: Rickie is very young. The direct and serious expression that the novelist offers us of the bent represented by such stories is in terms of a character, Stephen Wonham,

a man dowered with coarse kindliness and rustic strength, a kind of cynical ploughboy.

He is the illegitimate child (comes the shattering revelation) of Rickie's mother and a young farmer, of whom we are told

people sometimes took him for a gentleman until they saw his hands.

It is a Lady-Chatterley-and-the-keeper situation that is outlined, though Robert is too much idealized to be called a Lawrencian character. Stephen, product of a perfect passionate love (cut short by death), grows up among the villagers and shepherds a kind of heroic boor, devoid of the civilized graces and refinements, representative of physical and spiritual health:

> . . . looked at the face, which was frank, proud and beautiful, if truth is beauty. Of mercy or tact such a face knew little. It might be coarse, but. . . .

He loves horseplay and can be a drunken blackguard, but he is incapable of anything other than direct sincerity: he would, as Ansell says, "rather die than take money from people he did not love." He moves roughshod through the latter part of the action, violating suburban flowerbeds, outraging gentilities, and breaking through the pretences, self-deceptions and timid meannesses of respectability.

> He only held the creed of "here am I and there are you," and therefore class-distinctions were trivial things to him.

When Rickie, having suspected him of intent to blackmail, offers apology and atonement, this is how Stephen replies:

> "Last Sunday week," interrupted Stephen, his voice suddenly rising, "I came to call on you. Not as this or that's son. Not to fall on your neck. Nor to live here. Nor—damn your dirty little mind! I meant to say I didn't come for money. Sorry, sorry. I simply came as I was, and I haven't altered since. . . ." "*I* haven't altered since last Sunday week. I'm—" He stuttered again. He could not quite explain what he was. . . . His voice broke. "I mind it—I'm—*I* don't alter—blackguard one week—live here the next—I keep to one or the other—you've hurt something most badly in me I didn't know was there."

In short, it isn't easy to feel that the novelist in this essential part of his undertaking has attained a much more advanced maturity than the Rickie of the stories. Of course, what he has undertaken is something incomparably more difficult, and the weakness of the "poetic" element is made to look its worst by contrast with the distinction of what is strongest in the novel. Still, the contrast is there, and it is disastrous. What Mr. Forster offers as the centre of his purpose and intends with the greatest intensity of seriousness plainly cannot face the test of reality it challenges. Uninhibited by the passage about "knowledge of the world" and the "cup of experience" quoted above, the reader has to remark that Mr. Forster shows himself, for a writer whose touch can be so sure, disconcertingly inexperienced. An offence, even a gross one, against the probabilities, according to "knowledge of the world," of how people act and talk isn't necessarily very serious. But such a scene as that (Ch. XXVII) in which Ansell the Cambridge philosopher, defying headmaster, headmaster's wife, and prefects, addresses the assembled boys at Sawston School—

> "This man"—he turned to the avenue of faces—"this man who teaches you has a brother," etc.

—reflects significantly on the ruling preoccupation that, in the born novelist, could have led to anything so crudely unreal. And of all that in *The Longest Journey* centres in Stephen one has to say that, if not always as absurd, it is, with reference to the appropriate standard, equivalently unreal. The intention remains an intention; nothing adequate in substance or quality is grasped. And the author appears accordingly as the victim, where his own experience is concerned, of disabling immaturities in valuation: his attributions of importance don't justify themselves.

A ready way of satisfying oneself (if there were any doubt) that "immaturity" is the right word is to take note of the attitude towards Cambridge (after which one of the three parts of the novel is named). Rickie, a very innocent and serious young man, found happiness at Cambridge and left it behind him there, and that this phase of his life should continue to be represented, for him, by an innocent idealization is natural enough. But Rickie in this respect is indistinguishable from the author. And if one doesn't comment that the philosophic Ansell, representative of disinterestedness and intelligence and Cambridge, is seen through the hero-worshipping Rickie's eyes, that is because he is so plainly offered us directly and simply by the novelist himself in perfect good faith.

Howards End (1910), the latest of the pre-war novels and the most ambitious, is, while offering again a fulness and immediacy of experience, more mature in the sense that it is free of the autobiographical (a matter, not of where the material comes from, but of its relation to the author as it stands in the novel) and is at any rate fairly obviously the work of an older man. Yet it exhibits crudity of a kind to shock and distress the reader as Mr. Forster hasn't shocked or distressed him before.

The main theme of the novel concerns the contrasted Schlegels and Wilcoxes. The Schlegels represent the humane liberal culture, the fine civilization of cultivated personal intercourse, that Mr. Forster himself represents; they are the people for whom and in whom English literature (shall we say?—though the Schlegels are especially musical) exists. The Wilcoxes have built the Empire; they represent the "short-haired executive type"—obtuse, egotistic, unscrupulous, cowards spiritually, self-deceiving, successful. They are shown—shown up, one might say—as having hardly a redeeming characteristic, except that they are successful. Yet Margaret, the elder of the Schlegel sisters and the more mature intelligence, marries Mr. Wilcox, the head of the clan; does it coolly, with open eyes, and we are meant to sympathize and approve. The novelist's attitude is quite unambiguous: as a result of the marriage, which is Margaret's active choice, Helen, who in obeying flightily her generous impulses has come to disaster, is saved and the book closes serenely on the promise of a happy future. Nothing in the exhibition of Margaret's or Henry Wilcox's character makes the marriage credible or acceptable; even if we were to seize for motivation on the hint of a panicky flight from spinsterhood in the already old-maidish Margaret, it might go a little way to explain her marrying such a man, but it wouldn't in the least account for the view of the affair the novelist expects us to take. We are driven to protest, not so much against the unreality in itself, as against the perversity of intention it expresses: the effect is of a kind of *trahison des clercs*.

The perversity, of course, has its explanation and is not so bad as it looks. In Margaret the author expresses his sense of the inadequacy of the culture she stands for—its lack of relation to the forces shaping the world and its practical impotence. Its weaknesses, dependent as it is on an economic security it cannot provide, are embodied in the quixotic Helen, who, acting uncompromisingly on her standards, brings nothing but disaster on herself and the objects of her concern. The novelist's intention in making Margaret marry Mr. Wilcox is not, after all, obscure. One can only comment that, in letting his intention satisfy itself so, he unintentionally makes his cause look even more desperate than it need: intelligence and sensitiveness such as *Howards End* at its finest represents need not be so frustrated by innocence and inexperience as the unrealities of the book suggest. For "unreality" is the word: the business of Margaret and Henry Wilcox is essentially as unrealized as the business of Helen and the insurance clerk, Leonard Bast—who, with his Jacky, is clearly a mere external grasping at something that lies outside the author's firsthand experience.

And the Wilcoxes themselves, though they are in their way very much more convincingly done, are not adequate to the representative part the author assigns them—for he must be taken as endorsing Margaret's assertion to Helen, that they "made us possible": with merely Mr. Forster's Wilcoxes to represent action and practice as against the culture and the inner life of the Schlegels there could hardly have been civilization. Of course, that an intellectual in the twentieth century should pick on the Wilcox type for the part is natural enough; writing half-a-century earlier Mr. Forster would have picked on something different. But the fact remains that the Wilcoxes are not what he takes them to be, and he has not seen his problem rightly: his view of it is far too external and unsubtle.

At the same time it is subtler than has yet been suggested. There is the symbolism that centres in "Howards End," the house from which the book gets its title. Along with the concern about the practical insignificance of the Schlegels' culture goes a turning of the mind towards the question of ultimate sanctions. Where lie—or should lie—the real sources of strength, the springs of vitality, of his humane and liberal culture, which, the more it aspires to come to terms with "civilization" in order to escape its sense of impotence, needs the more obviously to find its life, strength, and authority elsewhere?

The general drift of the symbolism appears well enough here:

> The sense of flux which had haunted her all the year disappeared for a time. She forgot the luggage and the motor-cars, and the hurrying men who know so much and connect so little. She recaptured the sense of space which

is the basis of all earthly beauty, and, starting from Howards End, she attempted to realize England. She failed—visions do not come when we try, though they may come through trying. But an unexpected love of the island awoke in her, connecting on this side with the joys of the flesh, on that with the inconceivable. . . . It had certainly come through the house and old Miss Avery. Through them: the notion of "through" persisted; her mind trembled towards a conclusion which only the unwise have attempted to put into words.

Yes, but the author's success in the novel is staked on his effectively presenting this "conclusion" by means of symbols, images and actions created in words. And our criticism must be that, without a more substantial grasp of it than he shows himself to have, he was, as it turns out, hardly wise in so committing himself. The intention represented by Howards End and its associates, the wych-elm, the pig's teeth, old Miss Avery and the first Mrs. Wilcox remains a vague gesturing in a general—too general —direction, and the close of the book can hardly escape being found, in its innocent way, sentimental.

The inherent weakness becomes peculiarly apparent in such prose as this:

There was a long silence during which the tide returned into Poole Harbour. "One would lose something," murmured Helen, apparently to herself. The water crept over the mud-flats towards the gorse and the blackened heather. Branksea Island lost its immense foreshores, and became a sombre episode of trees. Frome was forced inward towards Dorchester, Stour against Wimborne, Avon towards Salisbury, and over the immense displacement the sun presided, leading it to triumph ere he sank to rest. England was alive, throbbing through all her estuaries, crying for joy through the mouths of all her gulls, and the north wind, with contrary motion, blew stronger against her rising seas. What did it mean? For what end are her fair complexities, her changes of soil, her sinuous coast? Does she belong to those who have moulded her and made her feared by other lands, or to those who have added nothing to her power, but have somehow seen her, seen the whole island at once, lying as a jewel in a silver sea, sailing as a ship of souls, with all the brave world's fleet accompanying her towards eternity?

Mr. Forster's "poetic" communication isn't all at this level of poeticality (which, had there been real grasp behind his intention, Mr. Forster would have seen to be Wilcox rather than Schlegel), but it nevertheless lapses into such exaltations quite easily. And the "somehow" in that last sentence may fairly be seized on: the intention that can thus innocently take vagueness of vision in these matters for a virtue proclaims its inadequacy and immaturity there.

In closing on this severe note my commentary on the pre-war novels I had perhaps better add explicitly (in case the implication may seem to have got lost) that they are all, as I see them, clearly the work of a significantly original talent, and they would have deserved to be still read and

remembered, even if they had not been the early work of the author of
A Passage to India.

In *A Passage to India* (1924), which comes fourteen years later (a remarkable abstention in an author who had enjoyed so decided a *succès
d'estime*), there are none of these staggering discrepancies. The prevailing
mood testifies to the power of time and history. For the earlier lyrical indulgences we have (it may fairly be taken as representative) the evocation
of Mrs. Moore's reactions to the caves ("Pathos, poetry, courage—they
exist, but are identical, and so is filth," etc. . . .). The tone characterizing
the treatment of personal relations is fairly represented by this:

> A friendliness, as of dwarfs shaking hands, was in the air. Both man and
> woman were at the height of their powers—sensible, honest, even subtle.
> They spoke the same language, and held the same opinions, and the variety
> of age and sex did not divide them. Yet they were dissatisfied. When they
> agreed, "I want to go on living a bit," or, "I don't believe in God," the
> words were followed by a curious backwash as if the universe had displaced
> itself to fill up a tiny void, or as though they had seen their own gestures
> from an immense height—dwarfs talking, shaking hands and assuring each
> other that they stood on the same footing of insight.

Of course, tone and mood are specifically related to the given theme
and setting of the novel. But the Indian sky and the Anglo-Indian circumstances must be taken as giving a particular focus and frame to the
author's familiar preoccupations (exhibiting as these naturally do a
more advanced maturity).

Fielding, the central figure in the book, who is clearly very close to the
author, represents in a maturer way what the Schlegels represented: what
may still be called liberal culture—humanity, disinterestedness, tolerance
and free intelligence, unassociated with dogma or religion or any very
determinate set of traditional forms. He might indeed (if we leave out all
that Howards End stood for) be said to represent what was intended by
Margaret's marrying Henry Wilcox, for he is level-headed and practical
and qualified in the ways of the world. His agnosticism is explicit. Asked

> Is it correct that most people are atheists in England now?

he replies:

> The educated thoughtful people. I should say so, though they don't like
> the name. The truth is that the West doesn't bother much over belief and
> disbelief in these days. Fifty years ago, or even when you and I were young,
> much more fuss was made.

Nevertheless, though Fielding doesn't share it, the kind of preoccupation he so easily passes by has its place in *A Passage to India* as in Mr.
Forster's other novels, and again (though there is no longer the early
crudity) its appearances are accompanied by something unsatisfactory
in the novelist's art, a curious lack of grasp. The first Mrs. Wilcox, that

very symbolic person, and Miss Avery may be said to have their equiva-
lents in Mrs. Moore and Ralph, the son of her second marriage. Mrs.
Moore, as a matter of fact, is in the first part of the book an ordinary
character, but she becomes, after her death, a vague pervasive suggestion
of mystery. It is true that it is she who has the experience in the cave—
the experience that concentrates the depressed ethos of the book—and
the echo "undermines her hold on life," but the effect should be to associate her with the reverse of the kind of mysteriousness that after her
death is made to invest her name. For she and the odd boy Ralph ("born
of too old a mother") are used as means of recognizing possibilities that
lie outside Fielding's philosophy—though he is open-minded. There is,
too, Ralph's sister Stella, whom Fielding marries:

> She has ideas I don't share—indeed, when I'm away from her I think them
> ridiculous. When I'm with her, I suppose because I'm fond of her, I feel
> different, I feel half dead and half blind. My wife's after something. You
> and I and Miss Quested are, roughly speaking, not after anything. We jog
> on as decently as we can. . . .

Our objection is that it's all too easy. It amounts to little more than
saying, "There may be something in it," but it has the effect of taking
itself for a good deal more. The very poise of Mr. Forster's art has something equivocal about it—it seems to be conditioned by its not knowing
what kind of poise it is. The account of the Krishna ceremony, for instance, which is a characteristic piece by the sensitive, sympathetic, and
whimsically ironic Mr. Forster, slides nevertheless into place in the general effect—there are more things in heaven and earth, Horatio—that
claims a proper impersonality. How radical is this uncertainty that takes
on the guise of a sureness and personal distinction of touch may be seen
in Mr. Forster's prose when a real and characteristic distinction is unmistakably there. Here is an instance:

> The other smiled, and looked at his watch. They both regretted the
> death, but they were middle-aged men who had invested their emotions
> elsewhere, and outbursts of grief could not be expected from them over a
> slight acquaintance. It's only one's own dead who matter. If for a moment
> the sense of communion in sorrow came to them, it passed. How indeed is
> it possible for one human being to be sorry for all the sadness that meets
> him on the face of the earth, for the pain that is endured not only by men,
> but by animals and plants, and perhaps by the stones? The soul is tired in
> a moment, and in fear of losing the little she does understand, she retreats
> to the permanent lines which habit or chance have dictated, and suffers there.

The touch seems sure in the first three sentences—in fact, but for one
phrase, in the whole passage. Consider, for instance, how different an
effect the second sentence would have out of its context: one would suppose it to be in satiric tone. Here, however, it is a means to the precise
definition of a very different tone, one fatigued and depressed but sym-

pathetic. The lapse, it seems to me, comes in that close of the penultimate sentence: ". . . plants, and perhaps by the stones." Once one's critical notice has fastened on it (for, significantly too, these things tend to slip by), can one do anything but reflect how extraordinary it is that so fine a writer should be able, in such a place, to be so little certain just how serious he is? For surely that run-out of the sentence cannot be justified in terms of the dramatic mood that Mr. Forster is offering to render? I suppose the show of a case might be made out for it as an appropriate irony, or appropriate dramatically in some way, but it wouldn't be a convincing case to anyone who had observed Mr. Forster's habit. Such a reader sees merely the easy, natural lapse of the very personal writer whose hand is "in." It may seem a not very important instance, but it is representative, and to say that is to pass a radical criticism.

Moreover, a general doubt arises regarding that personal distinction of style—that distinction which might seem to give Mr. Forster an advantage over, say Mr. L.H. Myers (to take another novelist who offers some obvious points of comparison). The doubt expresses itself in an emphasis on the "personal."

> Ronny approved of religion as long as it endorsed the National Anthem, but he objected when it attempted to influence his life.

> Sir Gilbert, though not an enlightened man, held enlightened opinions.

> Ronny's religion was of the sterilized Public School brand, which never goes bad, even in the tropics.

> Incurably inaccurate, he already thought that this was what had occurred. He was inaccurate because he was sensitive. He did not like to remember Miss Quested's remark about polygamy, because it was unworthy of a guest, so he put it away from his mind, and with it the knowledge that he had bolted into a cave to get away from her. He was inaccurate because he desired to honour her, and—facts being entangled—he had to arrange them in her vicinity, as one tidies the ground after extracting a weed.

> What had spoken to her in that scoured-out cavity of the granite? What dwelt in the first of the caves? Something very old and very small. Before time, it was before space also. Something snub-nosed, incapable of generosity —the undying worm itself.

A larger assemblage of quotations (there would be no difficulty but that of space in going on indefinitely) would make the point fairly conclusively: Mr. Forster's style is personal in the sense that it keeps us very much aware of the personality of the writer, so that even where actions, events and the experiences of characters are supposed to be speaking for themselves the turn of phrase and tone of voice bring the presenter and commentator into the foreground. Mr. Forster's felicities and his charm, then, involve limitations. Even where he is not betrayed into lapses of the kind illustrated above, his habit doesn't favour the impersonality, the presentment of themes and experiences as things standing there in themselves, that would be necessary for convincing success at the level of his highest intention.

The comparative reference to Mr. L.H. Myers thrown out above suggests a return to the question of Mr. Forster's representative significance. When one has recognized the interest and value his work has as representing liberal culture in the early years of the twentieth century, there is perhaps a temptation to see the weaknesses too simply as representative. That that culture has of its very nature grave weaknesses Mr. Forster's work itself constitutes an explicit recognition. But it seems worth while insisting at this point on the measure in which Mr. Forster's weaknesses are personal ones, qualifying the gifts that have earned him (I believe) a lasting place in English literature. He seems then, for one so perceptive and sensitive, extraordinarily lacking in force, or robustness, of intelligence; it is, perhaps, a general lack of vitality. The deficiencies of his novels must be correlated with the weakness so apparent in his critical and journalistic writings—*Aspects of the Novel, Abinger Harvest* —the weakness that makes them representative in so disconcerting a way. They are disconcerting because they exhibit a lively critical mind accepting, it seems, uncritically the very inferior social-intellectual milieu in which it has developed. Mr. Forster, we know, has been associated with Bloomsbury—the Bloomsbury which (to confine ourselves to one name) produced Lytton Strachey and took him for a great writer. And these writings of Mr. Forster's are, in their amiable way, Bloomsbury. They are Bloomsbury in the valuations they accept (in spite of the showings of real critical perception), in the assumptions they innocently express, and in prevailing ethos.

It might, of course, be said that it is just the weakness of liberal culture —"bourgeois," the Marxist would say—that is manifested by Bloomsbury (which certainly had claims to some kind of representative status). But there seems no need to deal directly with such a proposition here, or to discuss at any length what significance shall be given to the terms "liberal" and "culture." The necessary point is made by insisting that the weaknesses of Mr. Forster's work and of Bloomsbury are placed as such by standards implicit in what is best in that work. That those standards are not complete in themselves or securely based or sufficiently guaranteed by contemporary civilization there is no need to dispute: the recognition has been an essential part of the creative impulse in Mr. Forster. But that, in the exploration of the radical problems, more power than he commands may be shown by a creative writer who may equally be said to represent liberal culture appears well enough in *The Root and the Flower**—at least, I throw out this judgment as pretty obviously acceptable. And I cannot see how we can dispense with what they both stand

* By L. H. Myers. [ED.]

for. They represent, the spokesmen of the finer consciousness of our time, the humane tradition as it emerges from a period of "bourgeois" security, divorced from dogma and left by social change, the breakdown of traditional forms and the loss of sanctions embarrassingly "in the air"; no longer serenely confident or self-sufficient, but conscious of being not less than before the custodian of something essential. In these representatives it is far from the complacency of "freedom of thought," but they stand, nevertheless, for the free play of critical intelligence as a *sine qua non* of any hope for a human future. And it seems to me plain that this tradition really is, for all its weakness, the indispensable transmitter of something that humanity cannot afford to lose.

These rather commonplace observations seemed worth making because of the current fashion of using "liberal" largely and loosely as a term of derogation: too much is too lightly dismissed with it. To enforce this remark it seems to me enough to point to *A Passage to India*—and it will be an occasion for ensuring that I shall not, in effect, have done Mr. Forster a major critical injustice. For I have been assuming, tacitly, a general agreement that *A Passage to India*, all criticisms made, is a classic: not only a most significant document of our age, but a truly memorable work of literature. And that there is point in calling it a classic of the liberal spirit will, I suppose, be granted fairly readily, for the appropriateness of the adjective is obvious. In its touch upon racial and cultural problems, its treatment of personal relations, and in prevailing ethos the book is an expression, undeniably, of the liberal tradition; it has, as such, its fineness, its strength and its impressiveness; and it makes the achievement, the humane, decent and rational—the "civilized"—habit, of that tradition appear the invaluable thing it is.

On this note I should like to make my parting salute. Mr. Forster's is a name that, in these days, we should peculiarly honour.

E.M. Forster

by *Austin Warren*

The English novel has traditionally admitted of no exact definition, no generic purity. Written by all sorts and conditions of men, as was the poetic drama of the Elizabethans, it has been designed for as many kinds of readers. The responsibility of the nineteenth century novelist was to offer his readers a "story"; apart from that, and within the bounds of Victorian taste, he might provide what *extras* he would—sociological, psychological, moral. Sweeping his puppets aside, he might preach the new ethics, expound the nature of things, prophesy the future actions of his characters or the future of human character; returning again to his puppets, he was free to pass in and out of their minds, now seeing through this pair of subsidiary eyes, now through that, now exerting the omniscience of his own sight.

At the end of the century the popular novelists continued the practice; but George Moore and Henry James, both aliens to England, both trained in France, felt dissatisfaction at such looseness. A genre so readily susceptible of illustrated homily on prison reform or the loss of clerical faith lacked minimal aesthetic dignity. They busied themselves—James in particular—in devising an "art of fiction." Of this gospel the chief dogma was that of the "point of view." The novelist, James held, must preliminarily decide through whose eyes the proposed narration may, most profitably, be viewed. Or he may, instead, decide to use a series of instruments in turn: the ten books of *The Awkward Age* utilize the vision of as many persons. But there must be no mere convenient, unpremeditated transit. Further, the author must rigorously exclude himself as public commentator or "chorus." The only point of view inadmissible is that of the author.

James's technical experiments have, properly, commanded the respect of subsequent artists; and his influence upon them has been impressive.

"E.M. Forster." The first part of "E.M Forster"—Chapter VIII in *A Rage for Order: Essays in Criticism,* pp. 119-30. Published in 1948 by The University of Chicago Press; published in 1959 by The University of Michigan Press. Reprinted by permission of The University of Michigan Press. Copyright © 1959 by The University of Michigan Press.

Mr. Warren's argument continues into a discussion of Forster's "double vision," his sense of this world and of worlds behind.

Consciousness of form has marked the work of authors otherwise so various as Gide, Joyce, Hemingway, Mrs. Woolf. *Les Faux-Monnayeurs* is a novel analyzing the composition of a novel; each section of *Ulysses* employs a different method and a different style; Hemingway has removed from the novel all save its public or behavioristic device, its dialogue. Mrs. Woolf has subtracted almost all the banks which define the stream of consciousness; she has practiced the limited vision, successive instruments of vision; in *The Waves* she has offered in place of dialogue a series, symphonically arranged, of interior soliloquies. Like Proust's, like Huxley's *Point Counterpoint,* her work seems to aim at musical form—a pattern of recurrent and recurrently enriched motifs.

E.M. Forster has full and appreciative acquaintance with the work of Gide, Proust, Joyce, and Mrs. Woolf; but his personal masters are, rather, Jane Austen, Samuel Butler, and Dostoevski. In his *Aspects of the Novel* (1927) he expounds the Jamesian theory only to reject, or to minimize it. It is dangerous, he thinks, for the writer to take the reader into his confidence about his characters; but "to take your reader into your confidence about the universe is a different thing. It is not dangerous for a novelist to draw back from his characters, as Hardy and Conrad do, and to generalize about the conditions under which he thinks life is carried on." To be sure, the novelist must not anticipate, publicly, that future end of his characters which he must, out of elementary artistic decency, foresee. As the characters develop, the author interprets, concomitantly, their states of sensibility; he must keep his dramatic or factual surprises until they reach, and take on or off their guard, his persons. But it can impair no proper aesthetic faith that the novelist should articulate such observations and insights upon humanity at large as the conduct of his personae may suggest. Indeed, if the novelist be a man of wisdom as well as mimetic power, his imaginative self can assuredly, only with loss, be spared from the dramatis personae. He should move among his characters, though certainly not as man among dolls; he is to be cast as the most deeply seeing member of a company.

Both in theory and in practice Forster declines to restrict the novelist's ancient liberties. The richness of the novel, for him, lies in its range of levels. There is the "story"; then there are the persons of the story who act and speak; then there is the "inner life' of the characters, to be overheard and translated by the author; and, finally, there is the philosophic commentary of the author. Plot, characters, philosophy: each has a life of its own and threatens to expand until it menaces its competitors. If the novel restrict itself to action and speech, it does no more than reduplicate—and with the subtraction of mimes present "in person"—the drama or even the biography. To avoid being less, the novel must be more. "A memoir," says Forster, "is history, it is based on evidence. . . . And it is the function of the novelist to reveal the hidden life at its source: to tell us more than could be known. In daily life we never understand each other; neither complete clairvoyance nor complete confessional exists. . . . But people in a novel can be understood completely by the reader, if the novelist wishes; their inner vision as well as their outer life can be exposed." If, on the other hand, the "inner life" become all, then, like some parts of Proust's *À la Recherche,* the novel turns into a psychological treatise and the persons decompose into their constituent moods and "intermittences." The too intense self-consciousness, the self-consciousness divorced from action, dissolving its object, discovers no residual self. In *Howards End* the Wilcoxes are characterized as people incomplete because they eliminate the personal, cannot say "I"; but Helen Schlegel, overconcerned with the subconscious self, speaking of mankind as puppets whom an invisible showman twitches into love and war, herself risks, though by an opposite method, the elimination of the personal.

To Forster, then, the novel has its own function, that of a persuasive equilibrism: it must balance the claims of the existence and the essence, of personalities and ideas. To Forster, values are more important than facts; and the real values are friendship, intellectual exploration, insight and imagination, the values of the "inner life." But observation and interpretation, though terminal values, are, biologically, parasitic upon the body and the life of action. Forster's own work very satisfyingly preserves this equilibrium both in its repertory of characters and in its narrative method. Even more than the drama, the novel suits the mind which pushes beyond gossip and news but is unable or unwilling to accept a creed. Such a mind habitually generalizes its insights but, through indolence, self-distrust, or skepticism of absolutes, attempts no thoroughgoing system. It goes beyond judgments of John and John's attitude toward Jane to the conception of types—men like John and men who have such attitudes toward women like Jane; its propositions are not universals about men and women but linger halfway between John and "all men." Forster's essays, assembled in *Abinger Harvest* (1936),[1] document the conclusion that he has ideas but no "idea."

In *Howards End* he expresses the view that the complexity of the modern world offers to the best-prepared and best-intentioned but an option of alternative visions: seeing life steadily *or* seeing it whole. His own choice is clearly the latter; like Santayana, he has the excellent manners, the freedom from exaggerated emphases and extravagant exclusions, which traditionally have been the marks of the humanist. Santayana's

---

[1] Like the *Dickinson,* the book of essays is disappointing to a Forsterian. Its eighty constituent parts should, if their author deemed them all worth reprinting, have been collected in five or six thinnish volumes addressed rather to pockets than to library shelves. The two sketches of Howard Sturgis and Ronald Firbank are deft and discerning; "My Wood," a parable on the effects of owning property, is a little masterpiece; "Liberty in England," Forster's address before the International Congress of Writers at Paris, has a finely simple candor and dignity. But too many of the pieces, though stylistically meticulous, produce the impression of a coy sprightliness alien to the novels. Without a mask, pushed to the front of the stage to make his speech, Forster grows self-conscious.

Last Puritan showed unexpected lapses in comprehension. Though it saw value in man as animal (Lord Jim), as epicure (Peter Alden), as social creature (Mario), as high-minded spectator (Oliver), his catholicity failed to see any "life of reason" in New England Brahminism. Forster's range of "partial sympathies" is even greater. Though his cardinal virtues are courage, candor, sympathy, insight, disinterestedness, he can find worth in almost every quality except humbug and muddledom. People are "far more different than is pretended," says wise Margaret Schlegel, who loves her Philistine husband, to her sister Helen, an unmarried mother. "All over the world men and women are worrying because they cannot develop as they are supposed to develop. Here and there they have the matter out, and it comforts them. . . . Develop what you have; love your child. I do not love children. I am thankful to have none. . . . And others—others go further still and move outside humanity altogether. . . . It is part of the battle against sameness. Differences—external differences, planted by God in a single family, so that there may always be color; sorrow perhaps, but color in the daily grey." Only, different as human beings are, they have the common obligation of self-knowledge. Those who "follow neither the heart nor the brain, and march to their destiny by catch-words" are the truly benighted. "The armies are full of pleasant and pious folk. But they have yielded to the only enemy that matters—the enemy within. They have sinned against passion and truth, and vain will be their strife after virtue."

Forster's England is chiefly that of the upper middle classes and the intelligentsia of the universities and London, an England exempt alike from Lady Catherine de Bourgh and from the sadistic peasants of T.F. Powys, a world set on "gold islands." From this world, cruelty and lust are almost absent. The vice of the bourgeois, as Arnold and Carlyle never wearied of pointing out, is self-complacent, unimaginative respectability; the vice of the intelligentsia is another form of Phariseeism: the snobbery of "culture." Poor culture! We recall, as one of its exemplars, Miss Austen's Mary Bennett, who, "being the only plain one in the family, worked hard for knowledge and accomplishments, [and] was always impatient for display." In Forster's novels, "culture" appears as the Rev. Cuthbert Eager at Santa Croce, lecturing to English lady tourists with "prayer books as well as guide-books in their hands"; as Cecil Vyse, who acknowledges the truth of Lucy's impassioned analysis: "You may understand beautiful things, but you don't know how to see them; and you wrap yourself up in art and books and music, and would try to wrap me up"; as poor lower-class Leonard Bast, who read Mr. Ruskin, spouted R.L.S., tinkled a little Grieg, and "hoped to come to Culture suddenly, much as the Revivalist hopes to come to Jesus."

One of Forster's short fantasies concerns the "Celestial Omnibus," driven now by Sir Thomas Browne, now by Jane Austen, now by Dante, and conducting the candidly imaginative to the land of vicarious experi-

ence, where Achilles and Mrs. Gamp and Hamlet and Tom Jones disport
themselves companionably. A "boy" makes the journey in innocence, because he is too ignorant and wise to attribute the experience to his personal "merit." Not so Mr. Bons, Surbiton councilman who owns seven
copies of Shelley. Rich in his spiritual possessions and conscious of how
they set him above his fellows, Mr. Bons invokes the great Dante: "I have
honoured you. I have quoted you. I have bound you in vellum." But in
vain; for poetry is means and not end. Poetry is a spirit, not to be won
like a degree but to be cherished like a flame. And those who, like Mr.
Bons, do not *connect* their conduct with their "culture," will, like Mr.
Bons, topple from the precipice of heaven into a junk-heap of glittering
fragments.

Elementary "culture," the pathos of isolated aspirants, lists, with an
epithet or two apiece, the books it has read. "Give me a list of books,
worth-while ones," it bids the professor; "I want to improve myself."
"How whimsical Lamb is." "Henry James, how subtle." "Should I read
Thackeray next, or Tolstoi?" Culture is a list of books. Then there is
that more rarefied culture which keeps up with the newest ideas and the
latest names, which is allusive and light of touch, which, in order to play
dexterously about the peripheral, takes the central for granted—the
"clever" culture of people who live for books, concerts, art shows, and
chatter about them. "In spite of the season, Mrs. Vyse managed to scrape
together a dinner-party consisting entirely of the grandchildren of famous people. The food was poor, but the talk had a witty weariness. . . .
One was tired of everything, it seemed. One launched into enthusiasm
only to collapse gracefully, and pick oneself up amid sympathetic laughter."

The "real thing" of which "culture" is the parody or the pastiche appears in Forster's novels also. It is represented by Cecil and Tibby, more
completely by Philip, Rickie Elliot, and Mr. Beebe. These men are all
ascetics, scholars, aesthetes; are all, in varying degrees, detached observ-
ers, contemplatives. They are not, Forster makes clear, capable of passion
for women or indeed, perhaps, for persons at all. Tibby is a scholar for
whom the human is tiresome and crude, who desires the passionless air
of knowledge. Ansell is a professional philosopher, who believes it "worth
while to grow old and dusty seeking for truth though truth is unattainable, restating questions that have been stated at the beginning of the
world."

Cecil, the comic hero of *A Room with a View,* is a born curator. Wrong
in seeking to pervert the nature of others, wrong in being so ignorant of
his own nature as to "make love," in himself he is a genuine, if restricted
and indoor, person. The Middle Ages would have understood Cecil and
have made a place for him. "He was mediaeval . . . well educated, well
endowed, and not deficient physically, he remained in the grip of a cer-

tain devil whom the modern world knows as self-consciousness, and whom the mediaeval, with dimmer vision, worshipped as asceticism. A Gothic statue implies celibacy, just as a Greek statue implies fruition." Cecil does not fit "Nature": he is a muff at sports; he is to be imagined, thinks Lucy, as in a drawing-room, one with drawn draperies. His one attempt at love-making turns into high, rueful comedy. "As he approached her, he found time to wish that he could recoil. As he touched her, his gold pince-nez became dislodged and was flattened between them." Cecil's pince-nez was genuine; his passion, secondhand and temporary. Yet, ludicrous as this scene displays him, Cecil is absurd only as he pretends to a range of feelings denied him. Forster's books house few "flat" characters, to be summarized in a gesture or a recurrent phrase; for as we are just about to catalogue them, they turn toward us another side, a side which surprises us but surprises us in a way which is compatible with the sides' being sides of the same person. When Lucy eventually rebels against Cecil's attempt to mold a Vyse out of a Honeychurch, she treats him to a ruthless portrait of himself. He is unexpectedly, convincingly, honest and grateful. He cannot change his character; but, for the first time, he recognizes it.

Where Angels Fear to Tread offers Philip, a contemplative of larger stature. The short book is yet long enough to show Philip's growth from a culture-snob, vain of his taste for art and Italy, vain of his emancipation from British provincialism, into a man of insight and good will. Philip becomes capable of imaginative sympathy with persons as alien as the son of an Italian dentist; he grows in humanity. But his final triumph is self-awareness; and to this recognition he, like Cecil, is helped by a woman whom, in his ignorance, he fancies he desires. He sees all, "appreciates" all, but cannot act. To Caroline Abbott he confesses: "You would be surprised to know what my great events are. Going to the theatre yesterday, talking to you now—I don't suppose I shall ever meet anything greater. I seem fated to pass through the world without colliding with it or moving it—and I'm sure I can't tell you whether the fate's good or evil. I don't die—I don't fall in love . . . you are quite right; life to me is just a spectacle."

This is perhaps the best which "culture," singlehanded, can achieve. To know "the best that has been said and thought in the world"; to know with any fulness, to make one's own, the thought and experience of Aristotle, Lucretius, Racine, Montaigne, Bossuet, Goethe, Sophocles, Plotinus, Confucius, Aristophanes, Dante: that would be a formidable "task." The outlines of the knower's personality would grow vague; he would have no appetite left for life, no capacity for action, no energy for creation; he would be infected with a sense of personal futility. *"Tout est dit: et l'on vient trop tard depuis plus de sept mille ans qu'il y a des hommes, et qui pensent."*

There are times when, by reaction, Forster turns, temporarily, to primitivism—as Philip turns to Gino, as Rickie turns to that child of nature, his half-brother, Stephen. An animal is better than a prig, that parody of the saint; a child is better than a prude. But then Forster sees, too, the virtues of downright, unashamed, healthy extroverts like Henry Wilcox and Son, men devoid of intellectual curiosity and extra-domestic sympathy who can "do" and build. Himself a habituate of the "inner life," Forster feels, as must all half-men aware of their incompleteness, the attraction of his opposites: the child, the animal, the Philistine. Himself English, he has felt the fascination not only of Italy but of Italians—warm, spontaneous Italians, untroubled by scrupulosity or the miasma of introspection, affectionate by impulse not duty.

But Forster's humanity will know all: the earth, passion and friendship, thirst for the truth, and hunger for the Absolute. For him, the "Greek view of life" is the right one; and the problem of morality is not to set mind against body or soul against either, not to antithesize but to reconcile, by proportion and subordination to effect a harmony. In the language of metaphysics, Forster must be described as a "naturalist"; but he is a "naturalist" with wings and humanistic manners and balancing perceptions, one who, like Santayana, believes that everything ideal has a natural basis and that nothing in nature is incapable of an ideal fulfilment.

Is this balance attainable by the individual? That is to ask whether the individual can exemplify the universal man; and the answer seems clear: never completely; often not at all. Yet it is the undeniable nisus of large natures. Forster's character who most closely approaches universality is Margaret Schlegel: though she possesses her own personal mark and stamp, she can comprehend natures as diverse from her own as Mrs. Wilcox, Helen, and Henry; and she achieves the triumph not only of marrying a Philistine but of achieving with him a marriage of spiritual union. Then there is Forster's friend and hero, Lowes Dickinson, who admired the versatility of Goethe, who himself longed to be a poet, a scientist, and a dominating figure in European politics, yet who, doomed to dondom, expanded his vision through his friendships with men of affairs and philosophers and painters. "He solved his particular problem in later life by developing the power of entering into other people's positions while he retained his own. . . ."

Forster's "humanist," Mr. Jackson, warns Rickie that the Greeks were not broad church clergymen, that Sophocles was not a kind of enlightened bishop. If there is a "golden mean," it is not what so often passes for it—tepidity or compromise or apathetic good humor. "The business man who assumes that this life is everything, and the mystic who asserts that it is nothing, fail, on this side and on that, to hit the truth. 'Yes, I see, dear; it's about halfway between,' [the Schlegels'] Aunt Juley had hazarded in earlier years. No; truth, being alive, was not halfway between anything. It was only to be found by continuous excursions into either realm, and though proportion is the final secret, to espouse it at the outset is to insure sterility."

E.M. Forster

by D.S. Savage

Forster is a significant writer. But significant writers are of two kinds. There are those, and they are the greater ones, whose creative work proceeds from an achieved centre of being, and whose continual creativeness is the expression of the constant extension of their grasp upon and penetration into reality. And there are those others, necessarily more numerous, whose work takes its shape from the exteriorization of an inner conflict—which derives, that is to say, from a condition which is antecedent to an achieved inner integration. These latter writers work out, in the course of their art, a more or less significant personal logic, and with its conclusion, if they have not succeeded in achieving a valid inner integration which will remove them to the plane of the creators, they relapse into nonsignificance. Forster is a writer of the latter type, and it will be my purpose here to reveal the significant pattern which underlies his work and his silence. The interest of that pattern lies in the fact that it takes us to the heart of the liberal dilemma, the liberal confusion, and it is the interest of Forster's novels that they reveal very clearly to the perceptive eye the inner motions which preclude an attachment to the liberal outlook.

What are the characteristics of the liberal approach to life? First of all, the liberal mind is a *medium* mind, a mind which fears extremes and which therefore is predisposed towards compromise. It inhabits a middle region of life, that of people, and therefore its characteristic expression is a social and political one; but it is incapable of moving beyond people, as they appear on the social level, to an understanding of the principles and forces which govern their lives, and this incapacity applies both to spiritual and economic realities. The compromising tendency of liberalism causes it to give mental hostages both to the realm of ideals and to the world of affairs, but it is rooted in the latter and in a crisis it is the latter which proves the stronger. Liberalism is a half-hearted creed, born

"E.M. Forster." A slightly cut version of the essay in *The Withered Branch: Six Studies in the Modern Novel* by D.S. Savage. The essay originally appeared in *Now*, edited by George Woodcock; and a shorter version appeared in *Writers of To-Day*, edited by Denys Val Baker. Copyright © 1950 by Eyre and Spottiswoode (Publishers), Ltd. Reprinted by permission of Eyre and Spottiswoode (Publishers), Ltd.; George Woodcock; and John Farquharson, Ltd.

out of stable and comfortable material circumstances, in which it puts its main trust, making a gesture of greater or less sincerity towards spiritual values—but nothing more than a gesture, however sincere. Those spiritual values, however, tend to become something rather less than the ultimate and therefore terrifying ones. The absolute is carefully excluded from the liberal way of life. The gesture towards the spirit is arrested, and modified into a gesture towards culture; that, in turn, resolves itself into a salute to civilization, and in times of stress the process of deterioration will not always stop there. . . .

That "cultured, sensitive and democratic liberalism" is not so innocent, so admirable, and so pleasant as it would represent itself to be becomes apparent only upon a much closer examination than is usually accorded it. Such an examination will be implied in what follows. Liberalism rests upon a fundamental spiritual failure, a spiritual equivocation, a spiritual betrayal. It is the outcome of an absence of faith in the spiritual realities which lie at the back of the variable values to which it presents its dubious salutations. Forster, in *What I Believe,* cleverly attempts to discredit faith by attributing that quality to the blind collective hysteria of the dupes of totalitarianism, thereby making it responsible for the evil and violence in the modern world. This, an age of unfaith, and consequently of greedy materialism and the worship of brute force, is characterized by Forster as "an age of faith." "A child of unbelief," as he elsewhere names himself, he begins his liberal Credo with the sentence, "I do not believe in Belief," and wittily informs us that: "My motto is: 'Lord, I disbelieve—help thou my unbelief.' "

The point of departure for the liberal betrayal cannot be put more clearly than in these words.

I

E.M. Forster's first novel, *Where Angels Fear to Tread,* was published in 1905. In 1907 there appeared *The Longest Journey* and this was followed, in 1908, by *A Room with a View.* Each of these novels is concerned with the dual theme of personal salvation and the conflict of good and evil. Of the three it is *The Longest Journey* which is the most emotionally intense and personal, the others being more objectively conceived novels of social comedy, and here it may be convenient to consider the first and the third novels together—and perhaps this has even a chronological justification, for we are informed by Rose Macaulay that a draft of the first half of *A Room with a View* was made as early as 1903.

In each of these novels we have two opposed worlds or ways of life, and characters who oscillate between the two worlds. In *Where Angels Fear to Tread* the contrast and the conflict are between the world of "Sawston," that is, of smug, respectable conventionality, and that of "Italy," representing the free play of genuine natural feeling. Sawston is personified in Mrs. Herriton, insincere, calculating, cold, and moved by snobbery and her fear of public opinion; Italy by Gino, affectionate, impulsive and natural, a primitive whose very vulgarity has charm and warmth. In the drama that is played out between these opposites, it is Philip Herriton and Caroline Abbott who suffer the conflict between the two sets of values. Italy and the dramatic events which take place there have the effect of drawing out the nobility and passion of Miss Abbott's quiet nature, and it is through her that Philip, hitherto a man who has hovered distantly on the edge of existence, is drawn into life itself and given reality. . . .

In *A Room with a View*, the antithesis is similar, but this time, although the first part of the book is set against the background of Italy, it is the radical Emersons, father and son, who represent life, truth, sincerity. The heroine, Lucy Honeychurch, is torn between the values which they represent and those of the pretentious, bookish Cecil Vyse and the insincere and intriguing Charlotte Bartlett. Lucy has a moment of intense happiness in Italy when she is kissed against a prospect of primroses by George Emerson, but, a victim of the false proprieties as expounded and embodied by her cousin, Charlotte, she is implicated in a system of falsehoods. Persuading herself that she has been outrageously insulted by a "cad," she denies her natural feelings, and shortly after becomes engaged to Cecil Vyse. The Emersons, by a coincidence, come to live near Lucy's family in Sussex, and after a game of tennis, when an incident occurs to remind both George and Lucy of the previous episode in Italy, George kisses her again, and afterwards pleads for her love. Lucy deliberately repulses George, denying and suppressing again her genuine feelings, and that same evening breaks off her engagement to Cecil, after which, lifeless and empty—

> . . . She gave up trying to understand herself, and joined the vast armies of the benighted, who follow neither the heart nor the brain, and march to their destiny by catch-words. The armies are full of pleasant and pious folk. But they have yielded to the only enemy that matters—the enemy within. They have sinned against passion and truth, and vain will be their strife after virtue. As the years pass, they are censured. . . .

In each of these novels, there is a spiritual conflict. In Forster's words, describing Lucy's inner struggle,

> The contest lay not between love and duty. Perhaps there never is such a contest. It lay between the real and the pretended. . . .

The "real," however, seems to be associated with the natural; the "pretended," with the falsities of convention which deny and frustrate the natural impulses and passions.

Italy makes no appearance in *The Longest Journey* (according to Rose Macaulay, ". . . at once the most personal and the most universal of the five novels; and obviously the most autobiographical . . ."), which is divided into three sections, "Cambridge," "Sawston," and "Wiltshire." Once again, these localities have their counterparts in the personalities of certain of the characters. Cambridge, which clearly represents the author's naïve conception of the good life, has its counterpart in the figure of Stewart Ansell; Sawston, again representing insincere conventionality, pretentious "culture" and the worship of the false gods of prestige and success, has its human embodiment in the schoolmaster, Herbert Pembroke, and his sister, Agnes; while Wiltshire, which stands for the basic touchstone of nature, reality, the earth, is humanly projected into the figure of Stephen Wonham, the healthy, unreflective pagan. Rickie, the little lame hero of the book, is drawn in turn into the orbit of each of these worlds and undergoes an inward struggle which, although it is more desperate and emotionally intensified, is not unlike that of Lucy Honeychurch in *A Room with a View*. In many respects the theme of *The Longest Journey* recapitulates that of *Where Angels Fear to Tread* and *A Room with a View:* but its development is more complex, and the spiritual drama more intense. It is, no doubt, this intensity which gives the book its overcharged emotional atmosphere and its consequent queer iridescence as of something faintly morbid or perverse.

For the intensity does not seem justified by the terms of the drama. Which means that the drama itself is emotionally worked up to a point at which it becomes false to the terms of reference within which the mind of the novelist is operating. Throughout all of Forster's writings there is to be seen an unfortunate tendency to lapse, at moments when the author feels the necessity to indicate something beyond the level of human relationships in their social setting (a level upon which alone he is perfectly at ease), into "poetical" vagueness of the most embarrassing kind. An example of this is to be found early in *The Longest Journey*, when Rickie glimpses Agnes and her lover, Gerald Dawes, at a moment of erotic passion.

> Rickie limped away without the sandwiches, crimson and afraid. He thought, "Do such things actually happen?" and he seemed to be looking down coloured valleys. Brighter they glowed, till gods of pure flame were born in them, and then he was looking at pinnacles of virgin snow. While Mr. Pembroke talked, the riot of fair images increased. They invaded his being and lit lamps at unsuspected shrines. Their orchestra commenced in that suburban house, where he had to stand aside for the maid to carry in the luncheon. Music flowed past him like a river. He stood at the springs of creation and heard the primeval monotony. Then an obscure instrument gave out a little phrase. The river continued unheeding. The phrase was repeated, and a listener might know it was a fragment of the Tune of tunes. Nobler instruments accepted it, the clarionet protected, the brass encouraged, and it rose to the surface to the whisper of violins. In full unison was Love born, flame of the flame, flushing the dark river beneath him and the virgin snows above. His wings were infinite, his youth eternal; the sun was a jewel on his finger as he passed it in benediction over the world.

Creation, no longer monotonous, acclaimed him, in widening melody, in brighter radiances. Was Love a column of fire? Was he a torrent of song? Was he greater than either—the touch of a man on a woman?

Forster's books abound in passages of this sort, which, however, represent merely an intensification of his normal "sensitive" and "charming" style. The prevalence of this sort of false, overripe writing indicates some basic uncertainty in Forster's grasp of life, and to apprehend the roots of that uncertainty it is necessary to investigate the disparity between the religious drama which he unfolds and the ultimate principles to which it is referred.

What are the characteristics of this religious drama? First of all, it proffers the possibilities of salvation or of damnation, as we may see in the cases of Philip Herriton and Lucy Honeychurch in the other novels. Philip, granted a vision of "infinite pity and . . . majesty" (which, incidentally, had an erotic source), "underwent conversion. He was saved." Lucy, consequent upon a denial and a lie, joins "the vast armies of the benighted" and "the night received her." In *The Longest Journey* there are indications that the issue of salvation depends upon the acceptance or rejection of a "symbolic moment."

> It seems to me [says Rickie] that here and there in life we meet with a person or incident that is symbolical. It's nothing in itself, yet for the moment it stands for some eternal principle. We accept it, at whatever cost, and we have accepted life. But if we are frightened and reject it, the moment, so to speak, passes; the symbol is never offered again.

The symbol, for Rickie, was his illegitimate half-brother, Stephen. When his kinship with Stephen is revealed to him (although he is then under the mistaken impression that Stephen was the child of his father, whom he hated) he is inexpressibly shocked and disgusted, but his better impulse is to acknowledge him honestly and to inform him of the relationship. The impulse is quashed by Agnes, and Rickie succumbs inwardly to the false life represented by Sawston. When a later opportunity presents itself of acknowledging Stephen, and he again fails at the crisis, we are told that "he remained conscientious and decent, but the spiritual part of him proceeded towards ruin."

His inner ruination continues, but is interrupted by Stephen's appearance at Sawston, coincident with that of Ansell; who—when Stephen is callously turned away by Agnes—publicly denounces the inhumanity and hypocrisy of Rickie; and there follows Rickie's abandonment of the Sawston life and his reconciliation with Stephen, in which we must presumably see his movement towards "salvation."

Stephen, then, in this novel, is the touchstone of reality. He is the "elemental character" who "sees straight through perplexities and complications, who is utterly percipient of the reality behind appearance, both in matters of general truth and of incidents in the story," to quote from Burra's essay. . . . This is how Ansell sums him up . . . :

> A silence, akin to Poetry, invaded Ansell. Was it only a pose to like this man, or was he really wonderful? He was not romantic, for Romance is a figure with outstretched hands, yearning for the unattainable. Certain figures of the Greeks, to whom we continually return, suggested him a little. One expected nothing of him—no purity of phrase nor swift-edged thought. Yet the conviction grew that he had been back somewhere—back to some table of the gods, spread in a field where there is no noise, and that he belonged for ever to the guests with whom he had eaten.

This, then, is the touchstone of reality and of salvation which Forster proposes and it is not difficult to penetrate its glaring inadequacies: it in no way justifies the emotional intensity of the drama which is indicated as taking place in Rickie's soul. Between the poles of conventionality and naturalness there is room for drama of a sort, but not a drama insufflated with the highly pitched emotional excitement of *The Longest Journey*, or even indeed that of the other two novels. This is not to say that the drama which is proposed is intrinsically unreal; only that it is made unreal by being set in such limited and lateral perspectives: the drama is too intense for the slight terms of reference. A spiritual conflict is imported into a naturalistic framework, and the effect is one, inevitably, of sentimentality and falsification.

This confusion of the spiritual and the natural runs throughout the earlier novels. As in D.H. Lawrence (who, however, avoided Forster's irrelevant sweetness and charm), spiritual attributes are conferred upon biological phenomena. Thus in *Where Angels Fear to Tread*, Philip's "conversion" follows upon the erotic emotions stirred in Caroline Abbott by the frankly sensual Gino. Similarly, in *The Longest Journey*, not only is Rickie's personal drama initiated by his witnessing of the erotic passage between Agnes and Gerald Dawes, but the "acceptance" upon which his salvation depends centres around the result of his dead mother's illicit intercourse with her farmer lover—a Lady Chatterley situation. The importance which Forster confers upon sexual passion is shown both by the excessive excitement with which he approaches it, and the way in which he connects it with violent death—the finality of death being utilized to confer something of its own ultimate, absolute character upon the emotion stirred by sex.

To endow conventionality with all the attributes of the powers of darkness is, of course, grossly to overstate the matter. The world represented by the word "Sawston" has genuine undercurrents of evil which we are made to feel, but which are simply not explicable in the terms of Nature versus Convention which are proposed. When we encounter such a sentence as this—

Then he [i.e., Rickie] . . . prayed passionately, for he knew that the conventions would claim him soon . . .

we at once feel the somewhat ridiculous inadequacy of the antithesis which provides the frame of reference for the novel.

Not only in *The Longest Journey* is the question of salvation (raised in the action of the narrative and brought to an arbitrary conclusion there) left with a good many loose ends flying: the same is true of the other novels. What is to happen to Philip Herriton, now that his eyes have been opened to the wonder and beauty of life? What will happen to Lucy and George Emerson now that their difficulties are over and they are happily married? It is hard to see any more finality in their "saved" state than that implied in the insufficient and question-begging symbol, towards the end of *The Longest Journey*, of "Wiltshire"—the life of pastoral satisfactions.

The incompleteness and indeed the reversibility of Forster's moral symbolism is shown in his "realistic" confusion of the attributes of the "good" and "bad" types. Having said, as Burra says, . . . that Forster introduces an "elemental" character into each of his books, whose wisdom "puts into ironic contrast the errors and illusions of the rest," and having pointed out that "In the case of the men the stress is laid on the athletic, of the women on the intuitive," one can point to characters who possess the external evidences of these qualities, and who yet turn out to be on the wrong side of the moral fence. George Emerson, Gino and Stephen may be said to be athletic, and therefore on the side of the "real." But equally athletic, though by no means on the side of the real, are Gerald Dawes and Agnes, while Stewart Ansell, undoubtedly a touchstone of values, is not athletic at all. Similarly in the case of the "intuitive" women. Of them Mrs. Moore and Mrs. Wilcox and perhaps Mrs. Honeychurch are recognizably "good" characters, while Mrs. Failing, a woman of the same basic type, and who possesses the additional symbolical advantage of living in Wiltshire, is as recognizably "bad." One might compare also Cecil Vyse with Philip Herriton and Stewart Ansell. This confusion is true to life, no doubt, but it is not true to the symbolical pattern of the novels, and it is necessary to ask what are the reasons for this ambivalence.

The most plausible explanation of Forster's "realistic" confusion of good and bad types (a confusion which, it must be repeated, is out of place in a symbolical setting) lies in the very plain fact that the middle-class existence which Forster portrays, the life of the irresponsible, moneyed, parasitical bourgeoisie, is false, because it is based upon social falsehood, and nothing can ever be made really right within it. Consequently, no stable system of moral symbolism can be erected upon it.

This is not to say that his characters are by that fact deprived of the possibility of spiritual struggle; only that such a struggle which takes place within a spiritual arena circumscribed by its reference to the framework of their false social order, and whose outcome does not result in an overthrowing or a repudiation of the limits set around their lives by their privileged social and economic position, is thereby rendered devoid of real and radical significance. The life of Forster's characters, as members of the English upper-middle-classes, is based on falsehood because it is based on unearned income, derived from nameless and unmentioned sources, and all their independence, freedom, culture, "personal relationships" are only made possible by this fact. Their lives are lived in a watertight system abstracted from the larger life of society as a whole. They are out of touch with humanity, carefully, though for the most part unconsciously, preserving themselves, by means of their mental circumscriptions and social codes, from all encroachment of the painful and upsetting actualities which make their privileged existence possible. Unlike the rich of other times, their privileges carry with them no burden of responsibility, and thus possess no concrete social sanction. The penalty they pay for their social advantages is a heavy one—a fundamental unreality which vitiates the personal dramas which take place in the closed social circuit to which they are condemned. For an inner spiritual change which affects one's attitude to one or two other selected persons only, and does not extend itself to include every other human being irrespective of social distinction, is invalidated from the start. But at the point at which some attempt to deal with this question would seem necessary, Forster brings his stories to a close.

It is not difficult to perceive the connection existing between the false social circumstances which set limits to reality for the sake of their own perpetuation, and the inhibiting factors which prevent Forster from reaching out to ultimates for the validation of his religious drama. The novelist, despite his perception of the reality of personal struggle towards salvation, is himself unable to transcend the pattern imposed on reality by the self-interest of the class to which he belongs, and instead, therefore, of permitting the drama with which he is concerned to break through the pattern and centre itself within the perspectives of reality, he curtails the perspectives themselves and attempts to persuade himself and his readers that the drama takes place between the poles of Nature and Convention, with Nature filling the place of God, or the Absolute.[1] The novelist's own awareness that this will not justify a real spiritual dynamism in his characters must eventually follow.

[1] Of all the characters in the early novels who represent "the real" as against "the pretended," not one derives his sanction from any other than a natural principle. Stephen and Gino are a direct appeal to biological, not to say physiological, values. In the case of Stephen it is made clear that he is a crude atheist, while Ansell is evidently an ethical materialist. Old Mr. Emerson, a religious figure, is an old-fashioned agnostic radical. The clearest insight, however, into Forster's religiosity is to be derived from a study of his early short stories where Nature is deified as Pan and conventionalism is contrasted with the amoral universe of dryads, mermaids and satyrs.

II

It is possibly the realization of something of this which led Forster to abandon the narrow personal drama and to embrace the social issues which are clearly displayed in his fourth novel, *Howards End* (1910). There is no doubt whatever as to the social orientation of this novel and its characterization, nor as to its bearing upon the logic of Forster's development. From the point reached in *The Longest Journey* there were two possible paths for one in Forster's situation: either to affirm the reality of the spiritual, and thus to justify the drama of personal salvation, by placing the individual (and thus by inference his social circumstances) in the ultimate perspectives of existence; or to affirm the primary reality of the social and to reduce the spiritual to an epiphenomenon dependent upon the social pattern. The first alternative would have made possible a continuation and development of the personal drama; and thus, conceivably, the transformation of Forster into a genuine creator: the second could only have necessitated a transition from the personal to the social level, a movement from the centre to the periphery; which was, in fact, the result.

Howards End must be interpreted from this point of view. Here is an evidently allegorical contrast between the inner world of personal existence, represented by the cultured sisters Helen and Margaret Schlegel, and the outer world of the practical organization of living represented by the business-like, British-to-the-backbone, empire-building Wilcoxes. But before we move on to a consideration of the relationship between the two families, the focal point of the novel must be considered.

That focal point is money. Hardly are the Schlegels introduced before the subject of their investments is touched upon. Money, indeed, is the *leit-motif* which accompanies the Schlegels throughout the book. And it is poverty, in the character of Leonard Bast, which underscores their wealth and culture. The significance of this bringing to the surface of what, in order to permit the strictly personal drama, had hitherto been kept in concealment, hardly needs to be emphasized. *Howards End* is in one of its aspects a justification of economic privilege; but the recognition of the individual's dependence upon social circumstances destroys the possibility of the drama of personal salvation, and substitutes the drama of social relationships. . . .

The argument of *Howards End,* at all times implicit and at times declared, is that culture and the good life depend upon economic security, which in the capitalistic world of the time means privilege. "To trust people is a luxury in which only the wealthy can indulge; the poor cannot afford it"—such statements as this are intermittent in the early parts of the book. Because he does not enjoy the financial advantages of the Schlegels, Leonard Bast's aspirations towards culture are made to appear pathetic in their hopelessness. But the character of Leonard Bast

is not the result of authentic, disinterested observation of life; he is unconsciously falsified, in a manner which will be considered below, to fit
within the preconceived interpretation of reality which underpins the
structure of the novel. . . .

The respective positions of Leonard Bast and Henry Wilcox have an
obvious symbolic importance, in that the leanings of the Schlegel sisters
are divided between the two. The impulsive and idealistic Helen reacts
vehemently against Mr. Wilcox, and her reaction drives her towards
Leonard Bast, who has suffered as a result of the business-man's human
irresponsibility (and whose character as a *victim* is further emphasized
by the revelation that his bedraggled wife was once Mr. Wilcox's mistress).
Margaret, on the other hand, wiser and more level-headed, so we are
told, is drawn towards the Wilcox family and led to associate herself with
the values they represent.

> "If Wilcoxes hadn't worked and died in England for thousands of years,
> you and I couldn't sit here without having our throats cut. There would
> be no trains, no ships to carry us literary people about in, no fields even.
> Just savagery. No—perhaps not even that. Without their spirit life might
> never have moved out of protoplasm. More and more do I refuse to draw my
> income and sneer at those who guarantee it."

The dramatic action of the book develops out of the schism which
takes place between the Schlegel sisters as each moves further along her
chosen path, Margaret towards the acceptance of the "outer life," expressed in her engagement to the widowed Mr. Wilcox, and Helen towards her pursuit of a somewhat vaguely conceived "ideal." The scales
are, however, heavily weighted against Helen, who is used as a mere foil
to her sister's maturer wisdom. That Helen's antagonism to her sister's
engagement to Mr. Wilcox is a modified one, and that inwardly she is
reconciled to it and even approves of it, appears from a conversation between the sisters following an outburst of Helen's to Mr. Wilcox on the
subject of his responsibility for the misfortunes of Leonard Bast. . . .
The morality of the story and the conclusion we are supposed to draw
from it are plain. "Only connect . . ." exhorts the book's epigraph;
and Margaret it is, we are asked to believe, who accomplishes the connection.

In this novel, however, once again Forster's work suffers artistically as
the result of the confusion between the symbolical and the realistic treatment of his subject. A clearer and deeper mind, we can safely assume,
taking the theme of the relationship of the inner life to the outer, would
manipulate somewhat different symbols from "Wilcoxes" and "Schlegels"
and would reach somewhat different conclusions from those of *Howards
End*. For Forster has not in fact stated the real issue either helpfully or
sincerely. What he has succeeded in doing, and in doing quite clearly
enough, is to reveal, in the pre-determined and therefore falsified treat-

ment of his subject, the central predicament and equivocation inherent
in the compromising liberal mentality.

The crucial falsification is not that of the characters of the Wilcoxes,
who are presented honestly and objectively enough, but of the Schlegels
and Leonard Bast. And it is here, perhaps, that we touch upon the
psychological compulsion which inclined Forster's mind towards his
admixture of the symbolical and the realistic—namely, in its effect in
securing the falsification of symbolical truth necessary for the adaptation
of the realities represented by the words "culture" and "poverty" to the
far from disinterested preconceptions of the bourgeois liberal point of
view.

"It is private life that holds out the mirror to infinity; personal intercourse, and that alone, that ever hints at a personality beyond our daily
vision." Such, in characteristically Forsterian phraseology, is the Schlegel
viewpoint. Suppose we grant, then, what is so almost squeamishly
proffered—that, symbolically, the Schlegels represent the inner life of
personality in contrast to the outer life of organization represented by
the Wilcoxes. The question follows: Can there in fact ever be such a
reconciliation between the two as is symbolized by Margaret's marriage to
Mr. Wilcox? To speak more explicitly, can Culture only save itself from
inward debility by an alliance with the State, can the life of the spirit
maintain and strengthen itself only by a compromise with the Prince of
this world? [2] Is such a reconciliation, or compromise, a spiritual achievement or a betrayal?

From the spiritual, personal and cultural point of view it is clearly a
betrayal; it is the equivocal and deluded attempt to serve two masters
which is spoken of in the New Testament. That Forster is uneasy about
this is shown not only by his splitting of the Schlegel viewpoint into two,
but also by his hesitant treatment of the relations between Margaret and
Mr. Wilcox, for their relationship crashes on a critical issue, and is
only saved, rather unconvincingly, by the entirely fortuitous circumstances which make Henry Wilcox, at the last moment, a "broken man,"
and drive him humbly to his wife for protection.

What, indeed, is this "connection," but the bridging of the two worlds
which were, in the earlier novels, held apart as spiritual antitheses: the
world of falsity and convention and the world of the genuine and natural: the "pretended" and the "real"? Twists of presentation aside, in
what essential respect can the Wilcoxes be said to differ from the Pembrokes of *The Longest Journey*? Yet while, in the earlier novel, for the
sake of the personal drama which is enacted between those antitheses,
the Pembrokes are represented as something at all costs to be eschewed
and shunned, in the later book, where the personal drama gives place to

---

[2] *Vide* Chapter XXVII: "Talk as one would, *Mr. Wilcox was king of this world,* the
superman, with his own morality, whose head remained in the clouds." (My italics.)

the social, the same type, with a few changes, is represented as admirable and to be courted.

What is the reason for this change of attitude and the decision to compromise? The answer, it is not difficult to perceive, lies in the weakness and invalidity of the inner life, of "the real," as conceived by Forster, which, presented in naturalistic terms, has not sufficient inner vitality to maintain itself as a centre of spiritual energy in independence of the outer region of practical life. Forster's fundamental error consists of invoking the spiritual principle and then referring it for its ultimate sanction not to God, to the supernatural—a resort which would have had the effect of thoroughly disequilibrizing Forster's mental pattern and bringing it to a new and revolutionary centrality—but to Nature. That Forster's ethical naturalism will not bear the spiritual burdens which are placed upon it we have already seen. This inability to support the personal values represented by the Schlegels by an appeal to any higher order of being than that embodied in the mundanely "mysterious" figure of the first Mrs. Wilcox with her tiresome wisp of hay (with the dew still on it) deprives the antithesis between Schlegels and Wilcoxes of its absolute character and therefore of all real value as a statement of the relationship between the inner and outer realms of existence—or the realm of subjectivity and that of objectivization. For neither can the Schlegel sisters really be accepted as adequately symbolizing the life of the spirit, nor can Leonard Bast be regarded as a truthful representation of the urge towards culture unsupported by economic privilege. The Schlegels are simply what they are "realistically" represented to be— two specimens of the leisured bourgeois parasite upon culture. And all that the book leaves us with is a statement of the real relations between "cultured, sensitive and democratic' liberalism and the capitalistic structure of Edwardian society which permits and guarantees its harmless, ineffectual and even charming existence.

Here it is that Forster's confusion of symbolical and realistic treatment serves the purposes of so doctoring the issue that it conforms to the pre-requirements of an outlook obviously conditioned by its liberal bourgeois background. Forster's realistic presentation of the Schlegels enables him to get around the responsibility of declaring that his novel is an allegory of the inner life. Quite so. But if the Schlegels are only— the Schlegels, nothing more or less, then the book is deprived of inner significance. Forster's confused method enables him to retain the overtones of symbolical significance while presenting an apparently straightforward realistic narrative: it is no wonder that the book has been popular.

Perhaps we may exonerate Forster of the charge of sinister intent in deliberately falsifying his presentation of the Schlegels, at the price of denying them the symbolical significance which they are presumed to possess. But it is much more difficult to avoid making the charge in the case of his presentation of Leonard Bast; and there is the further reflection to which this leads, namely, that Leonard is presented in such a way as to emphasize the Schlegels' claim to symbolical significance as the bearers of cultural values and the inner life. For the implication of Leonard's failure, owing to inferior social advantages, to attain the inner life, is that the inner life itself is made possible only by the possession of social advantages such as those the Schlegels enjoy, and from this it follows that, in the author's mind, the Schlegels do therefore possess symbolical significance.

Forster's evident determination that Leonard Bast should be made to fit the preconception that culture is secondary to economic security leads him to draw a portrait which is the least convincing fabrication in the book, and the one which most plainly calls into question the author's fundamental seriousness and responsibility as an artist. Now, it simply is not true that an inferior social position automatically deprives its victim of the possibility of attaining to the inner life, any more than it is true that the possession of social advantages guarantees spiritual development. It is not even true that the average rich man is, as Forster states, more courteous, intelligent and lovable than the average poor man.

The wretched Leonard is a lay figure, an effigy made to walk and talk in such a way as to bolster up the liberal philosophy which inspires the book. For culture is *not* dependent upon wealth; it is only to the parasites of the spirit that it appears as an object which can be externally appropriated. Nor can Forster's pressing of this point home find any response in the mind of the genuine champion of the dispossessed, for the depth of his concern with the sufferings of the underprivileged masses may be judged from the fact that it is Henry Wilcox with whom Margaret, "keen to derive the modern capitalist from the warriors and hunters of the past," "connects."

Leonard is disposed of by death, and his elimination glossed over with an outburst of Forster's special lyricism:

> . . . the time for telegrams and anger was over, and it seemed wisest that the hands of Leonard should be folded on his breast and be filled with flowers. Here was the father; leave it at that. Let Squalor be turned into Tragedy, whose eyes are the stars, and whose hands hold the sunset and the dawn.

III

The foregoing delineation of the inner development of Forster's mind as revealed in his novels should have clarified the nature of the compromise or betrayal which lies at the root of "cultured, sensitive and democratic liberalism," a compromise which cannot but vitiate its perpetrator's grasp of reality and deprive his mind of creative purpose. But if my interpretation of the interior dialectic of Forster's novels has any validity, then it follows that *A Passage to India* (1924) must have its relation to it. What, briefly, is that relationship?

With the resolution of the conflict between what is called, in *A Room with a View,* "the real and the pretended," signified by the union of the Schlegels with the Wilcoxes, the novelist's own inner thought-conflict, expressing the inner conflict which lies at the bottom of all the novels, comes to an end, and there is no longer any imperative urge towards fictional creation. Forster has exhausted his theme, and the dramatic materials are lacking. More, his interest has moved outward, peripherally, from the personal drama to a concern with the generalized problems of society, and it is now possible to speak of him (*vide* Burra) as "an artist on the fringe of social reform." The only way in which the novelist can finally exploit his basic situation is by transporting his mechanical dramatic apparatus to some external situation which it happens approximately and fortuitously to fit. And so, in *A Passage to India,* we have the Anglo-Indian world of Turtons and Burtons on the one side and on the other that of Aziz and his compatriots, with Cyril Fielding, the liberal educationalist, in between, and Mrs. Moore, the counterpart of Mrs. Wilcox, anomalously bridging both worlds. But the apparatus hardly fits the drama, which, indeed, exiguous as it is, takes place, not in the battlefield of any individual soul, but on the plane of external action and political issues, where it is brought only to a precarious and inconclusive termination. The conflict is external to the author's mind.

A Passage to India is written at the extreme edge of Forster's creative impulse. It is hard to see how any but a mechanical and inwardly meaningless work of fiction could have succeeded it, and the fact that it has been followed by silence need cause us no great surprise. Certain features of the novel, however, have an interest in the light of the interpretation of Forster which I have proposed.

If the book can be said to have a hero, that hero must be Cyril Fielding, a character who evidently embodies his creator's own outlook upon life. In Fielding, we find a union of the qualities seen as separate in *Howards End*. Fielding is humane, cultured, enlightened, progressive, but he is also capable, reliable, and self-assured: he has a sense of the importance of "personal relationships" but he also has "grit" and his hands are definitely "on the ropes." Ideally, then, he should be an harmonious figure. Yet it seems that there is some dissatisfaction on his author's part with the finality of the values which he embodies.

> . . . he felt dubious and discontented suddenly, and wondered whether he was really and truly successful as a human being. After forty years' experience he had learnt to manage his life and make the best of it on advanced European lines, had developed his personality, explored his limitations, controlled his passions—and he had done it all without becoming either pedantic or worldly. A creditable achievement; but as the moment passed, he felt he ought to have been working at something else the whole

time—he didn't know at what, never would know, never could know, and that was why he felt sad.

Those feelings of self-dissatisfaction are again touched on at the end of the book, where Fielding is speaking to Aziz of his marriage to Mrs. Moore's daughter, Stella, who, he feels, unlike himself, is "after something"—the "something," whatever it is which is included in this vague gesture, being that, evidently, which is outside the scope of his limited, rationalistic scheme of life.

But the most significant factor in the novel is the emotional background provided by the Marabar Caves, around which the action centres. It is the visit of Aziz, Mrs. Moore and Miss Quested to the caves which precipitates the drama, and throughout the novel the echoing *"Boum-boum"* of the caves supplies an insistent undercurrent to the moods and thoughts of the characters.

The caves' horrible echo, is, however, a more elaborate repetition of something which has evidently lurked always at the edge of Forster's mind, for it has found expression in previous writings. It is indicated by the description of the infernal region in which a character in an early story finds himself after death, through his smug, unheroic life; and it is indicated also in the metaphor of the goblins "walking quietly over the universe" to describe the Beethoven Symphony in *Howards End*. ("Panic and emptiness," the message of the goblins, being the words which Helen has previously applied to the inner life of the Wilcoxes.) The caves reiterate the same message of meaninglessness and nullity, but more insistently and overpoweringly. The echo murmurs: "Pathos, piety, courage—they exist, but are identical, and so is filth. Everything exists, nothing has value." And the terror of the Marabar lay in the fact that it "robbed infinity and eternity of their vastness, the only quality that accommodates them to mankind." Not only does the echo of the caves prolong itself throughout the story to which it provides such a menacing undertone, but it has the effect of undermining and disintegrating Mrs. Moore's hold on life, and ultimately, of destroying her. When we recollect that Mrs. Moore is to *A Passage to India* what Mrs. Wilcox is to *Howards End*—that she is the "elemental character" who represents what appears to be the highest value to which Forster can appeal to sanction his interpretation of life, the metaphorical implications of her disintegration and its occasion are ominous, to say the very least. Nor is there anything in Forster's occasional and miscellaneous writings of the past twenty years to dispel the misgivings to which a consideration of the sequence of his novels, ending on this ominous note, gives rise.

Forster and the Liberal Imagination

by Lionel Trilling

E.M. Forster is for me the only living novelist who can be read again and again and who, after each reading, gives me what few writers can give us after our first days of novel-reading, the sensation of having learned something. I have wanted for a long time to write about him and it gives me a special satisfaction to write about him now, for a consideration of Forster's work is, I think, useful in time of war.

In America Forster has never established a great reputation. Perhaps his readers are more numerous than I suppose, but at best they make a quiet band, and his novels—excepting A Passage to India, and that for possibly fortuitous reasons—are still esoteric with us. In England, although scarcely a popular writer, he is widely known and highly regarded; still, it is not at all certain whether even in England he is properly regarded and truly known. Some of the younger writers—among them Christopher Isherwood and Cyril Connolly—hold him in great esteem and have written well about him; I.A. Richards' remarks about Forster are sometimes perceptive, Elizabeth Bowen has spoken of him briefly but well, and the late Peter Burra's essay (now the introduction to the Everyman edition of A Passage to India) is a sound appreciation. But both Rose Macaulay and Virginia Woolf, who write of Forster with admiration, perceive the delicacy but not the cogency of his mind. As for the judgment canonized in The Concise Cambridge History of English Literature, it is wholly mistaken; the "shy, unworldly quality" of work "almost diffidently presented" by a man who is "at heart a scholar" simply does not exist. The author of this comment has taken an irony literally and has misinterpreted a manner.

It is Forster's manner, no doubt, that prevents a greater response to his work. That manner is comic; Forster owes much to Fielding, Dickens, Meredith and James. And nowadays even the literate reader is likely to be unschooled in the comic tradition and unaware of the comic seriousness. The distinction between the serious and the solemn is an old one, but it must be made here again to explain one of the few truly serious novelists of our time. Stendhal believed that gaiety was one of the marks of the healthy intelligence, and we are mistakenly sure that Stendhal was wrong. We suppose that there is necessarily an intellectual "depth" in the deep tones of the organ; it is possibly the sign of a deprivation—our suspicion of gaiety in art perhaps signifies an inadequate seriousness in ourselves. A generation charmed by the lugubrious—once in O'Neill, Dreiser and Anderson, now in Steinbeck and Van Wyck Brooks—is perhaps fleeing from the trivial shape of its own thoughts.

Forster is not only comic, he is often playful. He is sometimes irritating in his refusal to be great. Greatness in literature, even in comedy, seems to have some affinity with greatness in government and war, suggesting power, a certain sternness, a touch of the imperial and imperious. But Forster, who in certain moods might say with Swift, "I have hated all nations, professions and communities, and all my love is for individuals," fears power and suspects formality as the sign of power. "Distrust every enterprise that requires new clothes" is the motto one of his characters inscribes over his wardrobe. It is a maxim of only limited wisdom; new thoughts sometimes need new clothes and the seriousness of Forster's intellectual enterprise is too often reduced by the unbuttoned manner he affects. The quaint, the facetious and the chatty sink his literary criticism below its proper level; they diminish the stature of his short fiction and they even touch, though they never actually harm, the five novels; the true comic note sometimes drops to mere chaff and we now and then wish that the style were less comfortable and more arrogant.

But while these lapses have to be reckoned with, they do not negate the validity of the manner of which they are the deficiency or excess. Forster's manner is the agent of a moral intention which can only be carried out by the mind *ondoyant et divers* of which Montaigne spoke. What Forster wants to know about the human heart must be caught by surprise, by what he calls the "relaxed will," and if not everything can be caught in this way, what is so caught cannot be caught in any other way. Rigor will not do, and Forster uses the novel as a form amenable to the most arbitrary manipulation. He teases his medium and plays with his genre. He scorns the fetish of "adequate motivation," delights in surprise and melodrama and has a kind of addiction to sudden death. Guiding his stories according to his serious whim—like the anonymous lady, he has a whim of iron—Forster takes full and conscious responsibility for his novels, refusing to share in the increasingly dull assumption of the contemporary novelist, that the writer has nothing to do with the story he tells and that, *mirabile dictu,* through no intention of his own, the story has chosen to tell itself through him. Like Fielding, he shapes his prose for comment and explanation, and like Fielding he is not above an explanatory footnote. He summarizes what he is going to show, introduces new themes when and as it suits him to do so, is not awed by the sacred doctrine of "point of view" and, understanding that verisimilitude, which more than one critic has defended from his indifference, can guarantee neither pleasure nor truth, he uses exaggeration and improbability. As a result, the four novels up to *A Passage to India* all suggest that they have been written after a close application to the dramatic principles of *The Winter's Tale*.

In all this Forster is not bizarre. He simply has the certainty of the great novelists that any novel is a made-up thing and that a story, in order to stand firmly on reality, needs to keep no more than one foot on probability. Against this belief is opposed our increasingly grim realistic prejudice: we have learned to believe that *The Winter's Tale* is great poetry but bad dramaturgy. Our literal and liberal intelligence jibs at an interruption of sixteen years, at what we are convinced is an improbability not only of event but of emotion—we think it wrong that Mamillius and Antigonus should die so casualty, or that anyone should "exit, pursued by a bear," or that Polixenes should fly into his brutal rage after having so charmingly taken part in Perdita's great flower scene, for it confuses us that good and evil should co-exist and alternate. To accept Forster we have to know that *The Winter's Tale* is dramatically and morally sound and that improbability is the guide to life.

This means an affirmation of faith in the masters of the novel, in James, Meredith, Dickens—and in Hawthorne, whose notion of the "romance" (for he was forced to distinguish his own kind of novel from the more literal kind) is here so suggestive.

> When a writer calls his work a Romance, it need hardly be observed that he wishes to claim a certain latitude, both as to its fashion and material, which he would not have felt himself entitled to assume had he professed to be writing a Novel. The latter form of composition is presumed to aim at a very minute fidelity, not merely to the possible, but to the probable and ordinary course of man's experience. The former—while, as a work of art, it must rigidly subject itself to laws, and while it sins unpardonably so far as it may swerve aside from the truth of the human heart—has fairly a right to present that truth under circumstances, to a great extent, of the writer's own choosing or creation.

Hawthorne is no doubt the greater artist and perhaps the greater moralist, yet Forster stands with him in his unremitting concern with moral realism. All novelists deal with morality, but not all novelists, or even all good novelists, are concerned with moral realism, which is not the awareness of morality itself but of the contradictions, paradoxes and dangers of living the moral life. To the understanding of the inextricable tangle of good and evil and of how perilous moral action can be, Hawthorne was entirely devoted. Henry James followed him in this devotion and after James, though in a smaller way, comes Forster, who can say of one of his characters that he was "cursed with the Primal Curse, which is not the knowledge of good and evil, but the knowledge of good-and-evil."

It is here that the precise point of Forster's manner appears. Forster's plots are always sharp and definite, for he expresses difference by means of struggle, and struggle by means of open conflict so intense as to flare into melodrama and even into physical violence. Across each of his novels runs a barricade; the opposed forces on each side are Good and Evil in the forms of Life and Death, Light and Darkness, Fertility and Sterility, Courage and Respectability, Intelligence and Stupidity—all the great absolutes that are so dull when discussed in themselves. The comic manner, however, will not tolerate absolutes. It stands on the barricade and casts doubt on both sides. The fierce plots move forward to grand simplicities but the comic manner confuses the issues, forcing upon us the difficulties and complications of the moral fact. The plot suggests eternal division, the manner reconciliation; the plot speaks of clear certainties, the manner resolutely insists that nothing can be quite so simple. "Wash ye, make yourselves clean," says the plot, and the manner murmurs, "If you can find the soap."

Now, to the simple mind the mention of complication looks like a kind of malice, and to the mind under great stress the suggestion of something "behind" the apparent fact looks like a call to quietism, like mere shilly-shallying. And this is the judgment, I think, that a great many readers of the most enlightened sort are likely to pass on Forster. For he stands in a peculiar relation to what, for want of a better word, we may call the liberal tradition, that loose body of middle-class opinion which includes such ideas as progress, collectivism and humanitarianism.

To this tradition Forster has long been committed—all his novels are politically and morally tendentious and always in the liberal direction. Yet he is deeply at odds with the liberal mind, and while liberal readers can go a long way with Forster, they can seldom go all the way. They can understand him when he attacks the manners and morals of the British middle class, when he speaks out for spontaneity of feeling, for the virtues of sexual fulfillment, for the values of intelligence; they go along with him when he speaks against the class system, satirizes soldiers and officials, questions the British Empire and attacks business ethics and the public schools. But sooner or later they begin to make reservations and draw back. They suspect Forster is not quite playing their game; they feel that he is challenging *them* as well as what they dislike. And they are right. For all his long commitment to the doctrines of liberalism, Forster is at war with the liberal imagination.

Surely if liberalism has a single desperate weakness, it is an inadequacy of imagination: liberalism is always being surprised. There is always the liberal work to do over again because disillusionment and fatigue follow hard upon surprise, and reaction is always ready for that moment of liberal disillusionment and fatigue—reaction never hopes, despairs or suffers amazement. Liberalism likes to suggest its affinity with science, pragmatism and the method of hypothesis, but in actual conduct it requires "ideals" and absolutes; it prefers to make its alliances only when it thinks it catches the scent of Utopia in parties and governments, the odor of sanctity in men; and if neither is actually present, liberalism makes sure to supply it. When liberalism must act with some degree of anomaly—and much necessary action is anomalous—it insists that it is acting on perfect theory and is astonished when anomaly then appears.

The liberal mind is sure that the order of human affairs owes it a simple logic: good is good and bad is bad. It can understand, for it invented and named, the moods of optimism and pessimism, but the mood that is the response to good-and-evil it has not named and cannot understand. Before the idea of good-and-evil its imagination fails; it cannot accept this improbable paradox. This is ironic, for one of the charter-documents of liberalism urges the liberal mind to cultivate imagination enough to accept just this improbability.

> Good and evil we know in the field of this world grow up together almost inseparably; and the knowledge of good is so involved and interwoven with the knowledge of evil, and in so many cunning resemblances hardly to be discerned, that those confused seeds which were imposed upon Psyche as an incessant labor to cull out, and sort asunder, were not more intermixed. It was from out the rind of one apple tasted, that the knowledge of good and evil, as two twins cleaving together, leaped forth into the world. And perhaps this is that doom which Adam fell into of knowing good and evil, that is to say of knowing good by evil.

And the irony is doubled when we think how well the great conservative minds have understood what Milton meant. Dr. Johnson and Burke and, in a lesser way at a later time, Fitzjames Stephen, understood the mystery of the twins; and Matthew Arnold has always been thought the less a liberal for his understanding of them. But we of the liberal connection have always liked to play the old intellectual game of antagonistic principles. It is an attractive game because it gives us the sensation of thinking, and its first rule is that if one of two opposed principles is wrong, the other is necessarily right. Forster will not play this game; or, rather, he plays it only to mock it.

This indifference to the commonplaces of liberal thought makes the very texture of Forster's novels and appeared in the first of them. The theme of *Where Angels Fear to Tread* is the violent opposition between British respectability and a kind of pagan and masculine integration. D.H. Lawrence, who played the old game of antagonistic principles for all it was worth—and it was worth something in his hands—gave us many characters like Forster's Gino Carella, characters who, like Gino, were cruel (the scene of Gino's cruelty is, incidentally, one of the most remarkable in modern fiction) or, like Gino, indifferent to the "higher" and romantic emotions. But here Lawrence always stopped; from this point on all his effort went to intensifying his picture, and by this he no doubt gained, as against Forster, in sheer coercive power. For the poor, lost, respectable British people, Gino may serve as the embodiment of the masculine and pagan principle, but Forster knows that he is also coarse, dull, vain, pretentious, facilely polite and very much taken with the charms of respectability.

And it is irritating to be promised a principle and then to be given only an hypothesis. The hypothesis, having led us to criticize respectability, is useful, but we had wanted it to be conclusive. And Forster refuses to be conclusive. No sooner does he come to a conclusion than he must unravel it again. In *A Room with a View*, to take another example, he leads us to make the typical liberal discovery that Miss Bartlett, the poor relation who thinks she is acting from duty, is really acting from a kind of malice—she has been trying to recruit the unawakened heroine into "the armies of the benighted, who follow neither the heart nor the brain." But Forster does not stop at this conventionality, even though in 1908 it was not quite so conventional. For when the heroine at last fulfills her destiny, deserts Miss Bartlett and marries the man she had unconsciously loved (this is, to all appearance, a very modest little novel), she comes to perceive that in some yet more hidden way Miss Bartlett had really desired the union. And we have been prepared for this demonstration of the something still further "behind" the apparent by the action of the tolerant and enlightened clergyman, Mr. Beebe, who has ceased to be the angel of light and has set himself against the betrothal.

Forster's insistence on the double turn, on the something else that lies behind, is sometimes taken for "tolerance," but although it often suggests forgiveness (a different thing), it almost as often makes the severest judgments. And even when it suggests forgiveness it does not spring so much from gentleness of heart as from respect for two facts co-existing, from the moral realism that understands the one apple tasted. Forster can despise Gerald of *The Longest Journey* because Gerald is a prig and a bully, but he can invest Gerald's death with a kind of primitive dignity, telling us of the maid-servants who weep, "They had not liked Gerald, but he was a man, they were women, he had died." And after Gerald's death he can give Agnes Pembroke her moment of tragic nobility, only to pursue her implacably for her genteel brutality.

So much moral realism is rare enough to be a kind of surprise, and Forster, as I have said, likes to work with surprises mild or great. "Gerald died that afternoon," is the beginning of a chapter which follows immediately upon a description of Gerald full of superabundant life. We have to stand unusually far back from Forster's characters not to be startled when they turn about, and the peculiar pleasure to be had from his books is that of a judicious imperturbability. He is always shocking us by removing the heroism of his heroes and heroines; in *A Passage to India*, Mrs. Moore, of whom we had expected high actions, lets herself

be sent away from the trial at which her testimony would have been
crucial; Cyril Fielding, who as a solitary man had heroically opposed
official ideas, himself becomes official when he is successful and married;
and Dr. Aziz cannot keep to his role of the sensitive and enlightened
native. It is a tampering with the heroic in the manner not of Lytton
Strachey but of Tolstoy, a kind of mithridate against our being surprised by life. Let us not deceive ourselves, Forster seems to say, it is with
just such frailties as Mrs. Moore and Mr. Fielding, and with and for such
unregeneracies as Dr. Aziz that the problem of, let us say, India must
be solved. The moments of any man's apparent grace are few, any man
may have them and their effects are not easily to be calculated. It is on
a helter-skelter distribution of grace that Forster pins what hopes he has;
but for years after *A Passage to India*—it is still his latest novel—he has
had the increasing sense of possible doom.

Perhaps it is because he has nothing of the taste for the unconditioned
—Nietzsche calls it the worst of all tastes, the taste that is always being
fooled by the world—that Forster has been able to deal so well with the
idea of class. The liberal mind has in our time spoken much of this idea
but has failed to believe in it. The modern liberal believes in categories
and wage-scales and calls these class. Forster knows better, and in
Howards End shows the conflicting truths of the idea—that on the one
hand class is character, soul and destiny, and that on the other hand class
is not finally determining. He knows that class may be truly represented
only by struggle and contradiction, not by description, and preferably by
moral struggle in the heart of a single person. When D.H. Lawrence
wrote to Forster that he had made "a nearly deadly mistake glorifying
those *business* people in *Howards End.* Business is no good," he was in-
dulging his own taste for the unconditioned. It led him to read Forster
inaccurately and it led him to make that significant shift from "business
people" to "business." But Forster, who is too worldly to suppose that
we can judge people without reference to their class, is also too worldly
to suppose that we can judge class-conditioned action until we make a
hypothetical deduction of the subject's essential humanity. It is exactly
because Forster can judge the "business people" as he does, and because
he can judge the lower classes so without sentimentality, that he can
deal firmly and intelligently with his own class, and if there is muddle
in *Howards End*—and the nearly allegorical reconciliation is rather
forced—then, in speaking of class, clear ideas are perhaps a sign of ignorance, muddle the sign of true knowledge; surely *Howards End* stands
with *Our Mutual Friend* and *The Princess Casamassima* as one of the
great comments on the class struggle.

To an American, one of the most notable things about Forster's work
is the directness and consciousness of its connection with tradition. We
know of Forster that he is a Hellenist but not a "classicist," that he loves
Greece in its mythical and naturalistic aspects, that Plato has never meant

much to him, perhaps because he mistrusts the Platonic drive to the
absolute and the Platonic judgment of the body and the senses. He dislikes the Middle Ages and all in Dante that is medieval. He speaks of
himself as a humanist and traces his descent to Erasmus and Montaigne.
He is clearly in the romantic line, yet his admiration for Goethe and
Shelley is qualified; Beethoven is a passion with him but he distrusts
Schumann. He has no faith in the regenerative power of Christianity and
he is frequently hostile to the clergy, yet he has a tenderness for religion
because it expresses, though it does not solve, the human mystery; in this
connection it is worth recalling that he once projected a book on Samuel
Butler. I list these preferences of Forster's not because I wish to bound
his intellectual life—so brief a list could not do that—but because enu-
merating them will help to suggest how hard it would be to name an
American novelist whose connection with intellectual tradition is equally
clear. In America the opinion still prevails, though not so strongly as it
once did, that a conscious relation with the past can only debilitate a
novelist's powers, dull his perceptions and prevent his experience of life.

Yet if we test the matter we must come to a contrary conclusion.
Sherwood Anderson, for example, though at first it may seem strange to
say so, had much in common with Forster. The original gifts of the two
men, so far as we can measure such things, might for purposes of argument be judged nearly equal. Each set himself in opposition to the respectable middle class of his own country and each found a symbolic
contrast in an alien and, as it seemed, a freer race. Each celebrated the
salvation of the loving heart, the passionate body and the liberated personality. Yet as Anderson went on, he grew more and more out of touch
with the life he represented and criticized, and it was as if, however much
he might experience beyond a certain point, he had not the means to
receive and order what he felt, and so ceased really to feel. In his later
years he became, as gifted men of a certain temperament tend to become,
symbolic and visionary, but, never understanding how to handle his
ultimate hopes and his obscurer insights, he began to repeat himself and
became increasingly vague. The vision itself began to fail when Anderson
could not properly judge its importance and could not find for it the
right symbols and the right language; and in his later years he made the
impression, terribly touching, of being lost and alone.

He was indeed lost and alone, though he need not have been. But the
men with whom he might have made community were not to be found
where he thought they were, in the stable and the craftsman's shop. The
men of Anderson's true community were the members of the European
tradition of thought. But Anderson was either indifferent to the past or
professionally contemptuous of it; he subscribed to the belief that American art must throw off the shackles of tradition and work only with
intuition and observation. Anderson saw "culture" as gentility; and he
saw it too, one feels, as a kind of homogeneous mass to be accepted or

rejected only in totality; he did not know that it was a collection of individuals much like himself with whom he might claim kinship and equality, nor did he know that what he was demanding for life had been demanded by other men time out of mind. Anderson's books, like so many other American books, had at first a great and taking power; then, like so many other American books that have astonished and delighted us, they fell out of the texture of our lives, they became curiosities.

Let us say the worst we can of Forster—that beside a man like Anderson with his tumble of emotions and child-like questions, Forster might seem to have something donnish about him. But then we must at once say that Forster has a sense of the way things go which Anderson, for all his great explicit impulse toward actuality, never had—the sense of what houses, classes, institutions, politics, manners and people are like. Forster knows, as Anderson never knew, that things are really there. All his training has helped bring his impulses to consciousness, and the play of consciousness over intuition and desire gives him his curious tough insight.

The great thing Forster has been able to learn from his attachment to tradition and from his sense of the past is his belief in the present. He has learned not to be what most of us are—eschatological. Most of us, consciously or unconsciously, are discontented with the nature rather than with the use of the human faculty; deep in our assumption lies the hope and the belief that humanity will end its career by developing virtues which will be admirable exactly because we cannot now conceive them. The past has been a weary failure, the present cannot matter, for it is but a step forward to the final judgment; we look to the future when the best of the works of man will seem but the futile and slightly disgusting twitchings of primeval creatures: thus, in the name of a superior and contemptuous posterity, we express our self-hatred—and our desire for power.

This is a moral and historical error into which Forster never falls; his whole work, indeed, is an implied protest against it. The very relaxation of his style, its colloquial unpretentiousness, is a mark of his acceptance of the human fact as we know it now. He is content with the human possibility and content with its limitations. The way of human action of course does not satisfy him, but he does not believe there are any new virtues to be discovered; not by becoming better, he says, but by ordering and distributing his native goodness can man live as befits him.

This, it seems to me, might well be called worldliness, this acceptance of man in the world without the sentimentality of cynicism and without the sentimentality of rationalism. Forster is that remarkably rare being, a naturalist whose naturalism is positive and passionate, not negative, passive and apologetic for man's nature. He accepts the many things the liberal imagination likes to put out of sight. He can accept, for example, not only the reality but the power of death—"Death destroys a man, but the idea of death saves him," he says, and the fine scene in *The*

Longest Journey in which Rickie forces Agnes to "mind" the death of Gerald is a criticism not only of the British fear of emotion but also of liberalism's incompetence before tragedy. To Forster, as to Blake, naturalism suggests not the invalidity or the irrelevance of human emotions but, rather, their validity and strength: "Far more mysterious than the call of sex to sex is the tenderness that we throw into that call; far wider is the gulf between us and the farmyard than between the farmyard and the garbage that nourishes it."

He is so worldly, indeed, that he believes that ideas are for his service and not for his worship. In 1939, when war was certain and the talk ran so high and loose about Democracy that it was hard to know what was being talked about, Forster remarked with the easy simplicity of a man in his own house, "So two cheers for Democracy; one because it admits variety and two because it permits criticism. Two cheers are quite enough: there is no occasion to give three. Only Love the Beloved Republic deserves that." He is so worldly that he has always felt that his nation belonged to him. He has always known that we cannot love anything bigger until we first love what Burke called "the little platoon" and so it has been easy for him to speak of his love for his country with whose faults he has never ceased to quarrel; and now he has no void to fill up with that acrid nationalism that literary men too often feel called upon to express in a time of crisis. He is one of the thinking people who were never led by thought to suppose they could be more than human and who, in bad times, will not become less.

Notes on the Uses of Coincidence
in the Novels of E.M. Forster

by Hyatt Howe Waggoner

I

"Death," wrote E.M. Forster in *Howards End*, "destroys a man, but the idea of death saves him." The imaginative realization of death, that is, can clarify one's view of life. It can make the parts fall into a meaningful pattern; it can save one, sometimes, from the kind of blindness born of concentrated egoism that theologians have called the worst of the sins, pride.

Though Forster is not a professing Christian, and indeed has treated the representatives of the church with ironical amusement and has commented often on the failures of religion, his novels suggest an essentially religious view of life. They suggest the seed of perspectives that will carry us beyond convention, beyond personal and individual instincts, desires, and ideas, beyond worldliness and subjectivity.

But this attitude of Forster's, though it forms a persistent thematic background, is never completely set forth in his fiction in the form of statement. His novels are, of course, "wise," but in them he never "sums up" any "philosophy." What may be called, perhaps without too great inaccuracy, his mystical naturalism emerges only as a totality of meaning, —complex, concrete, incapable of simple abstract statement. It emerges from the exercises in perspective that dominate the novels.

Since his technique is not that of the realist—and certainly not that of the naturalist—Forster does not attempt to present a transcription of "life as it is"; he is never under the illusion that he is recording the thing in itself of experience, whatever that metaphysical entity may be. He knows that, like the process of perception on which it depends, art is an act of assertion. Working in a way closely allied to that of the symbolists in poetry, he writes novels which put into permanent form, that is, into the

"Notes on the Uses of Coincidence in the Novels of E.M. Forster." Originally titled "Exercises in Perspective: Notes on the Uses of Coincidence in the Novels of E.M. Forster," from *Chimera*, III, No. 4 (Summer 1945), 3-14. Copyright © 1945 by Barbara Howes. Reprinted by permission of Barbara Howes and the author.

form of art, a part of his experience which to a degree did not exist before the act of creation began. He knows, as did Henry James, that in a very literal sense the novelist must be not only sensitive but creative; for the artist begins by cultivating awareness and ends by fashioning a segment of the world.

It is the distinction of Henry James not only that he strengthened the technical resources of the novelist but that he created a world of refined awareness within the general area of the already known. (The unknown, of course, lies both within and without the boundaries of the known.) He thought it the task of the novelist to be keenly aware of the subtle shadings in experience; and he succeeded magnificently in objectifying in fiction the movements of his refined sensibility. Yet if there is one outstanding limitation in most of the novels of Henry James it is that the rooms in which the characters talk so wittily and interestingly and analyze their emotions with such fine discrimination—that these rooms seldom have a *view*. The world of James' novels is ordinarily the drawing room, the salon, the library, a world of closed rooms. The mores of the social set, or of a segment of society, or, at most, of society as a whole, constitute the background and determine the perspectives.

James' stories are, perhaps, snapshots, or they are microscopic studies, or they are spectroscopic analyses in which values invisible to the eye are revealed by being passed through the prism of James' intelligence. But they are never aerial views. The lines of perspective seldom carry the eye beyond the social, perhaps never beyond the human. We are not made aware by James of the contours of the round earth itself, with all that such a setting implies for the conditions of human life.

E.M. Forster is not so fine a novelist as was Henry James—neither so productive nor, probably, so gifted. Yet there is one respect in which Forster's equipment as a novelist seems to some of us to excel that of James: Forster not only knows but feels that the earth is round, that the light from the stars is reaching us even on the clearest day. It is not only in *A Room with a View* that he arranges perspectives for our contemplation. Forster's views are always more inclusive than those of James, his sense of the pressure of the dark on the light is greater, his awareness of the uncharted areas in which the known is embedded like a tiny chain of islands in a vast untravelled sea is stronger. This awareness of the universal backdrop, against which human activities must be seen if they are to be seen in undistorted perspective, is one of the chief elements that give distinction to Forster's novels. Forster writes brilliant comedies of manners, and he is a penetrating analyst of what lies deeper than manners, the universally human; but one of his finest gifts is his ability to carry us through the social comedy, through and beyond human nature, to the natural and the eternal. The lines in his pictures converge in a reality more ultimate than that which brings the eye to rest in the works of James.

II

Forster embodies the universal backdrop in his novels in various ways, several of which have been discussed at length and quite adequately by his critics. His habit—archaic, as some see it—of interrupting his action with analytical asides, his comments on his characters when he describes them, his inveterate irony, an irony both stylistic and basic, which allows him to see no motive unmixed and no conclusion final—all these and other aspects of his novels help the reader to glimpse *sub specie aeternitatis* the patterns of conflicting interests and points of view that make up the stories. But there is another way in which Forster enlarges our vision, and it has received too little penetrating comment. Forster uses the device of coincidence purposefully—and, it seems to me, despite the arguments of a number of critics who consider this the weakest aspect of his work, effectively—to arrange perspectives.

It is mere coincidence, we often say, that it should have rained on the very day when we planned a picnic, and in such a dry month too. It is a mere coincidence that the tree should have fallen at just the moment when the car was passing below. But what do we mean by *coincidence?* That events are uncaused, unpredictable? That we live in a world of chance? To determine what we mean, or what we should mean, we must enter the realm of metaphysics, where Hume, Bergson, and Whitehead are better guides, however we may view their inadequacies, than any novelist. Yet the novelist, who works as an artist in the raw materials of judgment, may help us, by presenting aspects of experience which we are apt to forget or ignore, to think more clearly about such metaphysical problems. Both the artist and the scientist present the philosopher with data for synthesis. Because nothing that we experience, or may experience, is irrelevant for metaphysics, the novelist, though no substitute for the metaphysician, declares his philosophy, and perhaps its inadequacy, on every page that he writes. In the patterns of imagined experience that E.M. Forster presents in his novels, coincidence is significant both formally and philosophically. And form and content in literature must ultimately be studied integrally, for every artistic decision is also implicitly a moral and philosophical judgment.

Thus, for instance, the sudden deaths in Forster's novels, if they are viewed not as transcriptions of surprising events in life but as declarations of the artist's intention, assume a fresh importance. Their *suddenness* is largely a matter of presentation. They are frequently "sudden" because the novelist has not foreshadowed them, has, in fact, introduced them without preparation of any kind, as though he could assume that the reader would accept them without surprise as part of the natural order of things. When Mrs. Moore, for example, in *A Passage to India,* dies while journeying back to England through the intense heat, her death seems sudden to the reader but is not in fact either sudden or essentially a matter of chance, of coincidence. The apparently sudden and coincidental nature of it is a result of Forster's technique: the announcement to the reader comes unexpectedly in a fragment of trivial conversation. The death of the chief character occurs, that is, at a distance, under circumstances only partially made known to the reader; and it is announced with no emotion, in a situation completely lacking in dramatic "appropriateness." What from the social or the human points of view would have been a high point, probably the dramatic climax, in the book, has been played down until it assumes an importance comparable to that of human conversation in the caves, where all words, like all sounds of any kind, are echoed indistinguishably as a hollow booming.

And Forster has not had to resort to a romantic use of the improbable to achieve this perspective. He has pictured Mrs. Moore as old, in poor health, deeply depressed by her recent experiences. The season was a dangerous one for travellers of all but the most robust health. Perhaps we may even be justified in recalling, without pressing the point too hard, that the frequently mentioned ruddiness of Mrs. Moore's complexion may have indicated a condition that would make her more than usually liable to sunstroke or shock from intense heat.

But the point is not that the author has really made the death quite likely, however suddenly and casually he has introduced it into his narrative. It is rather quite the opposite: not that he has, in this instance, made death plausible, but that he has treated it as though it were a part of the natural course of things. Thus critics who draw careful distinctions between the "probable" and the "improbable" deaths in the novels are, it seems to me, missing part of the point: again, one should consider the deaths in context, as part of a pattern; and if one does so, one sees that all of them, from the death of Gino's baby in *Where Angels Fear to Tread* or of Rickie in *The Longest Journey* to the much more "likely" death of Mrs. Moore, have one thing in common. This feature common to all of them, this likeness in otherwise unlike circumstances, must constitute their significance as revelations of Forster's intention. And the feature which they share is the casualness of their presentation. They are sudden and shocking to the reader, and often to the other characters, but apparently not to Forster. Forster has naturalized death.

There is no need, I trust, to labor the point that Forster is not essentially misrepresenting life. All deaths except those due to lingering diseases or to senility are sudden to someone, to the deceased himself, to his friends and relatives, or to mere acquaintances, like Hamidullah and Fielding. Perhaps it is only because the secular liberalism of our times has carefully suppressed all awareness of death that we think of it as shocking, unusual, something to be excluded from our consciousness as not quite real. And if sometimes, as in the death of Gerald in *The Longest Journey,* Forster casually disposes of a character whose normal life-expectancy would be long, it is not, I think, that he has solved the problems of his novel too easily by having recourse to melodramatic coincidence but that he has deliberately focused our awareness on the intrusion of the unknown, the unpredictable, into our ordered and secure existence. The artist may legitimately consult other tables of probability than the actuarial.

But the order, the security, that the structure of the novels clearly suggests, is illusory. The artistic significance of the "coincidental" deaths in Forster is that they destroy the most carefully cherished illusion of our culture, the illusion of security. They imply that, despite the claims of those who pin their hope of salvation on the achievements of applied science or on politics or on social reform, we do not yet sufficiently control nature even to eliminate natural, to say nothing of moral, evil. Properly read, Forster's novels are disillusioning: they open up fissures in the structure of our secular faith, fissures through which we may glimpse the dark vistas that surround and contain our easy, well-lighted world of security through insurance policies and plans for post-war helicopters and television. They are as unkind—to shift the figure from the secular to the theological—to our illusion of salvation by works as they are to the opposite heresy of salvation by faith. They repeat, with many variations in many keys, the theme of Eliot's *Four Quartets*: "Dark, dark, dark, they all go into the dark."

So the sudden deaths in the novels help to supply the *view* which Forster has insisted is so necessary. And both the deaths and the other coincidences—even such really unlikely occurrences as the meeting of Henry Wilcox and Jacky in *Howards End*—have another implication. They suggest the endless web of *connections*, a web which, as Forster has said all through his novels, not only actually exists but which it is to our advantage to recognize and understand. Thus the theme of *Howards End*, "only connect the prose and the passion," is also, broadly interpreted, a theme in all of the novels. But to see just how this is so, we must revert to the term *coincidence* and to the experience which it symbolizes.

We mean when we say that something is a coincidence that we are unaware of the causes that brought together two "events"—which are themselves the result of the co-incidence of many other events—to form, in their *co-incidence*, a third event. We mean that we are not ordinarily aware of the crossing of two such chains of causality and thus have no pat "explanation" (in terms of prior events) ready to apply to the phenomenon. We do not seriously mean to assert that anything happens "without cause," even though we leave a place in our metaphysic for moral responsibility. The chain of causes that produced, say, an unusual meeting of former acquaintances whose lives have become widely separated may be too complicated and obscure for us to trace. But there are more things in heaven and earth than are dreamt of in our philosophy.

Forster's chance meetings and unexpected turns of fortune surprise us into awareness of the degree to which our lives hinge upon coincidence.

Just as, in Conrad's *Secret Sharer,* there would have been no tale to tell had it not been for the coincidences, the original irrationalities, of the captain's strangeness to his vessel, his unusual decision to stand watch himself and dismiss his crew, the crew's oversight in leaving the ladder down—so it is equally coincidental that the Schlegels should have met Leonard Bast at the concert, that they should have gone off by mistake with his umbrella, and that Leonard's wife, Jacky, should turn out to have been once Henry Wilcox's mistress. The last coincidence is not essentially different from the others, only more striking.

So in the famous handkerchief scene in *Othello* Shakespeare uses coincidence. It can be demonstrated that even without the episode Iago would have succeeded. Why then the handkerchief? At least one answer would be that the coincidence emphasizes the "inclusiveness" of the experience by giving Iago gratuitously, as it were, an extra dividend. Thus Shakespeare heightens the tragedy by introducing an element that takes us beyond the humanly controlled world. The fact that Shakespeare's plot does not depend upon the handkerchief episode to the extent that Forster's hinges upon Jacky's former connection with Henry Wilcox suggests only that Shakespeare has solved his problem with greater artistic finesse.

And it is by a series of comparable coincidences that one was born in America rather than in France or Malaya, white rather than black, normal rather than deformed; that one met and married this person rather than some other, that one was not killed by the speeding motorist. Our lives are involved in circumstances which are not only not under our control but of which for the most part we are entirely unaware. That there are causes of these circumstances we do not doubt, for we do not doubt the rationality of nature; but we do not know, nor can we ever find out, what all the causes are. Only when the unexpected fortune or misfortune jars us out of our routine do we become momentarily aware of the extent to which, though we are in some sense separate entities, personalities, souls, yet we are also foci of lines of coincidence. If it is easy, after realizing this truth, to espouse determinism or to dally with fatalism, it is not necessary to do so. Certainly Forster's novels never question the integrity of the individual, never cast any doubt on the reality of choice. But they do suggest the limitations within which choice is real.

Thus the coincidences in the novels help us to connect, to sense the interdependence of "matter" and "spirit," to see the behavior of the barnyard creatures and of Margaret and Henry Wilcox as somehow responsive to the same laws, though not entirely reducible to those laws. By suggesting some of the conditions to which will is subject, the coincidences present in clearer perspective the reality of freedom within necessity. And if we are thus led to see effects in terms of their causes, behavior in terms of environment and temperament, we may better understand, though we may remain powerless to modify, the *divisions* that, according to Forster, play so important and so unfortunate a part in our lives. To oversimplify, for the moment, a novel almost as complex as life itself, we may say that Mrs. Moore and Aziz are drawn together by the glimpse which each has had of himself and of others in the perspective afforded by the caves. And if Rickie had been better able to perceive the connections of which Mrs. Moore became aware, he might have managed his life more satisfactorily.

One further word on the artistic implications of the coincidences. They are more "accidental" from some points of view than from others. They are "coincidences" in the popular sense of the term chiefly from the point of view of the person who is accustomed to equate what is unusual in his experience with the inexplicable or the uncaused, from the point of view of some of the characters in the novels who are too immersed in the immediate details of their lives to understand what does not concern their supper or their success, from the point of view of all who lack vision. Forster's novels are elaborate tissues of interwoven, contradictory, mutually modifying perspectives. The perspective of the unenlightened person, that of the social class, that of the redemptive character, of a Mrs. Moore or a Mr. Emerson or a Mrs. Wilcox—all these are presented in the novels and allowed to work on and against each other. What is a mere coincidence to Lucy is natural to Mr. Emerson.

It is natural to him because he is constantly aware of the backdrop of human life. He has a view. Thus, unlike the conventionalists, he is aware of the natural causes of things, of man's life as inseparable either temporally or spatially from the universal process of which the stars and the quanta are as much a part as we. Where the Cuthbert Eagers see only disconnectedness, a world of spots and gaps in which all that might disturb their complaceny or challenge their vanity has been relegated to the realm of the unnatural or the coincidental, where it may safely be ignored, he takes a longer and steadier look and stands ready to admit the reality of the disapproved and the disenchanting.

But if Forster's novels are thus naturalistic in their implication, they represent a type of naturalism very far indeed from the naïve variety of the early practitioners of the form. If the novels suggest the dependence of ideals upon facts, they never make "facts" account for too much. One of the chief defects of such naturalists as Zola and Dreiser is that their philosophy was inadequate to experience. The world which they present for our inspection is nearly as unreal as the world in which Dr. Primrose suffered and was rewarded. For they labored under many illusions, chief of which we may abbreviate as the illusion of static materialism. (Zola's belief that physical science is essentially descriptive rather than essentially experimental is not the most damaging of his misconceptions; it is merely the most easily disproved.) Believing in a billiard ball world, and having no adequate notion of the necessary selectivity and ultimate subjectivity of art, they supposed that by describing painstakingly the details of their characters' physiques, their heredity, their experiences, they could fully account for them. Thus many naturalists have tended to write long, detailed, "unselective" chronicles of "fact," ruling out coincidence with the same assurance they exercised in deleting the spiritual. Dreiser's novels, for instance, declare on every page their author's intention of absolute objectivity and scientific probability. They once seemed daringly factual and concrete. But they are just as much illustrations of a doctrine, and of a doctrine that only imperfectly fits human experience, as the sentimental romances against which they were a reaction.

In contrast with this closed world built upon the fallacy of misplaced concreteness, in which the facts of physics are taken to be more real than the facts of value, the world of Forster's novels is open and dynamic. It may be thought of as a *process* in the Whiteheadian sense, a process in which there are neither gaps in the tissue of connections nor easy mechanistic answers to complex questions.

III

Forster's coincidences represent just one aspect of the maturity that distinguishes his work. If they naturalize the strange, it is equally true to say that they enlarge the natural to include all the possibilities. If they seem at times to suggest that he is using the method of romance rather than that of realism, they also carry within them the suggestion that they are used in the interest of truth to life, not only general, abstract truth in the sense that Hawthorne's "Ethan Brand" is true to life, but concrete, particular truth as well. They suggest an outlook naturalistic without inadequate dogmas, idealistic without groundless illusions. There is a sense in which it is meaningful to say that both Forster's thought and his technique are romantic. But insofar as he is a romanticist he is only asserting insights which are permanently valid. One can find in his work no tendency to "escape," no specious coloring, no blurring of distinctions essential to clear thinking. If his coincidences ally him with romantic thought and practice, they ally him no less clearly with modern relativism or, for that matter, with the seventeenth century's awareness of the skull beneath the skin.

It may still be true, of course, that he should have achieved his effects by some other means than the device of coincidence. Perhaps novelists should have nothing to do with the unusual and the unexpected, or, using them, should make them seem a part of the normal social pattern, so that they lose their wildness and become conventionalized. But whether or not they are effective for all his readers, Forster has woven his coincidences so completely into the structure of his novels that any tinkering with them in the interest of "realism" would destroy the integrity, and so the meaning, of the novels themselves.

And if the coincidences are not always "probable," who is to make the authoritative decision as to what is probable? A banker's calculus of probabilities is apt to be very different from E.M. Forster's or W.H. Auden's and may exclude much that is very probable indeed. Or if some of Forster's coincidences seem rather too improbable, too arranged, even to a sensitive, enlightened, and disciplined mind, still there is, I think, no valid reason why an artist may not work improbabilities into his pattern if he does so responsibly. Only a narrowly conceived credo of realism or a confusion of the commercial literary product with art would forbid the writer this freedom. Forster is neither a naturalist in the tradition of Zola nor a realist in the tradition of Maugham, Galsworthy, or Bennett; and he is not, of course, a contemporary experimentalist in the line of Joyce and the others—though in some respects he has more in common with them than many contemporary traditional realists have. His ties are with Hardy and Conrad, perhaps even more with Meredith. He manipulates his material. But so, we recall, does every artist. The difference is that Forster manipulates consciously, freely, fully aware of what he is doing and what he intends to achieve, while many realists and naturalists manipulate unconsciously, selecting and emphasizing, creating a world the pattern and features of which are determined by their acceptance of doctrines which they do not understand. Of the two ways, Forster's, it seems to me, is the better, if only because we have recently had so much of the other.

With no illusion that he is merely transcribing actuality, fully aware of the complexities of art, Forster arranges evocative symbols in shapes that are acceptable to a mind that is equally aware of facts, of paradox, and of mystery. The use which he makes of coincidence is a significant part of his declaration of intention.

Mr. E.M. Forster
as a Symbolist

by Frank Kermode

"A truly great novel is a tale to the simple, a parable to the wise, and a direct revelation of reality to the man who has made it a part of his being": so Middleton Murry, in a piece called "The Breakup of the Novel" which was published in 1924, the year of *A Passage to India*. A story, a parable, and at the same time an intuited truth, an image: anything less, it appeared, was only a bundle of fragments.

Whether or not *A Passage to India* provides "a direct revelation of reality," it certainly tells a story, and it also speaks, as it were in parable, for tolerance and liberalism. Indeed it does these things so well that it is admired by people who regard talk of "direct revelations of reality" as empty nonsense, and regret, as Roger Fry regretted, Mr. Forster's mystical tendencies. I think such readers are unlucky—I mean in their art rather than their religion—because, like Mr. Forster's character Fielding, they have the experience but miss the meaning. They miss a designedly inexplicable wholeness. Having, perhaps, every other gift, they want love—which, for Mr. Forster, can mean the power to read a book properly. "Our comprehension of the fine arts," he says, "is, or should be, of the nature of a mystic union. But, as in mysticism, we enter an unusual state, and we can only enter it through love." Love is the only mediator of meaning, because it confers and apprehends unity. The author in the act of composition is, according to Mr. Forster, in a condition of love. And clearly he had no difficulty in understanding the Rajah who said to him, "Love is the only power that can keep thought out." For "thought" here means that which analyses in this connection, douses reality in time, and misses the meaning.

To translate this into convertible critical currency, Mr. Forster is a kind of Symbolist. He declares for the autonomy of the work of art; for co-essence of form and meaning; for art as "organic and free from dead matter"; for music as a criterion of formal purity; for the work's essential anonymity. Like all art, he thinks, the novel must fuse differentiation into unity, in order to provide meaning we can experience; art is "the one orderly product that our muddling race has produced," the only unity and therefore the only meaning. This is Symbolist. But there are interesting qualifications to be made; they bear on the question of differentiation, of stresses within the unity—a question that would have interested the Cambridge Hegelians of Mr. Forster's youth, when the enemy, Bertrand Russell, was at their gates, brandishing what the Rajah called "thought."

The first qualification arises from Mr. Forster's celebrated insistence on the point that the novel tells a story—a low, atavistic thing to be doing if you claim the power to make direct revelations of reality. In the novel, the matter which seeks pure form is itself impure. This sounds like the old Symbolist envy of music; but we soon learn that Mr. Forster really values this impurity. He dislikes novels of the sort H.G. Wells attributed to James: "On the altar, very reverently placed, intensely there, is a dead kitten, an eggshell, a piece of string." He agrees with Wells that "life should be given the preference, and must not be whittled or distended for a pattern's sake." If "life" in this sense is pattern-resisting, impure, nevertheless our direct revelation of reality, pure as it is, must somehow include it. One thinks of Valéry, who said that no poem could be pure poetry and still be a poem. Unity implies the inclusion of impurity.

The second qualification again brings the French Symbolist to mind. "Organic unity"—art's kind of unity—has to be produced by a process coarsely characterised by Mr. Forster himself as "faking." "All a writer's faculties," he says, "including the valuable faculty of faking, do conspire together . . . for the creative act." "Faking" is the power he so greatly admired in Virginia Woolf. From the author's point of view the organism can look rather like a machine—a machine, as Valéry said, for producing poetic states. Eventually the author withdraws and lets the work lead its own anonymous life; but he must not do so too soon. The burden of Mr. Forster's criticism of Gide is that one can withdraw too soon, "introducing mysticism at the wrong stage of the affair." Later, the author may stand back and see what he has said; but first he must do his faking intelligently. Faking is what Valéry did in his multitudinous drafts; it is what makes the work of art different from oracular raving. "How shameful to write without a conception of the work's structure, caring little for *why* and still less for *how! Rougir d'être la Pythie!*" Organic and free of dead matter this direct revelation may be; but it contains impurity, and intelligence helped to make it. It is faked.

In this sense of the word, a novel not only fakes human relationships but also, working against muddle and chance, fakes an idea of order without which those relationships could have no significance. The fraud committed is, in fact, a general benefaction of significance. Nowadays, so

far as I know, nobody attempts faking on anything like Mr. Forster's
scale, and to this difference between then and now I will return. But first
I must have some sort of a shot at the task of illustrating how, in *A Passage to India,* where it is almost inconceivably elaborate, the faking is
done. The events it describes include the coming of Krishna, which makes
the world whole by love; and the novel's own analogous unity is achieved
by faking.

One can start at the opening chapter, indeed the opening sentence.
"Except for the Marabar Caves—and they are twenty miles off—the city
of Chandrapore presents nothing extraordinary." Easy, colloquial, if with
a touch of the guide-book, the words set a scene. But they will reach out
and shape the organic whole. Or, to put it another way, they lie there,
lacking all rhetorical emphasis, waiting for the relations which will give
them significance to the eye of "love." But they are prepared for these
relations. The order of principal and subordinate clauses, for instance,
is inverted, so that the exception may be mentioned first—"except for the
Marabar Caves." The excepted is what must be included if there is to be
meaning; first things first. First, then, the extraordinary which governs
and limits significance; then, secondly, we may consider the city. It keeps
the caves at a distance; it is free of mystery till nightfall, when the caves
close in to question its fragile appearance of order—an appearance that
depends upon a social conspiracy to ignore the extraordinary. Hence-
forth, in this novel, the word "extraordinary" is never used without reference to the opening sentence. It belongs to the caves. The last words of
the first chapter speak once more of "the extraordinary caves." Miss
Quested's behaviour in relation to the caves is "extraordinary."

It is a characteristically brilliant device; the word occurs so naturally
in conversation that its faked significance cannot disturb the story. The
characters say "extraordinary" but the novelist means "extra-ordinary."
In a sense, Fielding can measure the extraordinariness of Marabar by the
Mediterranean, the norm of his civilisation. But nobody can actually
say in what this extraordinariness consists. "Nothing, nothing attaches
to them, and their reputation—for they have one—does not depend upon
human speech. It is as if the surrounding plain or the passing birds have
taken upon themselves to exclaim 'extraordinary,' and the word has
taken root in the air, and been inhaled by mankind." Perhaps Professor
Godbole can explain in what they are extraordinary; Miss Quested asks
him at Fielding's tea-party:

"Are they large caves?" she asked.
"No, not large."
"Do describe them, Professor Godbole,"
"It will be a great honour." He drew up his chair and an expression of
tension came over his face. Taking the cigarette box, she offered to him and
Aziz, and lit up herself. After an impressive pause he said: "There is an

entrance in the rock which you enter, and through the entrance is the cave."

"Something like the caves at Elephanta?"

"Oh no, not at all; at Elephanta there are sculptures of Siva and Parvati. There are no sculptures at Marabar."

"They are immensely holy, no doubt," said Aziz, to help on the narrative.

"Oh no, oh no."

"Well, why are they so famous? We all talk of the famous Marabar Caves. Perhaps that is our empty brag."

"No, I should not quite say that."

"Describe them to this lady, then."

"It will be a great pleasure." He forwent the pleasure. . . .

We find out why he had to. The caves are the exception that menaces the city, the city of gardens and geometrical roads made by the English, the Indian city of unholy muddle. And sometimes it is possible to exclude them, to ignore them like the distance beyond distance in the sky, because, like God in the song of the beautiful ecstatic girl, they are without attributes.

In a sense, they *are* God without attributes; because his absence implies his presence. Therefore, says the Professor, we are entitled to repeat to Krishna, "Come, come, come." Without them there is no whole by which we may understand the parts. Fielding rejects them, and will never understand; he believes in "thought." Mrs. Moore accepts them, seeing a whole, but one in which love is absent; all distinctions obliterated not by meaning but by meaninglessness, the roar of the Marabar echo. Including the excepted does not necessarily result in felicity. But when we know the worst of Marabar—that it is of the very stuff of life, flesh of the sun, thrusting up into the holy soil of Ganges—we still have to observe that the last explicit mention of Marabar in the book, at the end of a petulant remark of Aziz, is drowned in the noise of rejoicing at Krishna's coming. An ordinary conversational remark, of course, with its place in the story, bears the weight of this piece of faking. Similarly, in the last pages, the rocks which, as in a parable, separate the friends Aziz and Fielding, are thrust up from the Indian earth like the fists and fingers of Marabar. Story, parable, coexist in the wholeness of the revelation.

Privation, the want of wholeness, may entitle us in life to say "Come, come, come"; but in the novel this appeal has also to be faked. Godbole first uses the words at the tea-party, after his statement concerning Marabar. In his song, the milkmaid asks Krishna to come; but he neglects to come. At Marabar the need of him is absolute; and even the road to the caves, where everything calls out "Come, come," remains what it is because "there is not enough god to go around." Resonant with the absence of Krishna, it confuses distinctions like that between love and animal feeling; so Miss Quested discovers. But it is not only Marabar; nothing is proof against the god's neglect, not even Aziz' poetry, for all it says about the Friend who never comes. What comes instead is the sun in April, the source of life and of Marabar; and the sun spreads not love but lust and muddle. Or, instead of Krishna, a British magistrate arrives: "He comes, he comes, he comes," says a satirical Indian. The lack of this coming is felt by the guests at the party who heard Godbole's song; they are unwell, with some malaise of privation; they are suffering from a deficiency of meaning, which cannot be cured until Love takes upon itself the form of Krishna and saves the world in the rain. The unity he makes is an image of art; for a moment at least all is one, apprehensible by love; nothing is excepted or extraordinary. The novel itself assumes a similar unity, becomes a mystery, a revelation of wholeness; and does so without disturbing the story or the parable.

But after this, does it, like the rejoicing at Krishna's coming, "become history and fall under the rule of time"? Like the birth of the god, the novel is contrived as a direct revelation of reality, of meaning conferred by a unifying and thought-excluding love; as—leaving gods out of it— the one orderly product. But does it still fall under the rule of time? Perhaps this mystical conception of order in art *was* more accessible to Mr. Forster than to his younger contemporaries. I rather bluntly called him a Symbolist; in fact the doctrines of that great sect were mediated to him in a peculiar way. Think how valuable, for instance, to a writer with this idea of order, was the ethics of G.E. Moore! I mean, in particular, the notion of overall unity analogous to that which gives significance to art; without such unity friendship itself is mocked by exception—beyond and beyond—and is only dwarfs shaking hands. All that civilisation excepts or disconnects has to be got in for meaning to subsist. Moore calls this unity "organic"—an analogy that surely reached ethics through aesthetics. Perhaps the *Principia* are never realisable except in novels; however this may be, a belief of this sort about human life as dependent on the orderly inclusion of the extraordinary, is clearly valuable to a novelist who holds the analogous aesthetic doctrine. The "one orderly product" can include life entire; good and evil, privation and plenitude, muddle and mystery—seen, for a moment, whole. The wholeness is made by love; nothing is excepted except what the Rajah called "thought."

The feeling that a work of art, a novel for instance, must be in this exalted sense orderly, survives; but, for whatever reasons, it seems less potent now. Perhaps you cannot have it very fully unless you have that "conviction of harmony" of which the Cambridge philosopher McTaggart used to speak in Mr. Forster's youth. For him, too, all meaning depended upon oneness. He had an argument to prove that it could never inhere in inductive thought; on the contrary, it depended upon what he called "love," meaning not sexual love nor benevolence nor saintliness nor even the love of God, but something like full knowledge and the justice and harmony this entails. McTaggart even allows the possibility of one's experiencing a mystic unity which is not benevolent, not indeed anything but "perfectly simple Being"—without attributes—"difficult, if not impossible, to distinguish from Nothing." He is thinking of Indian mysticism. Marabar is perhaps Being under that aspect; however, Godbole can distinguish between presence and absence, and it is Mrs. Moore who cannot, and who therefore becomes a saint of Nothingness.

These remarks about the intellectual climate at the relevant period are meant to be suggestive, but not to suggest that Mr. Forster as a novelist is a conscious disciple of any philosopher. I do think, though, that the wonderful years at Cambridge enabled him to prepare the ground for a creation of order—gave him the secure sense of organic unity that made possible those feats of faking, and allowed him to see that, properly viewed, the human muddle could itself be mystery. Only in some such way can I account for the marvellous ease with which story, parable and image here coexist. There was a "conviction of harmony," a belief in order. Perhaps that has fallen under the rule of time.

We, in our time, are, I think, incapable of genuinely supposing a work of art to be something quite different from *A Passage to India;* it is, in this sense, contemporary and exemplary. In another sense, though, it does fall under the rule of time, because any conviction of harmony we may have will be differently grounded. Of these two facts, the first seems to me of incomparably greater importance. It is a consequence that we cannot know too much about the remarkable *inclusiveness* of the book. We continue to have our illusions of order, and clever faking; but this book reminds us how vast the effort for totality must be; nothing is excepted, the extraordinary is essential to order. The cities of muddle, the echoes of disorder, the excepting and the excepted, are all to be made meaningful in being made one. This will not happen without the truth of imagination which Mr. Forster calls "love"; love cheats, and muddle turns into mystery: into art, our one orderly product.

E.M. Forster's Comic Spirit

by Frederick C. Crews

Forster's preoccupation as an artist . . . has been with finding a viable symbolism. The symbolist wants to see universality and timelessness within his temporal experience, but he runs the risk of shallowness when this desire presses him too urgently. He must learn to "immortalize" only those moments in which the real world is naturally suffused with meaning. The trouble with Rickie Elliot's short stories, and equally with Forster's own, is an overbalance of meaningfulness at the expense of represented life—a preponderance of "unearned" symbolism. That this imperfection is less conspicuous in Forster's novels is largely due, I think, to the operation of a contrary feeling, his sense of the comic. Comedy provides the counterweight to keep the symbolist from slipping too far toward allegory; it continually refreshes his awareness of the world's intractability to private patterns of meaning.

In saying this I do not mean that comedy and symbolism, taken as literary methods, are opposites. Forster's Italian novels, with their purposeful selectivity of detail and their almost geometrical structure, are also highly comic; the recurrent symbols or rhythms can appear with equal plausibility in scenes of tragedy and of farce. This is made possible, however, by the fact that Forster's sense of irony governs the world of these novels. To a great extent the meaning he wants to create is ironic meaning; the significant moments are usually the ones that confound our surface expectations and those of the comically wrong-headed characters. A fictional world of this kind is patently artificial, for its details are chosen for their usefulness to the author's practical jokes. There is no urgency here to the characters' task of extracting "symbolic moments" from the chaotic world, for the represented world is not chaotic at all; it has already been severely trimmed to suit the purpose of the plot.

The opposition between symbolism and comedy pertains rather to the author's own search for meaning. If he is a humanist in the sense we have described—a man who disbelieves in all authority and order not verified by himself—he will be tempted to *perceive* the world in terms of his private values in order to protect himself from total disorder. As an artist he must reject this impulse; his symbolism has communicative power only insofar as it is grounded in the objective world known to his readers. The comic mode of vision is thus a helpful restraint upon the writer's zeal for meaning. In reminding him that there will be cakes and ale whether we accept his values or not, comedy insures him against facile self-importance and obscurantism.

This checks-and-balances notion of the writer's mind is the keynote of *Aspects of the Novel.* Forster's position on every question of theory is a middle one, involving a vital balance between extremes that threaten to "tyrannize" the novel. A novel should exist simultaneously in a world of time and a world of value, without giving itself wholly to either measure. It must be "sogged with humanity" (*Aspects of the Novel*, p. 43*), but must possess formal unity. It must be beautiful without aiming at beauty; impressive, but never at the expense of truthfulness. Pattern is desirable, but not beyond the point where it begins to restrict "the immense richness of material which life provides." (p. 233) And a great part of this richness, for Forster, is unavailable to logical categories; it falls under the heading of "muddle," and is hence perceivable only by a sense of the incongruous. For this reason the "charmed stagnation" of *Tristram Shandy* is more congenial to Forster's taste than the relentless purposefulness of *The Ambassadors.* "The army of unutterable muddle" (p. 164) lies behind Sterne's masterpiece and provides its appeal. Or again, though Forster admires "prophetic" works like *Billy Budd,* he regrets that they require a suspension of the sense of humor (p. 211), for a sense of humor is needed to round out any vision of life, however glorious or intense it may be.

Forster's respect for muddle may help us to see the limitations of a fictional technique that he employs in most of his allegorical tales but generally eschews in his novels, namely, fantasy. Fantasy is, in Forster's definition, the "muddling up the actual and the impossible until the reader isn't sure which is which." (*Two Cheers,* p. 222) It consists of violating the conventions of plausibility without wholly dismissing them, so that the reader must take up two problematical views of reality instead of a single unquestioned one. The peculiar advantage of this technique (as of fantasy in its psychoanalytical meaning) is that it frees the writer from being strictly accountable to a world of distasteful facts. His wish for a more congenial order is projected onto an otherwise realistic narrative, thus sparing him a hopeless antagonism to his subject-matter. Though Forster wrings comic effects from his use of fantasy,[1] the technique is

---

* Page references throughout this essay are to the American editions. [ED.]

[1] See, e.g., "The Story of a Panic," "The Other Side of the Hedge," "The Celestial Omnibus," and "The Curate's Friend," in the *Collected Tales.* Each of these stories embodies a sweeping criticism of accepted institutions or ideas, but each can remain good-humored because the satirized world is not the only one available.

obviously not a tool of the comic spirit as I have defined it. Fantasy, we might say, is symbolism that has seized control of reality; it is the extreme luxury of self-indulgence which the true symbolist will try to avoid. In many of his tales Forster uses fantasy to manifest his belief in freedom and passion—in the typical situation a comically inhibited character is confronted with an ideally "free" world which he fails to comprehend—but the technique itself suggests an inflexible dogmatism of attitude. Since it undermines plausibility, we are not surprised to find that it plays only a minor part in Forster's relatively realistic longer fiction.[2]

Forster's sense of muddle, his willingness to admit violations and ab-surdities into his moral universe, is really quite opposite in spirit to his use of fantasy. It is one thing to produce effects of muddle by thwarting the expectations of narrow-minded characters—fantasy is well suited for this—but something else again to allow one's own values to be softened or qualified by a feeling for comedy. As a creator of fantasy Forster aligns himself with the Swift of *Gulliver's Travels* and the Butler of *Erewhon:* that is, with contrivers of schematic machinery for satirizing attitudes that are opposite to their own. His writing is also distinguished, however, by comedy in the restraining, self-critical sense. Like the Butler of *The Way of All Flesh,* Forster usually manages to satirize intolerant people without losing his characteristic modesty and nonchalance; he does not fall into the tone of the saint or the misanthrope. I return to Butler be-cause Forster has confessed to a strong temperamental sympathy with him—not only with his common sense and intelligence, but with his good temper, graciousness, and "willingness to abandon any moral standard at a pinch." (*Two Cheers,* p. 221) This last quality suggests a healthy respect for the comic discrepancy between black-and-white values and the actual complexity and unpredictability of experience. Butler's influence on Forster, which was considerable,[3] was perhaps nowhere so great as in helping to fix his dominant attitude of self-belittlement, his application of comic irony to his own position as a moralist.

[2] Forster does occasionally create a vague atmosphere of fantasy in his novels when he wants to suggest that the realm of value is asserting its claims over drab temporality. In *A Room with a View* this is the case in the murder-scene and in the dreamlike con-clusion to the Fiesole episode, and we may regard the theoretical presence of "ghosts" in *Howards End* and *A Passage to India* in a similar light. However far he may drift toward fantasy, though, Forster the novelist always remains anchored to the familiar and the tangible.

[3] Forster's specific borrowings from Butler, as well as some general similarities of opinion, are listed by Lee Elbert Holt, "E.M. Forster and Samuel Butler," *PMLA,* LXI, September 1946, 804-19. After Holt's article appeared, Forster produced an essay on Butler in which he confirmed the deep influence of Butler's eclecticism, and noted that he lectured on Butler "somewhere about 1910" and had contracted to write a book about him when the war broke out. Butler, he summarizes, "stands for the un-dogmatic outlook, for tolerance, good temper, good taste, empiricism, and reasonable-ness." See Forster, "The Legacy of Samuel Butler," *The Listener,* XLVII, June 12, 1952, 955f.

We can best describe the operation of the comic spirit in Forster's novels if we place him beside Jane Austen, his favorite novelist. As in her works, Forster's comedy is usually generated by ironic contrasts between what is superficially "proper" and what is truly reasonable. Characters like Cecil Vyse and Jane Austen's Mr. Collins are figures of fun because they lack self-knowledge; though Lucy Honeychurch and Elizabeth Bennett do not hesitate to tell us what to think of these stuffy gentlemen, the real satire is conveyed through verbal ironies within a narrow social context. And our standard of comic judgment in both cases is not a Puritanical concern for rectitude but simply an Augustan love of good sense. When the author has succeeded in exposing all the pride and prejudice, not only in these flagrant cases but also in the reformable central characters, the social structure remains intact. We have not been persuaded that family, class, and nation are bad, but that in order to live comfortably with these institutions one must see the modesty of one's place in the total scheme. Elizabeth Bennett, for all her caustic railing against hypocrisy, finally takes her privileged place in the social world, and so in a lesser degree does Lucy Honeychurch; the self-knowledge that has made them aware of their affections also tells them not to expand their revolt to Swiftian dimensions.

Where Forster's comedy chiefly differs from Jane Austen's is in the acceleration of its witty reversals, the greater density of thematic irony, and the greater freedom with which Forster moves his focus from the world of his characters to that of general human nature. The "double vision" that Lowes Dickinson found in his friend's work, and which James McConkey wisely takes as his starting-point in discussing Forster, is exercised almost incessantly. For illustration, let us see how the Fiesole outing in *A Room with a View* draws to its climax. Jane Austen would never offer us such an episode of complex disorder as this one; we seem to be closer to the world of Fielding or of Smollett. Neither Fielding nor Smollett, however, would press so much thematic meaning from his scene. In Forster the comic chaos is only apparent, for underneath it there always runs a discernible thread of logic, a reason in madness, that leads us straight to Forster's moral position.

The trip to Fiesole, we remember, culminates in the first kiss between George and Lucy, a "good" result in terms of the total plot of *A Room with a View*. It is introduced, however, by a series of comic mistakes, confusions, and petty social grudges among the English characters on the outing, who pride themselves on their national virtues of self-control and fair play. The broad irony of the sequence of events is obvious: the blunt and unsociable George Emerson will introduce Lucy to the possible harmony of her inward life, her true self, after the specious harmony of "society" has broken down. The elder Mr. Emerson helpfully states the theme, "Non fate guerra al Maggio," and adds, after his free translation of Lorenzo's line is pedantically contested by the Reverend Eager,

"Do you suppose there's any difference between Spring in nature and Spring in man?" (*A Room with a View,* pp. 103f.) The day's voyage into the blooming Italian spring, against which the inhibited characters try unsuccessfully to "make war," brings Lucy and George to their own personal springtime of emotion. Through several patently symbolic devices, including the amorous sporting of a carriage driver and his sweetheart whom Forster calls "Phaethon" and "Persephone," Forster ensures that even the most obtuse reader will see the real drift of the scene.

What makes this episode distinctively Forsterian, however, is not simply its thematic weight but the multiplicity of its social ironies, which lead causally to the "celestial irony" (p. 97) of George and Lucy's encounter. The prospective lovers are together on this day only because the Reverend Beebe, who considers himself more "advanced" than the equally provincial Reverend Eager, has invited the Emersons without the latter's knowledge. The conversation during the drive consists of such appropriate remarks as Mr. Eager's observation that English tourists in Italy seem "quite unconscious of anything that is outside Baedeker," and the timidly adventuresome Miss Lavish's agreement that "the narrowness and superficiality of the Anglo-Saxon tourist is nothing less than a menace." (p. 98) A few moments later the same Mr. Eager is found berating the carriage driver for his loose morals while Miss Lavish is heroically trying to take a bohemian view of the case. The driver, with seeming implausibility, appeals to Lucy for support; like the murder-victim in the Piazza Signoria, he seems to be endowed with a special knowledge of her inner life. When "Persephone" has been exiled over Mr. Emerson's protests and the two carriages have arrived at their destination, the ironies of plot begin to quicken. Social antagonisms cause the party to split into three groups and then into stray individuals. Lucy, for instance, is set apart with Miss Lavish and Charlotte, but feels obliged to leave them when a fuss is made over the distribution of two mackintosh ground-cloths among the three ladies. The petty machinery of social form malfunctions so completely that Lucy is free to meet George unchaperoned.

Lucy, however, does not know that she wants to find George; she goes off in search of the two clergymen. In halting Italian she asks the carriage driver where the two "buoni uomini" can be found. The driver, who has been given a cigar by the *simpatici* Emersons, understands perfectly; he leads her straight to George. Lest we miss the implication that this is Lucy's buried wish, Forster now heightens the air of hidden meaningfulness in his narrative. Italians, he says, "are born knowing the way"; finding the right people is "a gift from God." (p. 108) From this point on Lucy increasingly rejoices in the contagious "influence of the Spring," until, when she is about to find George, Forster resumes the novel's central pun: "The view was forming at last." (p. 109) As Lucy stumbles into the bed of violets where George is waiting, the driver calls out *in English:* "Courage! Courage and love" (p. 110), suggesting to us, as a last turn of irony, that Lucy's fortunate inability to communicate her surface meaning to him has been due to her tourist's grasp of the Italian language. Had she been more articulate, like the Reverend Eager and Miss Lavish, or less so, necessitating a conversation in English, she might not have been led to George. Altogether, Forster has arranged things so that his thematically inevitable climax is produced through a quick series of trivial comic surprises—each of which, however, is realistically justifiable in terms of the personalities involved. I can think of no other novelist who unravels his strands of social irony with such deft rapidity and complexity as this.

However believable any one of Forster's coincidences of plot may be, the hand of the puppet-master is clearly in view above his "meaningful" scenes of comedy. The Italian novels are so rigidly governed by thematic irony that their plots give a total effect of fantasy; we find ourselves in a world where error is always punished with ironic appropriateness. And this fact may suggest the name of another novelist whose influence on Forster seems hardly less important than Butler's or Jane Austen's. I am thinking of George Meredith, whose popular theory of comedy seems to be, if anything, more relevant to Forster's novels than to Meredith's own. Meredith insisted that the province of comedy was quite different from that of ordinary, plausible realism:

"Comedy is a game played to throw reflections upon social life, and it deals with human nature in the drawing-room of civilized men and women, where we have no dust of the struggling outer world, no mire, no violent crashes, to make the correctness of the representation convincing. Credulity is not wooed through the impressionable senses; nor have we recourse to the small circular glow of the watch-maker's eye to raise in bright relief minutest grains of evidence for the routing of incredulity. The comic spirit conceives a definite situation for a number of characters, and rejects all accessories in the exclusive pursuit of them and their speech. For being a spirit, he hunts the spirit in men; vision and ardor constitute his merit; he has not a thought of persuading you to believe in him." [4]

Instead of recording things as they are, Meredith's comic spirit focuses on human egoism and sees that it is justly punished. The comic plot assumes the function of a moral scourge, a purposeful agent of retribution against all forms of self-importance. And this can be said equally of Forster's own plots, particularly the early ones. Each of them enforces the proverb from Ecclesiastes that Anthony Failing expands to read, "Cast bitter bread upon the waters, and after many days it really will come back to you." (*The Longest Journey*, p. 157)

It is in the gentleness and impartiality of his comic spirit that Forster is more Meredithian than Meredith. In his famous *Essay on Comedy* Mere-

[4] George Meredith, *The Egoist* (New York, 1951), p. 3.

dith laid special stress on the necessity for "a most subtle delicacy" [5] in the comic writer. His laughter must be both thoughtful and polite: neither charged with pathos like the humorist's nor barbed with malice like the satirist's. True comedy, for Meredith, involves the reader and even the author in the follies it exposes; as a tool of "clear reason" and common sense, it avoids the note of contempt that would place its user beyond comic criticism himself. "You may estimate your capacity for Comic perception," says Meredith, "by being able to detect the ridicule of them you love, without loving them less: and more by being able to see yourself somewhat ridiculous in dear eyes, and accepting the correction their image of you proposes." [6] It is very questionable, however, whether Meredith can pass his own test of objectivity. No reader of *The Egoist* can fail to sense the vengeful scorn that is heaped on the comic victim, Willoughby Patterne, and we search in vain through Meredith's novels for evidence that the author could laugh urbanely at himself. Forster, in contrast, remains both tolerant and affectionate toward his characters with "undeveloped hearts." His politeness, instead of being a surface manner which checks a savage indignation, is intrinsic to his benevolent and selfcritical approach to human nature.

The fact remains, however, that Forster's early plots are closely bound to the Meredithian formula of thwarting egoism. The role of Monteriano in *Where Angels Fear to Tread* is to administer comic justice to the English egoists. Egoism, in Meredith's terms, covers all forms of pretense and self-deception; not only Harriet Herriton, but also Philip, Caroline, and Lilia are tainted with egoism, for each is partly blind to his own nature. Philip and Caroline, the most flexible characters, are chastened and enlightened in the course of the plot. They are brought sharply against the truth of their desires and limitations, and they have to conclude that the world is larger and more complicated than they once thought. Lilia, whose susceptibility to infatuation stems from an unawareness of anything beyond her immediate passions, must live out the prosaic reality of her "romantic" marriage and finally die in childbirth. It is not because she is romantic that she is punished—Forster surely agrees with Meredith that the comic spirit "is not opposed to romance" [7]—but because her grasp of reality is weakened by sentimentalism. Harriet, who lacks "the very slightest sense of the ludicrous" (*Where Angels Fear to Tread*, p. 102), suffers a nervous breakdown after her abortive kidnapping. She has not really learned anything, but she has been severely chastened for her pretense of moral superiority. And the fact that a sense of the comic is a sign of self-knowledge also lies behind the farcical opera scene, which, for all its boisterous foolishness, is offered to the reader as a highly signifi-

---

[5] George Meredith, *Miscellaneous Prose* (New York, 1910), p. 3.
[6] *Ibid.*, p. 41.
[7] *The Egoist*, p. 5.

cant occasion, a moment of transformation for Philip. It is his escape from egoism toward Mr. Failing's principle that "nonsense and beauty have close connections—closer connections than Art will allow." (*The Longest Journey*, p. 13c) Harriet's inability to stand the zany antics of the Italian opera audience is consistent with her later indifference to a father's love for his son, and is thus the sign of a cardinal flaw of character that must be avenged.

Meredith's comic formula is more overtly the basis for Forster's treatment of Cecil Vyse in *A Room with a View*. Cecil himself is a great fan of Meredith's, and he regards himself as the agent of Meredith's Comic Muse. "George Meredith's right," he announces, "the cause of Comedy and the cause of Truth are really the same." (*A Room with a View*, p. 180.) Cecil, of course, is the egoist whose own machinations produce his downfall. By bringing the Emersons to Windy Corner "in the interests of the Comic Muse and of Truth" (p. 182), he hastens Lucy's realization that George Emerson is the man she really loves.[8] It is significant, too, that Cecil's insensitivity to the ludicrous is directly involved in Lucy's awakening. His absence from the "baptism" scene at the woodside pool, where the idea of salvation is again involved in an episode of farce, is as meaningful as George's presence there, and it is Cecil's refusal to make an ass of himself by joining a tennis match that suddenly persuades Lucy how "absolutely intolerable" he is. (p. 257) The plot of *A Room with a View* rescues Lucy herself from the form of egoism to which Charlotte Bartlett has already succumbed, that of setting herself above the vulgarity of sexual love.

In *The Longest Journey* we have a more complex and more serious novel, but one which nonetheless punishes its egoists à la Meredith. Rickie suffers for his effort to repudiate his physical nature, and Herbert and Agnes are rebuffed for their humorless self-importance. Mrs. Failing, it is true, seems to be spared by the Comic Muse, but her life is already devoid of comforting illusions. *The Longest Journey* also takes up another of Meredith's comic ideas, that of the "hero" as it is ironically developed in *The Ordeal of Richard Feverel*. Stephen Wonham strikes Mrs. Failing as a hero, whose chief characteristics, she explains, "are infinite disregard for the feelings of others, plus general inability to understand them." (*The Longest Journey*, p. 121) As in Meredith's novel, this definition is of crucial importance, for in both cases (and in *The Egoist* as well) the resolution of the plot depends on whether a certain character is accepted in his "heroic" role or as an ordinary man. Stephen is idolized by Rickie

---

[8] At this point in his career Forster is unabashedly taking the role of Comic Muse himself. "The Comic Muse," he writes, "though able to look after her own interests, did not disdain the assistance of Mr. Vyse. His idea of bringing the Emersons to Windy Corner struck her as decidedly good, and she carried through the negotiations without a hitch." (*A Room with a View*, p. 183.)

in the same sense that Richard Feverel and Willoughby Patterne are idolized by Lucy Desborough and Laetitia Dale. Stephen is truly heroic, however, only by fits and starts, and when Rickie is forced to see his self-indulgent side, he turns against Stephen altogether. "To yield to temptation," Forster explains, "is not fatal for most of us. But it was the end of everything for a hero." (*The Longest Journey*, p. 318) Our last view of Stephen, however, refutes the opposite simplification, that of Mrs. Failing. The consummately normal Stephen, who shows himself to be an affectionate husband and father, has escaped from the categories of both hero and mock-hero.

In bringing his Meredithian theme to this conclusion Forster is not simply going beyond Meredith's pattern of inflicting vengeance on the false hero; he is also, it seems, questioning the legitimacy of that pattern. The Meredithian narrator who reserves for himself the luxury of exploding the myth of the hero becomes a character in Forster's novel (Mrs. Failing) and is subjected to Forster's criticism. Mrs. Failing's iconoclasm takes its place alongside Rickie's symbol-making as a falsification of the real world. I think we can see this, plus the fate of the Meredithian humorist Cecil in *A Room with a View*, as a kind of declaration of independence from Meredith's comic vogue. Forster makes free use of the current literary fashion of Meredithianism, but he is careful to show us that he is aware of its facility. By the time of *Aspects of the Novel*, certainly, Forster was ready to dissociate himself from Meredith altogether: "What with the faking, what with the preaching, which was never agreeable and is now said to be hollow, and what with the home counties posing as the universe, it is no wonder Meredith now lies in the trough." (*Aspects of the Novel*, p. 136)

In view of this, we are not surprised to find that the idea of comic justice becomes progressively less relevant to our understanding of Forster's two final novels. Forster retains his satirical attitude toward egoists, of course, but his plots are not primarily concerned with exposing them. As moral questions become subordinate to questions about the ultimate meaning of human existence, the plot necessarily loses its function of superintending private morality. Indeed, the very possibility of a Meredithian comic plot diminishes as Forster's total attitude toward life becomes more conspicuous. That attitude, we remember, is one of extreme skepticism about the existence of a providential order. Such skepticism naturally precludes belief in a mechanical system of retribution against egoists; a novel based on such a system must be offered with a certain facetious flair. [But Forster's two last novels] resume the effort, gingerly undertaken in *The Longest Journey*, to reflect the real poignancy of man's isolation from meaning. Forster's plots remain comic in that the characters are handled ironically, but his comic distance from them begins to take on a sober philosophical import—until, in *A Passage to*

India, the comic vision accurately conveys Forster's view of human pretensions in general. Forster remains comic, but in somewhat the same way that Chaucer is comic at the end of *Troilus and Criseyde,* where human tragedy is seen from the belittling perspective of divine indifference to our imperfect and undignified lives.

Forster's Humanism
and the Nineteenth Century

by H.A. Smith

"I belong," said Forster in a broadcast of 1946, "to the fag-end of Victorian liberalism." The tone of comic-rueful self-deprecation is typical and also misleading, since it soon becomes clear that Forster is by no means throwing away the values with which he grew up, although he recognises that it was not only inevitable, but right, that the economic basis which had given them an appearance of stability should have been undermined. This essay will be concerned only incidentally with the politics and economics of his liberalism, and will, as far as possible, avoid that highly equivocal word itself. It will be directed to two questions: (1) how illuminating is it to consider Forster as coming at the end of a tradition?; and (2) how far is it justifiable to explain the slightness and indeterminacy which genuine admirers have found in his work in terms of the fact that he came not only at the end of a tradition, but at the fag-end of it—at a time when its energies, if not actually at their last gasp, were burning low?

Literary traditions are complex things, and merely to sketch in the outlines of one, and indicate a few of its landmarks, is liable to do injustice to its richness and variety. But in this case the line of development, which must surely have had a profound influence both upon the pattern of values to be found in the novels and (even more patently) on the method used to deploy it, is a very familiar one, and it is only Forster's association with it which seems to have been insufficiently acknowledged. His strategy in all five of the novels is basically a simple one, and may be summed up in the word "confrontation." He presents a society which has been depersonalised by materialism, philistinism, some of the more inhibiting forms of puritanism and, most of all perhaps, by a blinding complacency engendered by a confident sense of its own entrenchment. The small-town or suburban world of the first three novels is greatly extended in the other two, and now brings in some of the makers of wealth and wielders of power, but the Sawston attitudes survive happily enough in the metropolitan wilderness of London, and do not budge (they are not of the budging sort) even when transplanted to Chandrapore. And the spokesmen for this world, whether they be Pembrokes, Herritons, Wilcoxes, Callendars, or Turtons, all use essentially the same language. But this language is sharply challenged in all of the novels, and here an element of complication comes in, since the Sawston voice is opposed not by one voice, but by two. The two voices are akin in that they are both on the side of ' Life"—on the side, that is, of a clearer, richer and deeper perception of human personality and human relations than Sawston cares about or can comprehend. They therefore almost invariably combine against Sawston, but at times, too, they can only salute one another from a distance, or even come into regretful conflict with each other. At the risk of some simplification, the one voice may be summed up in the term applied to Mrs. Wilcox, "instinctive wisdom,"[1] and the other in terms used to describe Fielding's attitude: "good will plus culture and intelligence." And the genuine but uneasy relationship between them finds rather crude allegorical expression in *The Longest Journey,* where Stephen punches Ansell in the mouth before making friends with him, and later Ansell defends him against the Pembrokes with a sharp articulateness which Stephen himself could not supply.

Forster invokes these two voices, and explores the virtues and limitations of each, throughout the novels, and to the modern reader, who would not, of course, lose the variegation provided by the social comedy, but who recognises that with the decline in authority of the Sawston *mores* it is bound to lose some of its relevance and force, it may well seem that it is here that their chief interest lies. At times Forster may seem to be coming down on one side or the other, but the final effect is one of holding the balance, while delicately discriminating between the two. It is indicated, for instance, in *The Longest Journey,* that Stephen is "in touch with Nature" (although Forster characteristically makes play with the cant phrase); this is obviously equally true of the Emersons and Ruth Wilcox, and when we remember all those celebrations of Pan in the early stories, it may well seem that Forster is upholding Nature and Instinct as the ideal. But his attitude is surely equivocal. It is true that there is a Dionysian element, more or less strong, in all the novels. It is there in the whole portrayal of Stephen, in the bathing-scene in *A Room with a View* (where the Silent Pool in the woods near Forster's village of Abinger in Surrey becomes a "Sacred Lake"), in the splendid gaiety of the opera in *Where Angels Fear to Tread,* in the

---

[1] I use Forster's key words or phrases as a convenient descriptive shorthand, while noting that they are not, of course, philosophical statements but, in the broad sense, poetic ones—in that they draw most of their validity from the total pattern and rhythm of which they form a part.

"flaming ramparts" of Beethoven's Fifth in *Howards End,* and in the
entire Temple festival in the last section of *A Passage to India.* But in all
this divine merriment and superhuman joy, Forster is liable to find (although not, of course, in the Beethoven) an intermixture of "muddle";
his aesthetic sense is disturbed by the absence of order, proportion, and
form, and his religious sense, too, is jolted: in the Hindu festival he sees
the human spirit suffering a "desperate contortion" in its attempt to
"ravish the unknown." And the individual protagonists of the instinctive life are all, with the exception of Ruth Wilcox, to some degree
flawed; Stephen is barbarous, Gino cruel, Aziz, for all his "secret understanding of the heart," suffers an unnecessary alienation from Fielding
because he allows his feelings to get the better of his sense of evidence.
Even Mrs. Moore, who has Mrs. Wilcox's kind of instinctive wisdom, and
whose spirit, like hers, broods as a religious presence over the book after
she is dead, loses hold on her vision at a crucial moment, with George
Emerson, too, we are told that it is "touch and go."

But it cannot be said that Forster is any more satisfied with his
protagonists of the life of reason and intellectual culture. Some of them
have the culture and intelligence *without* the goodwill, and then, in
their contemptuous indolence and their rejection of the human, they
come near to being ranged with the forces of darkness rather than light.
Tibby Schlegel betrays the Basts to the Wilcox wolf-pack; Philip Herriton could have saved Gino's baby; and Cecil Vyse, in spite of his scorn
for many of the Sawston values, is in effect at one with them in his
turning away from "the Spirit of Life." Stewart Ansell does not lack
goodwill, but there is an obscure ineffectualness about him which affects
not only his career but his dealings with his friends. He has his one
magnificent (if, in realistic terms, wholly incredible) outburst, but apart
from this he is oddly silent and withdrawn when Rickie most desperately
needs his help. And what of Fielding? Here clearly there is no absence of
the capacity to act when action is needed, and his generous good sense
sustains both Adela and Aziz through the major crisis of the book. But,
like his very much less admirable predecessors, Fielding will 'travel
light" if he can, and, in particular, he would prefer to escape the complete involvement required either by affection or by what Forster calls
"the unseen." It is greatly to his credit that he recognises that "travelling
light is less easy as soon as affection is involved," and when he faces its
demands, whether from Aziz or from Stella, his earlier easy optimism
about personal relations fails him. But the religious sensibility which
links Aziz, Godbole, and Mrs. Moore is beyond his grasp. When Mrs.
Moore (surely speaking for Forster) says, "I like mysteries but I rather
dislike muddles," Fielding's reply comes sharp, "A mystery is a muddle";
and when he says with the same kind of bluntness, "I don't believe in
God," the reader, as well as his hearers, is likely to find the words "too
definite and bleak," since, with all their truthfulness and impatience with

cant, they exclude so much. Later, when the disaster of the caves has
opened up not only the depth and bitterness of human animosities but
a glimpse of Ancient Night and the undying worm itself, he is willing to
admit that "perhaps life is a mystery, not a muddle"—but, we are told,
he had not the apparatus for judging. And although he is aware of the
echo of evil which had haunted and confused Adela and defeated Mrs.
Moore, he cannot come to terms with it: "it belonged to the universe that
he had missed or rejected." Hence, when together with Adela he tries to
face the tragedy that had overwhelmed her, he finds that, "sensible,
honest, even subtle" though they both are, they have no adequate words.
In the presence of a displaced world, they are as dwarfs shaking hands.

But suppose that the two voices—instinct and intelligence, Culture
and Nature, reason and religious insight—could be combined in one
person? Rickie Elliot has something of both, but not enough of either.
Helen Schlegel has more force and articulate intelligence than Rickie,
but her impulsiveness upsets the balance. But it appears to be Forster's
intention that Helen's sister Margaret should serenely combine the two,
and that she should therefore be able to "connect" on a deeper level,
perhaps, than any of the overt statements in the book would suggest. I
said earlier that Ruth Wilcox is the only one of the "instinctive" protagonists who is not inadequate, and it could be argued in support of
this that it is sufficient for Ruth that, like a poem, she should not mean
but be. And yet she is inadequate in the sense that she needs Margaret to
complete her, to realise her potentialities, to turn a diffused radiance into
a beam of light. Margaret possesses intellectual culture, but it is not this
that attracts Ruth to her; in fact in the presence of Ruth her clever
friends seem like gibbering monkeys. But she has imaginative culture as
well, and it is this—admirably summed up by Forster as a "profound
vivacity"—which binds the two women together. I feel obliged to add
that, if I have interpreted Forster's intentions correctly, I am by no
means always satisfied that Margaret's actions fulfil them, and even after
allowing for the fact that she is a person as well as a symbol, and that
persons make mistakes, my dissatisfaction remains. But if the attempt to
connect "the prose and the passion" is only partially successful, she does,
I think, connect the positive values which Forster has studied, on their
varying levels, throughout the novels, and her quality of mind can perhaps be summed up in a term of Matthew Arnold's: "imaginative reason."

We may now turn to the nineteenth century. I shall suggest (1) that
in his attack upon "the inner darkness in high places which comes with
a commercial age" Forster arrives late in a long succession of writers;
(2) that the principal method used to confront this "inner darkness" was
already long established when Forster began to write; (3) that the positive
alternative offered by many of these writers to an alien civilisation takes
the form of a humanism which has very much in common with Forster's

own; and (4) that in a few at least of the writers this humanism has the equivocal quality—the two voices, the "double vision"—which we have already found in Forster himself.

The attack in fact antedates the Victorian age, but it is appropriate to begin with Carlyle, who was born in the same year as Keats but lived on to be one of the most influential of the Victorians. In *Sartor Resartus, Chartism, Past and Present,* and those two very striking early essays, "Signs of the Times" and "Characteristics," he is concerned with one central problem: what the new industrial order, and the social and economic assumptions lying behind it, have made of man. In "Signs of the Times" he makes a plea for the recognition of the wholeness of man, and for him, as for Forster, this includes an element of mystery. He speaks of "the primary, unmodified forces and energies of man, the mysterious springs of love, and fear, and wonder, of enthusiasm, poetry and religion, all which have a truly vital and infinite character." In the new society, however, man has been belittled and degraded into a mere getting-and-spending animal, and the bonds, both natural and supernatural, which at one time joined men together have been replaced by the entirely impersonal relationship of what he calls the "Cash-Nexus." To emphasize this point, Carlyle uses the method of confrontation: in *Past and Present* he sets the spiritual chaos and anarchy of his own day against the ordered world of the twelfth century Abbot Samson. Ruskin employs essentially the same method in his chapter on "The Nature of Gothic" in *The Stones of Venice,*[2] he too cares about "the human being in its wholeness," and he compares the creative freedom of the medieval craftsman, who was able not only to enjoy his skill but to pursue his aspirations and appease to some extent the "restlessness of the dreaming mind" (there is the same religious emphasis, it will be noted, as in Carlyle), with the modern fragmentation of labour which produces also a fragmentation of life, so degrading the operative into a machine. In our modern industrial cities, he says, "we manufacture everything . . . except men; we blanch cotton, and strengthen steel, and refine sugar, and shape pottery; but to brighten, to strengthen, to refine, or to form a single living spirit never enters into our estimate of advantages." William Morris's revolt against modern civilisation[3] is even more forthright than

---

[2] Not, incidentally, the one we see Leonard Bast reading. That was Chapter II of the second volume, whereas this is Chapter VI. But this is certainly just as "famous."

[3] I recognise, of course, that in *Howards End* Forster is urging us (or himself) not to revolt against civilisation, but to come to terms with it. But I find the attempt unconvincing, and Forster seems to me to have come here under the alien influence of Shaw. There is quite a close thematic parallel between *Howards End* and *Major Barbara* (1905), in that Culture, in the person of Cusins, and Religion, in the person of Barbara, "connect" with Money and Power, in the person of Undershaft. Nearly all the talk about money in *Howards End* closely echoes Shaw. I do not quarrel with the statement that cash is "the warp of civilisation," but only with the attempt to persuade us that it is a good thing that it should be so. (Even the applauded "grit" of the Wilcoxes

Ruskin's, and like Forster he is dismayed by its "eyeless vulgarity" and its betrayal of beauty. He too, in *A Dream of John Ball* and *News from Nowhere,* creates dream-worlds of the past and future which are in sharp contrast to the "counting-house on the top of a cinder-heap" which he sees as the possible end-product of the dull squalor surrounding him. The phrase about the counting-house has a (designedly) Dickensian ring, and in turning now briefly to Dickens we find not only parallels in spirit with Forster but some possible actual anticipations. The Cash-Nexus is a very potent force in Dickens's novels dealing with the contemporary commercial world, and it may be convenient to note at this point that it is still operating in all its crudity in Forster's Sawston. When the Pembrokes want to be rid of Stephen, they hope to write him off with a large cheque. Gino is offered a thousand lire in exchange for Lilia; later, the Herritons are willing to pay all they have for Gino's precious child (although they don't care for it), and when it cannot be bought, it is stolen. Mr. Wilcox "was a little apt to think one wanted to get something out of him," and on the two occasions when Margaret tries to face him with the kind of personal betrayal involved in his liaison with Jacky, the blank wall of his obtuseness prevents his personality from being touched, but his pocket and his reputation (based on money) can be touched, and each time he barks out: "Blackmail." It must be acknowledged that the sinister force of the Cash-Nexus troubles the imagination more deeply in Dickens than anything in *Howards End,* but the resemblances are there. Mr. Wilcox is foreshadowed in Mr. Dombey, whose powerful tentacles stretch through the City and over the oceans beyond, but whose personal life, and personal dealings both with Edith and Florence, are characterised only by blindness and emptiness. And there is perhaps a somewhat similar sentimentality in the endings of the two books; Dombey is a broken man at the end, and is reconciled with Florence, just as Henry is reconciled with Margaret, but a broken Dombey or Wilcox does not mean that the power of Dombeyism or Wilcoxism has been conquered. A rather closer parallel, in some respects, may be traced between *Howards End* and *Hard Times.* Gradgrind, too, is a broken man at the end of the novel, and for substantially the

---

breaks down under stress.) It is true that Forster tries to set the balance right by introducing Leonard Bast. Margaret makes a regular connection with the "hero" of modern civilisation, while her sister Helen makes an irregular one with the man who is both literally and symbolically his victim. There were highly interesting possibilities here, but if they were to be satisfactorily developed, it was essential that the author's sympathies should be fully (although not, of course, uncritically) engaged with the victim. But we are told that the very poor are unthinkable, and that the poor man is not as intelligent or healthy or lovable as the average rich man. (Could any one be much less lovable than Charles Wilcox?) Once again I have the sense of Shaw's bright hard paradoxes overlaying Forster's natural sensibilities, which might otherwise have been able to surmount the class barrier, just as later he was able to overleap the race barrier to portray his Indians. After such an unpromising start, it is not surprising that Leonard Bast should be Forster's one outstanding failure.

same reason as is Henry Wilcox. Both of them have sons who are much more objectionable than they are themselves, and both sons are responsible for the death of an inoffensive man who has been treated with unjustifiable harshness simply because he is poor. The resemblance here is probably fortuitous, but Dickens also attempts in this novel the method of confrontation; against the cold hard world of Utilitarian fact and Malthusian calculation, he places the cheerful generous world of Sleary's Circus—and whatever else the Slearys may lack, they certainly do not suffer from what Forster calls "the undeveloped heart." But while Dickens is here upholding the life of personal relations, not only in the Slearys but in Sissy Jupe, his alternative has none of the philosophical strength and subtlety which we find in Carlyle and Ruskin, and for a final example of confrontation we may turn to something quite different: Arnold's poem "The Scholar Gipsy." Forster writes with particular affection of this poem, and the scholar-gipsy combines Nature and Culture in a manner very close to Forster's own.

It should perhaps be noted that the method I have been describing is never purely allegorical; fully formalised allegory is rare in the period, and Butler's *Erewhon* is probably the only significant example. It works rather by an apposition which advances to the edge of allegory, and this is Forster's method too. It may also be noted that whereas all the nineteenth century examples I have quoted are conceived in terms of time (usually past versus present), Forster's appositions are presented in terms of place: Wiltshire, Howards End, Italy, India—or, in some of the stories, Greece. But the underlying intention remains much the same.

Invoking, again, the help of Forster's nineteenth century heritage, we may now look rather more closely at the nature of his humanism. Broadly speaking, we may distinguish two main forms of humanism in the modern world. (There were of course others earlier, but they need not concern us.) There is a rational, sceptical humanism, which stems from the Enlightenment, and an imaginative (and often religious) humanism which draws its sustenance primarily from the Romantic Movement.[4] Clearly something of both of these are to be found in Forster, but there can be no doubt as to where his sympathies essentially lie. When, in the essay "What I Believe," he makes his well-known statement, "I do not believe in Belief," and goes on to declare his allegiance to Erasmus and Montaigne (which may be matched with his high praise, elsewhere, for Gibbon and Voltaire), he may appear at first sight to be ranking himself with the sceptical rationalists. But when we see the human endowments which he picks out for special praise: "the heart" (as so often), creativity in all its forms (and we may recall a statement made in a

---

[4] The two were already clearly distinguished at the beginning of the Victorian period, by J.S. Mill in his classic essays on Bentham and Coleridge. For further discussion of Forster's connection with Romanticism, see J.B. Beer, *The Achievement of E.M. Forster* (London: Chatto & Windus, Ltd., 1962).

wartime broadcast, also reprinted in *Two Cheers for Democracy*: "Creation means passionate understanding. Creation lies at the heart of civilisation like fire in the heart of the earth"), a rejection of the creeds of
religion but an acceptance of its "indwelling spirit"; and when we find
that the ideal which he sets before himself, however unattainable, is
"Love, the Beloved Republic," then it becomes clear that his humanism
is both romantic and, in a perfectly acceptable sense of the word, religious.

We are told in *Howards End* that "it is private life that holds out the
mirror to infinity," and that "any human being lies nearer to the unseen
than any organization." The kind of religious attitude implied here,
with its emphasis on the "inward witness" and its acknowledgement of
the possibility of a "faith beyond the forms of faith," can perhaps be
regarded as the ultimate expression of Protestantism, and W.R. Inge, in
his book on *Protestantism,* speaks of "the transition from authority to
experience" as a typical phenomenon of the mid-nineteenth century.
Certainly we find it in a host of Victorian authors: Carlyle, Tennyson,
Browning, Arnold, Clough, "Mark Rutherford,"[5] and many more. In
the ninth chapter of *A Passage to India* Aziz recites a poem. Forster hears
it as "a passing reminder, a breath from the divine lips of beauty, a
nightingale between two worlds of dust," and he adds, "It voiced . . .
our need for the Friend who never comes yet is not entirely disproved."
The phrase looks back to Arnold (to the famous essay where he says that
religion, when the fact has failed it, must find expression through its
poetry), and forward to *Godot,* and only an agnostic could have made it.

[5] Besides the same kind of interest in what they both call "the unseen," there may well
be a closer link between "Mark Rutherford" (William Hale White) and Forster. The
resemblances between Mark Rutherford's last novel, *Clara Hopgood* (1896), and *Howards
End* are sufficiently striking to suggest, if not actually prove, some direct influence. For
the two Hopgood sisters—Clara, the elder, objective, steady, but not without "radiance,"
and Madge, the younger, more attractive, passionate and impetuous—"thought was
vocal"; they were educated in Goethe's Weimar, and like the Schlegel sisters drew
much of their culture from Germany. Madge thinks herself in love with a rich young
businessman, Frank Palmer, who has the Wilcox grit without their grittiness, and in
her first (albeit reluctant) admiration for him she becomes a little weary of "culture,"
and decides that the man who shapes events must be more highly prized than the
"babbler about literature" (cf. the Schlegel's fear of "sloppiness"). But it soon appears
that Frank, although "wise" about his business, has no inner resources or sharpness of
perception (like Lucy Honeychurch, he is devoted to music, but "there was a curious
lack in him . . . of correspondence between his music and the rest of himself"), and
both sisters become impatient with his "smiling latitudinarianism," which blurs distinctions which seem essential to them. His sexual attraction, however, is still strong
for Madge, and in a moment when he has tried hard to meet her at her own level,
and failed, a strong sense of compassion and compunction impels her to give herself
to him; the same motivation—surely a rare one in literature—draws Helen, for the
one night, to Leonard Bast. But—while the same problem is central to both novels—
Hale White has none of Forster's confidence that disparities can be connected. Madge
is sure that there can be no meaningful union between her passion and Frank's prose,
and although she is bearing Frank's child, she refuses to marry him.

But it is a reverent agnosticism, quite different from the bleak definiteness of Fielding's avowal of disbelief. Fielding is Forster's main spokesman for the rational, sceptical kind of humanism, and he is an admirable one, but the universe which he has missed or rejected impinges on all the novels, and gives them much of their special quality.

I have spoken chiefly so far about Forster's links with the Victorians, but his links with the Romantics are perhaps even firmer and more significant. Like all writers of comedy, Forster deals with illusion and reality, but his characters are not measured, primarily, against a commonly accepted social norm; they are judged, rather, by the ideal standards of the "Beloved Republic." (This explains, no doubt, why, mingling with the laughter, we find that curious apocalyptic note, so unlike Jane Austen. Harriet, stealing the baby, appears grotesque, almost a monster; the "terrible cousin" Charlotte appears as a portent, "brown against the view"; Lucy Honeychurch is not simply a conventional girl making too much fuss over a kiss on the cheek from a fellow-tourist, but is ranged with the "armies of the benighted"; Charles Wilcox wields his foolish sword and the oracular Miss Avery cries out "Murderer!") The human failure which Forster is most at pains to attack and expose is "stupidity" or "obtuseness." His "good" characters are transparent, in that they can see into themselves and others, and usually have some insight into "the unseen" as well, while his "bad" characters are opaque. (And some of them, like Caroline Abbott and Lucy Honeychurch, move rather uncertainly from opacity to transparency.) The failure delineated here is a failure of imagination—both of the penetrative imagination which can see beyond the surface of things, and the sympathetic imagination which has a "passionate understanding" into the hearts of others—and we can find an apt comment on it in Blake's aphorism, "If the doors of perception were cleansed every thing would appear to man as it is, infinite." The great trouble with Pembrokes and Wilcoxes is that their doors of perception are sorely in need of cleansing, or are beyond it. Blake's statement has of course religious overtones, and so too has an equally famous statement by Keats: "I am certain of nothing but of the holiness of the heart's affections, and the truth of imagination." This declaration was obviously of central importance to Forster,[6] and it is referred to directly at least three times in his writings. (Each time, as it happens, it is misquoted or paraphrased. We find "the Holiness of the Heart's Affection" in *What I Believe*, "the holiness of the heart's imagination" in Section XXVI of *The Longest Journey*, and "One is certain of nothing but the truth of one's own emotions" in Chapter XIX of *Howards End*.) The great *sin*, for Forster, is the "sin against affection," but only those with imaginative perception can fully realise what affection demands, and

---

[6] There is no space to develop the point, but Forster may well have found that the support given to his central concepts by Keats was reinforced by his reading of Moore's *Principia Ethica*, particularly the last chapter. There are clearly recognisable parallels.

fully respond to it. And the major dividing line in the novels, as we have noted, is between those who have this perception and those who lack it.

But although the claims of Love and "passionate understanding" are constantly reasserted, it was inevitable that Forster's hold on them should be less sure than that of his Romantic predecessors. The Romantic philosophy was firmly rooted in the idea of a beneficent Nature, and in *The Prelude* Wordsworth associates and even identifies Imagination with the "Intellectual Love" which is at the centre of things. It is true that, in Shelley's phrase, there is an "unwilling dross" in "the dull dense world" which may check its flight (for Forster this is "the rubbish that cumbers the world"), but the Spirit of Love must eventually triumph. But in the Victorian age, even before the advent of Darwin, the concept of Nature's benevolence was rudely disturbed. In an early sonnet, ironically entitled "In Harmony with Nature," Arnold observed that "Nature is cruel," and this was reinforced in some of the most painful, familiar, and influential stanzas of *In Memoriam*. Admittedly, the cult of Nature enjoyed some revival in the last years of the century and the earlier years of this; Edward Carpenter's *Towards Democracy* ran through many editions, and Meredith, in such poems as "The Woods of Westermain," attempted to accommodate a Romantic natural piety with Darwinian science. Forster acknowledges the influence of Meredith on his youth, and the vehement innocence of old Mr. Emerson's plea for a "return to Nature" is strongly reminiscent of Carpenter.[7] But although Nature plays an important or even a major part in three of the novels, Forster's attitude towards it was bound to be equivocal. In *The Longest Journey* he echoes Arnold's phrase about Nature's cruelty, yet in *Howards End* he says specifically, "The Earth as an artistic cult has had its day." The net product of this indeterminacy is a curious whimsicality. At the beginning of the book Ruth Wilcox appears trailing wisps of hay, at the end Helen rejoices in a grand crop of hay—but the male Wilcoxes and Tibby suffer from hay fever! Mrs. Wilcox and Howards End retain their force as poetic symbols, but the whimsicality surely tends to dissipate if not discredit it.

In the same novel Forster looks forward sadly to the time when "trees and meadows and mountains will be only a spectacle, and the binding force that they once exercised on character must be entrusted to Love alone." And he adds, "May Love be equal to the task!" The attitude here is again strongly reminiscent of Arnold (who, Forster tells us, "is of all the Victorians most to my taste"). When, in *A Room with a View*, he speaks of the "armies of the benighted" (those who have denied Love), he is surely recalling the "ignorant armies" which "clash by night" in Arnold's *Dover Beach*, and in this poem Arnold offers love as the only

---

[7] In a recent letter to one of my students, Forster denies any identification between the two, but he knew and admired Carpenter, and respected his work.

sure solace for the incertitude which follows the ebbing of the Sea of Faith. But Arnold too feels obliged to ask, "Is even Love too weak?"—too weak, that is, to release the "buried stream" of the imaginative life, and allow men the free exercise of their sympathies and perceptions. At one important point in Forster's novels Love does fail. Mrs. Moore is unable to help Aziz and Adela because her faith in affection and everything else has been undermined by her nightmare experience in the Marabar Caves. The caves "robbed infinity and eternity of their vastness," and it appears that that other universe, which, as I have said, Forster invokes in all the novels, may after all close in upon us and have nothing clear to say to us; beyond arch after arch there may be only silence. The experience so powerfully depicted here is, again, not new. Arnold says that "all men in a brazen prison live," and he was very familiar with "the twilight of the double vision" which troubles Forster. In a letter written to Clough on March 6, 1848, Arnold discriminates clearly between the two kinds of humanism I have been discussing: "Our weakness is that in an age where all tends to the triumph of the logical absolute reason we neither courageously have thrown ourselves into this movement . . . nor yet have driven our feet into the solid ground of our individuality as spiritual, poetic, profound *persons*. . . . How long halt ye between two opinions?" Arnold says that the second of these two lines was the natural one for him, and so it was too for Forster; his humanism was predominantly of the imaginative and religious kind. But in the absence of any firm sanctions for the imaginative life, the rational, sceptical spirit is liable to make very severe inroads into it, and the inroads clearly became sharper as Forster grew older. The faith, central to *Howards End,* not only that the two kinds of humanism can be united, but that their combined force may even transform civilisation, has declined or even disappeared in *A Passage to India,* and it may not be entirely fanciful to see the parting of the ways between Aziz and Fielding at the end of the novel as symbolic, not only of the gap between East and West, but of the growing gulf between the two voices. It should be noted, however, that in spite of the Marabar nightmare Forster does not surrender his imaginative faith. In the last pages of the book Fielding says that his wife's ideas (she is Mrs. Moore's spiritual heir) seem ridiculous when she is away from him, but when she is with him he feels half dead and half blind by comparison. As I have suggested earlier, Fielding is by no means to be identified with Forster, but Forster must surely have known this double awareness: a sense of the absurdity of "the unseen," and a sense of inadequacy in its presence. In the face of the irreconcilable, one can only jog along as decently as one can, seeing life steadily and, at times, in spite of the surrounding uncertainty, seeing it whole.

Imagination and Moral Theme
in E.M. Forster's *The Longest Journey*

by John Harvey

E.M. Forster's *The Longest Journey* has left many of his critics puzzled and a little uneasy. Lionel Trilling's general comment on the book is a good example of this kind of reaction. He grants that it is "by conventional notions the least perfect—the least compact, the least precisely formed," but immediately he goes on to claim that "it is perhaps the most brilliant, the most dramatic and the most passionate of his works." He admits "that the book is not a perfect whole" but feels "that it does not so much fall apart as fly apart; the responsive reader can be conscious not of an inadequate plan or a defect instructure but rather of the too-much steam that blows up the boiler." [1]

One feels here that Trilling's metaphor has betrayed him into a crude division between, on the one hand, form or technique, and, on the other, substance or the pressure of experienced material. The two, of course, cannot really be separated—or if they can, some defect in the work of art is indicated. But ideally, technique and form are not merely the means by which experience is discovered to us; they are inseparable from the experience itself. What one sees is also the way in which one sees it—this, one of the themes of Forster's novel, can also provide a useful entry into critical discussion of it. The purpose of this essay, then, is to maintain that structural flaws, technical defects are not mere superficial blemishes but are the inevitable correlatives of a confused or inadequate vision of life, and that by an examination of the novel's form we can best approach an evaluation of its "substances," of the experience being offered us.

It would, perhaps, be more orthodox to begin by asking what the novel is about. But questions of this sort too often tempt the critic into isolating one of the main themes and insisting that this is the major

"Imagination and Moral Theme in E.M. Forster's *The Longest Journey*." From *Essays in Criticism*, VI, No. 4 (October 1956), 418-33. Copyright © 1956 by the editors of *Essays in Criticism*. Reprinted by permission of the editors of *Essays in Criticism* and the author.

[1] Lionel Trilling, *E.M. Forster* (London: The Hogarth Press, 1944), p. 67.

unifying principle of the book. If the critic does this, he is liable to falsify the total work; the need for lucidity and emphasis in his analysis
may tempt him to make coherent, simple and intellectually consistent
what in the novel itself may be sprawling, complicated or confused.
Trilling does not wholly escape this trap; for him *The Longest Journey*
is a novel about appearance and reality; granted this postulate, his job
then seems to be one of tidying up, of making the various elements of
the novel fit in with its central theme, though—unlike less scrupulous
critics—he does not actually suppress or distort those elements that do
not square with the general pattern he has already abstracted from the
book. Nevertheless the result is ultimately misleading; *The Longest
Journey,* as it comes to us through the filter of Trilling's critical intelligence, appears to have a shapeliness of form and a clarity of outline
that it does not in fact possess.

Trilling is undeniably right in stressing the importance of "appearance
and reality" as a thematic element in *The Longest Journey;* the book
directs us to this problem in the opening pages, by the philosophic discussion on the existence of the cow. We may even accept Trilling's narrowing down of the theme to the problem of appearance and reality as
it confronts the imaginative man, for the imaginative nature of Rickie
is equally heavily stressed at the outset of the book. While the other undergraduates argue whether the objective reality of the cow can be distinguished from one's subjective perception of it, Rickie is lost in a
dream about cows, a vision where:

> The darkness of Europe was dotted with them, and in the far East their
> flanks were shining in the rising sun. Great herds of them stood browsing in
> pastures where no man came nor need ever come, or plashed knee-deep by
> the brink of impassable rivers.   (p. 9) [2]

If we accept this much, then we shall probably agree that a crucial
passage in the book is the scene where Rickie accuses his intellectual
friend, Ansell, of philosophic inconsistency in that Ansell has refused to
acknowledge the real presence of Agnes Pembroke. Ansell replies:

> Did it never strike you that phenomena may be of two kinds; *one,* those
> which have a real existence, such as the cow; *two,* those which are the sub
> jective product of a diseased imagination, and which, to our destruction,
> we invest with the semblance of reality?   (p. 24)

For Trilling, everything in *The Longest Journey* derives from this
passage. Rickie's imagination *is* diseased and he literally destroys himself
by investing subjective illusions with the semblance of reality. In terms
of character and action, he does this by idealizing three people—his dead
mother; Agnes Pembroke, whom he marries; and Stephen Wonham, his

---

[2] All page-references are to the pocket edition of *The Longest Journey,* published by
Edward Arnold & Co., London, 1947.

half-brother. This undoubtedly is an important thread in the whole book and it has been unravelled so fully and so carefully by Trilling that it would be superfluous to repeat it. Trilling is persuasive as well as perceptive, and his analysis of *The Longest Journey* almost convinces the reader that the book is as shapely and as lucid as his essay implies it is. But the book itself is at once richer and untidier than Trilling suggests; he has, after all, unravelled only one thread and we must not mistake the single strand for the entire cord. In particular it is important to decide whether the cord is patterned into an intricate knot or whether it remains a hopeless tangle; to discover, if possible, when, how, and why a proper and necessary complexity slides into confusion.

We may accept Trilling's analysis as the starting-point of such an exploration. Rickie is at the centre of the novel and around him are grouped various opposing forces in patterns that are significantly, even suspiciously, neat. These patterns can perhaps best be defined in terms of sight and blindness. If we accept for the moment Forster's vague term "reality" as the thing it is important to see clearly, as the value that should demand one's allegiance, then there are various modes of insight depicted in the book and, similarly, various kinds and degrees of blindness. On one side are lined up the forces of insight—Ansell the philosopher, the intellectual man, whose favourite haunt is the reading-room of the British Museum:

> There he knew that life was not ignoble. It was worth while to grow old and dusty seeking for truth though truth is unattainable, restating questions that have been stated at the beginning of the world. Failure would await him, but not disillusionment.   (pp. 199-200)

Aligned, though contrasted with him, is Stephen, the natural child and the child of nature, the man of intuition who knows so instinctively what is real and what is right that he does not even know he knows. His is a natural sympathy, expressed sometimes in impulsive action, sometimes simply by being alive.

> He was scarcely a fashionable horseman. He was not even graceful. But he rode as a living man, though Rickie was too much bored to notice it. Not a muscle in him was idle, not a muscle working hard. When he returned from a gallop his limbs were still unsatisfied and his manners still irritable. He did not know that he was ill: he knew nothing about himself at all.   (pp. 126-27)

On the other side are Herbert and Agnes Pembroke, stultified by convention, ignorant even of their ignorance of reality, and Mrs. Failing who, because her choice of the powers of darkness and unreality is one of conscious intellect as a deliberate act of the will, is thereby the more actively malicious. The minor characters also arrange themselves according to this pattern; Jackson and Mr. Failing on the one side, Gerald and Rickie's father on the other. Rickie is the focus, the point of balance of these opposing forces; his imagination is a valid mode of insight but a vulnerable one; it can be perverted into creating false images or it can be blinkered and stifled by convention.

This pattern defines itself in the book by a highly elaborate network of parallels and contrasts, anticipations and recollections; sometimes between members of the same group, sometimes between members of opposing groups. There is, for example, all the difference in the world between Gerald's conventionally indignant reaction to the naive but benevolent offer of money by Rickie and Stephen's rejection of the bribe held out to Agnes. Rickie's apparently friendly scuffle with Ansell at Cambridge in fact conceals the parting of two friends; Ansell's fight with Stephen at Sawston is the beginning of an alliance between two people who see the same things, though in vastly different ways. Just as these two ally themselves after initial conflict so Agnes and Mrs. Failing join forces after quarrelling. And so on—examples of this kind of organization could be multiplied indefinitely; some of them will emerge later in a consideration of the book's symbolism.

There are two important points to notice about this kind of pattern. Firstly, it is clearly directed and controlled by a moral intention. Only occasionally does this intention approach the obviousness of direct statement; Rickie's momentary view of Herbert Pembroke is as nearly explicit as anything in the book:

> What was amiss with Herbert? He had known that something was amiss, and had entered into partnership with open eyes. The man was kind and unselfish; more than that, he was truly charitable, and it was a real pleasure to him to give pleasure to others. Certainly he might talk too much about it afterwards; but it was the doing, not the talking, that he really valued, and benefactors of this sort are not too common. He was, moreover, diligent and conscientious; his heart was in his work, and his adherence to the Church of England no mere matter of form. He was capable of affection; he was usually courteous and tolerant. Then what was amiss? Why, in spite of all these qualities, should Rickie feel that there was something wrong with him—nay, that he was wrong as a whole, and that if the Spirit of Humanity should ever hold a judgment he would assuredly be classed among the goats? The answer at first sight appeared a graceless one—it was that Herbert was stupid . . . for all his fine talk about spiritual life he had but one test for things—success; success for the body in this life or for the soul in the life to come. And for this reason Humanity, and perhaps such other tribunals as there may be, would assuredly reject him.   (pp. 187-88)

This division of humanity into the sheep and the goats, the open-eyed and the blind, the good and the evil, is constant in Forster; it underlies the similar grouping of characters that we find in his other novels. And were this intention the sole motivating principle of *The Longest Journey* it would indeed have had the clarity and firmness of outline that Trilling's essay suggests; it would have been a morality play with the forces of good and evil contending for the soul of Rickie. This simple moral division is always a temptation to Forster and when he succumbs to it, as in some of his short stories, the results are generally lamentable. But in his novels the moral impulse is usually held in check, because, having accepted the framework of social comedy as his literary mode, he must to some extent fulfil the expectations aroused by that framework and, more important, because his own sense of what life is like tells him that such a crude division of humanity into black and white would, if enforced, only arouse the hostility of the reader. The morality play could easily slide into melodrama—indeed melodrama is never far below the surface of Forster's work: consequently he must insist that the sheep and the goats partake of each other's nature; thus in the book:

> Rickie suffered from the Primal Curse, which is not—as the Authorized Version suggests—the knowledge of good and evil, but the knowledge of good-and-evil.   (p. 194)

Correspondingly Forster himself insists upon the good-and-evil of the human world; he is careful to blur the moral edges of his characters so that we shall not adopt a simple and single attitude towards them but shall acknowledge through them the richness and complexity of life itself. Thus in the judgment on Herbert Pembroke quoted above, Forster is careful to emphasize Herbert's many good points; thus Agnes Pembroke is capable of being jolted by Rickie out of her convention-ridden life into a moment of intense passion and grief for the dead Gerald; thus Mrs. Failing is similarly complicated by the novelist so that:

> Rickie was impressed by her loneliness, and also by the mixture in her of insight and obtuseness. She was so quick, so clear-headed, so imaginative even. But all the same she had forgotten what people were like. Finding life dull, she had dropped lies into it, as a chemist drops a new element into a solution, hoping that life would thereby sparkle or turn some beautiful colour. She loved to mislead others, and in the end her private view of false and true was obscured, and she misled herself.   (p. 307)

The opposing group of characters is treated in a similar manner; thus Ansell is shown to have his limitations and behind Ansell the whole world of Cambridge friendship which sometimes seems to be advanced by the book as a type of the ideal life. These undergraduates, too, have their blind-spots, the moments when they lose touch with reality; thus, early in the book, one of them is betrayed into tactlessness:

> Widdrington was crimson too. In his wish to be sprightly he had used words without thinking of their meanings. Suddenly he realized that "father" and "mother" really meant father and mother—people whom he had himself at home.   (p. 28)

This is later expanded into a generalized comment; Rickie

was only used to Cambridge, and to a very small corner of that. He and his
friends there believed in free speech. But they spoke freely about general-
ities. They were scientific and philosophic. They would have shrunk from
the empirical freedom that results from a little beer.   (p. 129)

The same thing happens with Stephen; Forster is careful to emphasize
his sulkiness, clumsiness, occasional insensitivity; he is for a time seduced
by shallowly rationalistic pamphlets, while at one point he touches his
counterpart in the opposing camp:

> The boy had a little reminded him of Gerald—the Gerald of history, not
> the Gerald of romance. He was more genial, but there was the same brutal-
> ity, the same peevish insistence on the pound of flesh.   (p. 123)

We must make allowances here for Rickie's limited viewpoint (his
imagination is already deceived) but nevertheless this impression of
Stephen does remain with us—remains with us so strongly, in fact, that
we are reluctant to accept the positive values that Forster insists are embodied in him. This local difficulty about Stephen is only a particular
instance of the general view of the novel I should wish to maintain—that
in *The Longest Journey* Forster's moral intention, his impulse to divide
and judge, comes into conflict with his sense of what life is really like.
On the one hand he is tempted by the clarity and decision of the
morality, on the other he is acutely aware that human beings are not so
simple, that they will constantly elude his moral categories. The content
of the novel, in other words, is not amenable to the form he wishes to
impose upon it and the fact that he imposes rather than elicits form—
indeed, that any division between form and content should exist—suggests that the novel is not a completely successful work of art. Basically,
the problem is one of the author's skill in manipulating and directing
the reader's responses, and our responses to this novel are often confused
and contradictory; we are torn between the impulse to decide, to judge,
and the impulse to withhold, to qualify. This tension is never successfully
resolved in the novel.

Let us examine more closely the moral problems involved and the
methods employed by Forster. There are, of course, many local successes
and these generally occur when Forster is content to work within the
framework of social comedy. Forster notably scores with Herbert Pembroke. He is a master of irony by juxtaposition; consider, for example,
how he deflates Pembroke in the scene in which the schoolmaster is
waxing eloquent to his assembled pupils:

> He told them that this term, the second of his reign, was *the* term for
> Dunwood House; that it behoved every boy to labour during it for his
> house's honour, and, through the house, for the honour of the school. Tak-
> ing a wider range, he spoke of England, or rather of Great Britain, and of
> her continental foes. Portraits of empire builders hung on the wall, and he
> pointed to them. He quoted imperial poets. . . . And it seemed that only a

short ladder lay between the preparation-room and the Anglo-Saxon hegemony of the globe. Then he paused, and in the silence came "sob, sob, sob," from a little boy, who was regretting a villa in Guildford and his mother's half-acre of garden.   (pp. 178-79)

or the ironic, because unconscious, self-betrayal of:

"It is true that I vote Conservative," pursued Mr. Pembroke, apparently confronting some objector. "But why? Because the Conservatives, rather than the Liberals, stand for progress. One must not be misled by catchwords."   (p. 184)

But beyond these particulars the social comedy is successful in that it carries a good deal of the general moral burden of the novel. It does this by revealing, in terms of character, situation and symbol, firstly, the wrong demands society makes upon the individual, and, secondly, the wrong demands individuals make upon each other. The first of these is conveyed largely through the important role given to convention in the lives of the blind, convention which, with its attendant stock responses, platitudes and clichés, chokes up the springs of personal feeling and darkens the world with "the shadow of unreality." This is made most explicit at the end of the book in the final conversation between Rickie and Mrs. Failing, but it is implicit throughout. Thus, at the very outset, when Rickie is apologizing to Agnes for Ansell's behaviour:

"Ansell isn't a gentleman. His father's a draper. His uncles are farmers. He's here because he's so clever—just on account of his brains. Now sit down. He isn't a gentleman at all." And he hurried off to order some dinner.

"What a snob the boy is getting!" thought Agnes, a good deal mollified. It never struck her that those could be the words of affection—that Rickie would never have spoken them about a person whom he disliked.
                                         (pp. 12-13)

Agnes, that is, translates everything into terms of *social* relationship—she rarely perceives the *human* relationships that lie beneath. When she does, her tendency is to retreat, to withdraw; thus, of a moment of personal feeling between brother and sister, Forster can write: "Their tenderness soon passed. They exchanged it with averted eyes. It embarrassed them."

Those characters blinded and hidebound by convention are generally described in mechanical terms; Sawston school is more than once called a "benevolent machine" while Agnes is described by Ansell and one of his friends in these terms:

"My cousin thinks Mrs. Elliot one of the most horrible women he has ever seen. He calls her 'Medusa in Arcady.' She's so pleasant, too. But certainly it was a very stony meal."

"What kind of stoniness?"

"No one stopped talking for a moment."

"That's the real kind," said Ansell moodily, "the only kind."

"Well I," he continued, "am inclined to compare her to an electric light. Click! she's on. Click! she's off. No waste. No flicker."   (p. 201)

We notice the force of "Medusa in Arcady"—for to accept the way of life that Agnes stands for is to become petrified, to lose one's identity; similarly of her brother, Herbert, it is said that:

> In three years Mr. Pembroke had done much to solidify the day-boys at Sawston school. If they were not solid they were at all events curdling.
>
> (p. 167)

This links the world of social convention with the world in which individuals make improper claims upon each other. The great sin of the spiritually blind is to deny the autonomy of human beings, to impose upon them a pattern of one's own making, to mould them and organize them. Herbert Pembroke is eminently of this kind:

> His technical position was that of a master to a form low down on the Modern side. But his work lay elsewhere. He organized. If no organization existed he would create one. If one did exist, he would modify it. "An organization," he would say, "is after all not an end in itself. It must contribute to a movement." When one good custom seemed likely to corrupt the school, he was ready with another; he believed that without innumerable customs there was no safety, either for boys or men. Perhaps he is right, and always will be right. Perhaps each of us would go to ruin if for one short hour we acted as we thought fit, and attempted the service of perfect freedom.   (p. 52)

But Pembroke is merely a slave to the machine he has helped to create; the two more actively malignant characters in the book, Mrs. Failing and Mr. Elliot (Rickie's father), see themselves as puppet masters in a comedy of life, whose characters they can manipulate for their own amusement. It is part of Rickie's spiritual illness that he attempts to impose his own ideal patterns upon human life; at the end of the book Agnes's attempt to bribe Stephen with money is paralleled by Rickie's attempt at moral blackmail, when he forces Stephen to promise that he will not get drunk. When Stephen asserts himself and does get drunk, Rickie is left disillusioned:

> Rickie said, "May God receive me and pardon me for trusting the earth."
>
> "But Mr. Elliot, what have you done that's wrong?"
>
> "Gone bankrupt, Leighton, for the second time. Pretended again that people were real. May God have mercy on me!"
>
> Leighton dropped his arm. Though he did not understand, a chill of disgust passed over him.   (p. 311)

This is the tragic crux of Rickie's perverted view of the world: that the framework of social comedy can be stretched to include such a theme indicates how far Forster is successful. Nevertheless his success is fatally limited in that whatever is alive in the book derives from his insight into the world of the spiritually blind or into the ways in which spiritual insight may be so far perverted that values are reversed and "true" and "false," "pretence" and "reality" change sides and turn into their opposites. All this may be called the negative vision of the book; but negation, sickness, unreality all imply—and in a novel, demand—their opposites. It is when Forster attempts to portray the positive side of his theme, the norm which some characters deny and others pervert, that the book becomes confused.

So long as Forster confines himself to suggesting the good life, either by symbol or by dramatic contrasts of human response and attitude, the book is successful. The two cannot be separated; I mean, for example, the constant use of the Greek past—whether heroic or pastoral—as a standard of reference whereby characters may be tested. The differing responses of the two schoolmasters, Jackson and Pembroke, to the classical past reveals the truth about both of them. Rickie's degeneration can be accurately measured in such terms, while Stephen is the very incarnation of that past and as such is contrasted with Gerald who merely "had the figure of a Greek athlete and the face of an English one." Or again, one may contrast Stephen's deep and abiding communion with nature with Mrs. Failing's attitude, which was:

> severely aesthetic—an attitude more sterile than the severely practical. She applied the test of beauty to shadow and odour and sound; they never filled her with reverence or excitement; she never knew them as a resistless trinity that may intoxicate the worshipper with joy.   (p. 119)

It is when Forster refuses obliquity, when he rejects symbol for statement and drama for assertion, that the trouble begins. There is a good deal of talk in the novel about Truth, Freedom and Love and these abstractions never find an adequately concrete correlative, they never make contact with the imaginatively experienced and dramatically expressed content of the book. The crucial concept, however, is Reality; the book stands or falls by the way in which the Real is made actual in terms of the felt life transmitted to us through character, action and symbol. It is the recognition and acceptance of the real that constitute spiritual insight, perversion and refusal that constitute blindness and spiritual sickness. The Real, therefore, is at the moral centre of the book and, as such, it is imperative that it should be brought to imaginative life. Forster's failure to do this, the presence in the book of a stubborn gap between the abstract concept and the particular facts of life presented dramatically, represents the essential failure of *The Longest Journey*.

Forster's language betrays him; consider one of the key passages of the novel, the revelation to Rickie of the love that exists between Gerald and Agnes and his reaction to this discovery:

He only looked for a moment, but the sight burnt into his brain. The man's grip was the stronger. He had drawn the woman on to his knee, was pressing her, with all his strength, against him. Already her hands slipped off him and she whispered, "Don't—you hurt—" Her face had no expression. It stared at the intruder and never saw him. Then her lover kissed it, and immediately it shone with mysterious beauty, like some star.

Rickie limped away without the sandwiches, crimson and afraid. He thought, "Do such things actually happen?" and he seemed to be looking down coloured valleys. Brighter they glowed, till gods of pure flame were born in them, and then he was looking at pinnacles of virgin snow. While Mr. Pembroke talked, the riot of fair images increased. They invaded his being and lit lamps at unsuspected shrines. Their orchestra commenced in that suburban house, where he had to stand aside for the maid to carry in the luncheon. Music flowed past him like a river. He stood at the springs of creation and heard the primeval monotony. Then an obscure instrument gave out a little phrase. The river continued unheeding. The phrase was repeated, and a listener might know it was a fragment of the Tune of tunes. Nobler instruments accepted it, the clarionet protected, the brass encouraged and it rose to the surface to the whisper of violins. In full unison was Love born, flame of the flame, flushing the dark river beneath him, and the virgin snows above. His wings were infinite, his youth eternal; the sun was a jewel on his finger, as he passed it in benediction over the world. Creation, no longer monotonous, acclaimed him, in widening melody, in brighter radiances. Was love a column of fire? Was he a torrent of song? Was he greater than either—the touch of a man on a woman?   (p. 49)

This is, or should be, one of the peaks of the novel; its relevance to the central theme lies in the fact that Forster constantly suggests to us that what is real—and really important—is the intense, passionate moment of perception when human relationships are seen to be what they really are. This is such a moment—but how is it conveyed to us? To be blunt, by a purple passage that would be more at home in a woman's weekly magazine than in the work of one of the great modern novelists. It is a lamentable and vulgar piece of writing—depending on the clichés of popular romance ("the sight burnt into his brain"), on a tumult of over-heightened, florid and cloudy associations, completely divorced from life as we know it and collapsing at the end into a welter of rhetorical questions. Of course, it may be objected that what we are being given here is the moment as perceived by Rickie, as filtered through his sensibility, that it is in fact, a dramatic passage, appropriate to the character who experiences this moment. That has its own truth; but as an objection it may be answered in two ways. Accepting it as true, then the quality of Rickie's imagination is coarsened and the whole moral theme of the novel thereby diminished. Secondly, one still uneasily feels the presence of Forster behind his character; we are certainly meant to endorse the values implied by this moment of perception, all the power of the rhetoric being directed to this end. But the rhetoric defeats itself; this is supposed to be a moment of intense awareness of personal experience but the style, by its evasion of experience, contradicts what it is meant to enforce. This second point is reinforced by the presence in the novel of a number of passages where Forster is speaking directly to the reader without the refuge of an intervening dramatic sensibility, passages which display the same stylistic defects; a notable example is the short chapter which concludes the Sawston section of the book.

This is but one example of Forster failing at just those points where it is most important he should succeed. Other, and more extended, examples could be quoted; in particular, Stephen Wonham, as a human being, is incapable of bearing those moral values he is meant to convey to us. This brings us back to the clash between the moral intention of the novelist and his sense of what life, in all its complexities and contradictions, is really like. It is just those sections of the book which are most vividly realized by the author—the sections centering upon the Pembrokes—that he must insist are unreal, if the book is going to make its moral point. Again, the reader is torn between assenting to the world presented to us and assenting to the denial of that world which is demanded of us by the author. The moral emphasis and the dramatic power of the book not only do not coincide; they are in direct conflict with each other. This would seem to be more than an aesthetic confusion. We have noticed that in his attempt to be fair to Herbert Pembroke, Forster allows that "it was the doing not the talking, that he really valued." Yet how is this real value to be distinguished from the reality accessible to Ansell or Stephen? Other criteria must be involved but they are never adequately realized in the book itself.

One way in which Forster attempts to resolve these difficulties is his elaborate and insistent use of symbolism. This obtrudes with an explicitness quite unusual in his work; frequently the characters themselves point out how this scene or that action is symbolic. That this explicitness weakens the effectiveness of the symbol is probable but the symbolism of *The Longest Journey* demands an essay to itself. We may notice, however, that frequently it conflicts with, instead of reinforcing, some other element in the book. Thus Ansell's initial refusal to acknowledge the existence of Agnes Pembroke may be symbolically acceptable, even necessary, but viewed in the context of social comedy and naturalistic detail, it is, to say the least, clumsy.

The Longest Journey, then, despite—or perhaps because of—its local successes is a failure as a whole. The disparate elements of which it is composed are never brought together into any kind of unity; at best they lie uneasily side by side; more often they actively quarrel with each other. One feels that Forster's ambition has outrun his technical resources; sometimes he sees life steadily, and sometimes he sees it whole; but never both at the same time. It is not until *A Passage to India* that he harmonizes and unifies those "heterogeneous ideas" which in *The Longest Journey* are "yoked by violence together."

Howards End

by Malcolm Bradbury

I

One problem in the discussion of fiction—a problem that arises from the considerable variety of modes of presentation, and of human experience, that a single novel can by reason of its length and prose character contain—is that of reaching an effective description of the direction or unifying principle of a single work. Critics and novelists alike have agreed that works of fiction must have unity, a unity in which the parts of the action exist in some necessary relationship one with another, so contributing to the shape or emotional character of the whole. In fact, when it comes to the point of distinguishing and condemning violations of this unity, the judgment of the critic is usually prescriptive —novels must not have episodes, or novels must not have variations of tone, or novels must be subject to the test of reality (is it probable, does this follow from that?). There are many famous critical instances of the problem, such as the "Man on the Hill" episode in *Tom Jones,* and the "History of a Self-Tormentor" episode in *Little Dorrit*; and some of E.M. Forster's fiction presents us with a sophisticated version of the same difficulty. In this case, the problem is not that of interposed episodes, introducing secondary narrative into the primary one, but of an unusual range of tone.

A number of critics of Forster have distinguished two modes in his fiction, and have argued that they exist at odds with each other. The two modes are usually described as those of social comedy and visionary writing; and it is not infrequent for critics to praise Forster's success in one and condemn the intrusion of the other. Lord David Cecil makes the criticism in a general way when he says that Forster as a novelist is a romantic comedian, satirizing and commenting on his materials not from the point of view of common sense but of uncommon sensibility, and that this perspective leads him into a technical defect.[1] Forster does not, Cecil claims, succeed in harmonizing realism and symbolism, and the

"Howards End." Revised from "E.M. Forster's Howards End," by Malcolm Bradbury, in *The Critical Quarterly*, IV, Autumn 1962, pp. 229-41. Copyright © 1962, 1965 by Malcolm Bradbury. Reprinted by permission of the editors of *The Critical Quarterly*.

[1] Lord David Cecil, in *Poets and Story-Tellers* (London: Constable, Ltd., 1949).

symbolic episodes are sometimes too improbable for the reader to maintain his illusion of everyday reality (as an example, he cites Helen
Schlegel's unlikely seduction of Leonard Bast in *Howards End*). Virginia
Woolf, too, has a similar criticism to make; she argues, in her essay on
Forster, that he is a novelist much concerned with present conditions,
with social reality, but that he wants also to address a message to the
soul. "It seems, then, that if he is to succeed in his mission his reality
must at certain points become irradiated. . . ." Yet it is at these moments when the uncompromisingly solid should become the luminously
transparent that he fails, because the conjunction of the two realities
casts doubt upon both.[2]

In his essay on Forster, F.R. Leavis puts a like argument in a much
more sophisticated way—a much more sustainable way, because we can
see more clearly what his premises about fiction are. He argues that the
kind of life that Forster appears, in *Howards End,* to value, and toward
which Margaret is reaching, is not satisfactorily achieved in the marriage
of Margaret and Mr. Wilcox; and this constitutes "a perversity of intention" which derives in part from too great an attentiveness to the
schematic design of the book, and not enough to the particular reality
in the situation. The immediacy of experience in the novel is at odds
with the symbolic structuring and the poetic gestures the novel seeks to
make. We can "explain" the book, then, in symbolic terms, but in terms
of the actual life conveyed something is missing.[3] Leavis is distrustful
of the vague, the ambiguous, the whole mode of the poetic as Forster
uses it; and if we depend on fiction to make everything come alive for us
in its particularity then we may share his disquiet. But it is of course possible to argue that the metaphysical and transcendental dimensions of
the novel could scarcely be got by other means, and that these, too, are
among the things we take pleasure in. And it is also possible to argue
(though this would not meet Leavis's order of objection) that the elements which critics have tended to define as contradictory and at odds
are very much more in accord than many critics have tended to suggest.
A fuller description of the kind of literary activity taking place in the
novel might, then, make it easier for us to avoid seeing it as a social
novel with flawed elements, or a visionary novel with too much social
detailing, or even as simply a novel that is striving toward the same conclusion as Margaret Schlegel reaches toward—as Leavis's account of it
seems to suggest. This would seem to involve asking questions about the
kind of comedy there is in the novel, and in what ways it is related to the
"poetic" or visionary features of the work. And this in turn can lead us
to ask whether the development of the action doesn't itself contain ele-

[2] Virginia Woolf, in *The Death of the Moth, and other Essays* (London: The Hogarth
Press, 1942).
[3] F.R. Leavis, in *The Common Pursuit* (London: Chatto & Windus, Ltd., 1952). (Essay reprinted in this volume.)

ments of irony which are associated with that comedy, and so create a greater unity in the novel than is often supposed.

Howards End is, I take it, a novel, treated in the comic mode, about the circumstances in which the moral life, which is also the full life of the imagination, can be led in society, about the compromises which it must effect with itself if it is to do so, and about the moral and imaginative value of making certain such compromises. It is to this sort of theme that we refer when we talk of Forster as a "liberal" novelist—to his concern with what is decent, human, and enlarging in daily conduct, to his concern with personal relationships and responsiveness to life, to his desire to find that truth and goodness coincide. But it is also a novel in which the moral life is concerned with transcendence, with questions about the way in which reality may be known. And this fact may lead us to give a very positive reading of the novel—to say, that is, that it postulates an end that can be achieved, a contact with the infinite. There is, it is true, a lot that is Platonic about Forster; life is grey unless it partakes of infinity, and intimations of the infinite can reside in personal relationships, in harmonious living, in contact with the earth. His liberalism finally justifies itself when it mirrors infinity; and Margaret Schlegel's "sermon" to her "lord," Mr. Wilcox: "Live in fragments no longer" is undoubtedly part of the ideal proposed by the book. In this sense, the book can be read as a metaphysical novel, and Cyrus Hoy has in fact offered a remarkably intelligent reading of it at this level, seeing it as solving a multiplicity of dualities and intimating "the comprehensive and harmonious vision of experience wherein the earthly partakes of the eternal, the particular testifies to the universal, and multiplicity becomes but another attribute of the one." [4] To read it in this way is, however, to miss accounting for some of the book's most striking features: its concern with society, the irony of its plot, and the striking ambiguity of the ending. It is also a novel concerned with the necessary conditions of this kind of liberal hope, concerned with social history and the possible developments of the future, concerned in fact with those "great impersonal forces" that Mr. Wilcox appeals to so complacently when he wants to eliminate the personal from conversation. And because it is so concerned, we must, I think, recognize that Forster tends, more than we often care to believe, to look quizzically at the things he is usually supposed to stand for. One of the main functions of the comic tone in the book is to enforce this feeling, to enable Forster to introduce a mode of scepticism about *himself*. *Howards End*, I am suggesting, is a good deal more ironic than most of the positive interpretations we can look up suggest, and a book more deliberately "limited" than is often supposed. The irony is in fact of the essence; it is present in the social comedy and in the

---

[4] Cyrus Hoy, "Forster's Metaphysical Novel," *PMLA*, LXXV, March 1960, 126-36.

poetic or visionary sections of the work, so creating more unity in the book than is usually found there.

What follows here is an attempt to give a description of the novel, which represents all the complications of the imitation and suggests something of the way in which the ironic tone works in the novel. This kind of description, necessary to—though it precedes—literary criticism, involves looking at as many of the parts of the myth as possible—taking *myth* to mean the total invention, the total effect the novelist seeks to produce. This is surely particularly necessary in the case of *Howards End* because it is tonally a very various novel, and this has meant, as I have suggested, that it can be read in radically different ways.

II

The substantial action of *Howards End* does not in fact begin until we are half-way through the novel. The reason for this is surely that what first must be established are the complexities by which it may be judged. When that action begins, it tells of a girl, imaginative, intellectual, middle class, of German stock, who becomes engaged to an English businessman, a widower with children, unimaginative, practical, effective. During their engagement they are confronted with a moral dilemma in that a chain of indirect responsibility links them both, he more than her, with the misfortunes of a lower-middle-class clerk and his wife. Because of the hero's unimaginativeness and the heroine's deference toward her fiancé, they do not immediately disentangle this responsibility, and in consequence the heroine's sister, a moral romantic, sleeps with the clerk as an act of sympathy. When she becomes pregnant, the issue of responsibility emerges in a new form; and the couple, now married, become openly divided, the wife insisting on the primacy of the standard of personal sympathy, the man on the standard of social propriety. Ensuing events, involving accident and coincidence, support the wife's point of view; this the husband is forced into accepting, and the action ends with the child of the unconventional union becoming heir to a part of the hero's estate in preference to his own children. It will be apparent that the action turns on a moral issue, though in fact the person for whom it is an issue— Wilcox—never completely recognizes this; thus the action infers the authorial view not only that persons bear a responsibility for those whose misfortunes they can be held remotely accountable, but also that they have an obligation to recognize this responsibility whether they have been trained to or not, and whether this violates their social duties or not. Further, the resolution of the action concerns a social matter—inheritance—but breaks the accepted conventions governing it by indicating that a moral or spiritual right to inherit precedes familial right; the worthiest people shall inherit the earth.

In short the novel is both tendentious and symbolic, and it would thus seem to support the notion held by the heroine, Margaret, that "any human being lies nearer to the unseen than any organization" and that personal relationships precede public ones. On the other hand, one might say that the fact that the heroine marries the hero and makes choices in his favour at many points in the action points to a countervailing principle. The hero is unimaginative, but he is effective and productive; the heroine's sister is a moral romantic who commits a foolish action. The whole action thus bears complex interpretation, and is treated in a complex way. Indeed, as I have indicated, the slowness with which the novel begins is directly related to the complexity of the interpretative apparatus the author wishes to create. The novel is dominated by two distinct kinds of tone, one comic, one poetic; it is also symbolic and tendentious; it contains a moral action conducted within a framework of the unseen in competition with the seen, the public with the private, and a social action conducted within an equally broad speculative framework, its question being who shall inherit England. One can say indeed that *Howards End* is a novel in which the events themselves are less important than the apparatus by which they are perceived and interpreted, and that the apparatus is one for conveying sensitivity, significance, a sense of large and formidable issues often not perceived even by the characters themselves. And to this end the development is delayed, turned from its chronological order, treated from various points of view, presented by indirection, in order to create a subtle questioning tone—modulating between two main modes, the comic, which refers chiefly to the social events of the book, and the poetic, which refers chiefly to the moral and spiritual events of the book.

Howards End sets out to present several different interpretations of the world, to show the social conditions which produce and may damage them, and to indicate how *all* in their different ways fall short of any complete account of experience; it also tries to show what that experience is that all must answer to. The opening chapters, prior to the entrance of Bast, present plainly two of these interpretations, one which insists on the public aspect of actions and events, another which insists on the personal aspect. These two interpretations are associated with families, groups of people—the Wilcoxes and the Schlegels. Both have their own distinctive history, circumstances and milieu which make them what they are. The Wilcoxes, in business, belong to a world of "telegrams and anger"; they describe the world as being organized towards given ends. They are sharp towards the lower orders, deferential towards social formalities, respectful towards machinery. Predominantly practical, predatory, expansionist, their spirit is the spirit of Whiggery, their economics and social philosophy are *laissez faire*. Their household is masculine and has all the energy associated with the male principle. When Helen Schlegel goes to stay with them at Howards End, she is attracted by and falls in love with the Wilcoxes as an institution because of this energy:

> The energy of the Wilcoxes had fascinated her, had created new images of beauty in her responsive mind. To be all day with them in the open air, to sleep at night under their roof, had seemed the supreme joy of life, and had led to that abandonment of personality that is a possible prelude to love. She had liked giving in to Mr. Wilcox, or Evie, or Charles; she had liked being told that her notions of life were sheltered or academic; that Equality was nonsense, Votes for Women nonsense, Socialism nonsense, Art and Literature, except when conducive to strengthening the character, nonsense. One by one the Schlegel fetishes had been overthrown, and, though professing to defend them, she had rejoiced. When Mr. Wilcox said that one sound man of business did more good to the world than a dozen of your social reformers, she had swallowed the curious assertion without a gasp, and had leant back luxuriously among the cushions of his motor-car.

The Wilcoxes, whose motor-car becomes a symbol of their practicality, their ceaseless urge to motion, their power to put things to use, are played off against the Schlegels and their "fetishes." The Schlegel household is predominantly female; the girls are emancipated, modern, humane, thoughtful, concerned with the arts for more or less their own sake, responsive to the plight of those less fortunate. The Wilcoxes are associated with a practical English heritage, the Schlegels with an intellectual, *deraciné* one. Their German background gives them a certain distance from English life and they draw on the international idealism of their father, of whom it is said that if one classed him at all it would be "as the countryman of Kant and Hegel, as the idealist, inclined to be dreamy, whose Imperialism was the Imperialism of the air." His life had been active and he had fought for his culture, but the discovery that this culture was too much devoted to commercial and political imperialism had deracinated him. "It was his hope that the clouds of materialism obscuring the Fatherland would part in time, and a mild intellectual light re-emerge." The juxtaposition of these two different principles, and the consciousness of the wide terms of their difference, animates the book. By throwing them into contrast, a mass of intellectual, moral, philosophical and social questions are raised; a dialectic is created in which the national contests with the international, the seen with the unseen, the practical with the romantic, the prose with the poetry and the passion; and the expectation that the book raises from its early pages is of conflict and possible synthesis, in which the terms of the dialectic are extended and laid bare. One is reminded of the structure of *The Magic Mountain,* which is likewise a dialectical novel in which the principles of order and disorder, bourgeois practicality and a Slavic anarchy, tolerance and intransigence contest, synthesize and form a new thesis for the next stage in the dialectic. The difference is that Forster's own values are deeply involved at each stage in the fiction.

The novel is concerned with developing relationships which heighten and illustrate the moral and intellectual principles brought into play. These relationships occur within a small and circumscribed area. The number of characters in the book is small; many are linked by kinship; most know one another before the novel begins. The settings are largely domestic; the kinds of crisis and choice that occur in this world are whether or not to marry this person, whether or not to help that one. It is a world in which kisses are felt with some impact and where the death of an individual has the greatest force. But the events take place in an elaborate social and intellectual context, and this is largely determined by the Schlegels. Though the settings are domestic, there is a great deal of travel and movement, within England and outside it in Europe. Though the number of characters is small, there are many different kinds of relation between them. Though many of the scenes are indoor ones, there are a number of highly important accidental meetings in the street, at concerts, and the like. The novel is set in the Edwardian period, and covers a number of years over which considerable social change occurs. This was the period in which female emancipation was an issue, when modern urban society was spreading widely over the countryside, when the stirrings of war with Germany were already being felt but when the great process of imperial and commercial expansion was still active. It was a time when the intellectual heritage of romanticism was undergoing some strain, when intellectuals were moving from liberalism to socialism, when G.E. Moore's *Principia Ethica* was influential and when, as Desmond MacCarthy put it, there was discussion about "those 'goods' which were ends in themselves; and these ends, for which the rest of life was only a scaffolding, could be subsumed under three heads: the search for truth, aesthetic emotions and personal relations—love and friendship." We feel all these things in the novel. It is not that it is a period piece but that it is responsive to the social dimension, and indeed what is happening in society has the largest relevance to the plot.

We have in the book three main milieux, the intellectual urban milieu of the Schlegels, the country commuter's world of the Wilcoxes, the suburbia of Leonard Bast. In all these milieux we are conscious of social development, social change, urbanization. Rebuilding, moving house, is a major activity in the book. Wickham Place, where the Schlegels live, is made into blocks of flats. "To be parted from your house, your father's house—it oughtn't to be allowed. . . . Can what they call civilization be right, if people mayn't die in the room where they were born?" asks Mrs. Wilcox. But the "civilization of luggage" insists on movement, and even the Schlegel's cultivation is Londonish and impermanent, as Margaret comes to realize. Hilton, the station for Howards End, shows the same process—it is a village that has escaped rural decay because it is near

enough to London to be residential to it: "The station, like the scenery,
like Helen's letters, struck an indeterminate note. Into which country
will it lead, England or Suburbia? It was new, it had island platforms
and a subway, and the superficial comfort exacted by business-men. But
it held hints of local life, personal intercourse, as even Mrs. Munt was to
discover." The interpretative action of the book shows itself in the distinction between England and suburbia; the novel is *against* this movement, and in this context the condemned Leonard Bast's basement flat
on Camelia Road is not England but suburbia. Buildings are used indeed with an interpretative force that builds up during the novel, as we
become conscious of the symbolic significance that is attached to the place
Howards End—permanently linked with privilege, yes, but also with
culture and cultivation in a consistent and *stable* context.

So we become conscious of a changing England and an altering economic structure. We are also conscious of a world of ideas causally related to economics. The novel evokes England, urban and rural; we are
given many settings and landscapes. It also seeks to evoke the economic
and intellectual life of the west as a whole. The agents in the novel are
aware of Europe and its intellectual, social and economic history. In all
of their lives ideas and culture play some part. Cultivation and taste are
part of their natural experience; it is no mistake that the points at which
characters interrelate with one another tend to be cultural occasions, that
the Schlegels meet the Wilcoxes looking for a Rhineland cathedral and
Leonard Bast at a concert in the Queen's Hall. They are all concerned
for art and ideas, but to each person these have different degrees of relevance—the different interpretations which the Beethoven Fifth Symphony evokes in the various members of the audience are an amusing
instance of the way art is used as a touchstone in the novel. We are most
conscious of the difference between Margaret and Helen Schlegel when
we see their different responses to the symphony. We are equally responsive to the strange situation in the Camelia Road flat when Leonard Bast
reads Ruskin on Venice; it is true that Ruskin seems to us terribly irrelevant to Bast, but what strikes us hardest is that Bast is terribly irrelevant
to Ruskin. So what we are concerned with are the middle reaches of society, with those who go to concerts, read and discuss, take their holidays
in Europe, live pleasantly in large houses, have servants, buy shares and
are financially in the position to act on whim. Their social habits range
from the arrogantly conventional, in the case of the Wilcoxes, to the degree of unconventionality involved in Helen's affair with Bast, an unconventionality that goes so far as to say that personal relationships come
first and that social risks should be taken to make sure that they do. But
there is much common feeling between Wilcoxes and Schlegels, a community of feeling based on wealth and class, and hinted at in the way that
they have met. And this kinship is shown more clearly by the introduction of Leonard Bast, who comes from a different class or rather the lower

reaches of the middle class ("We are not concerned with the very poor") and becomes a central figure for the plot, since he draws out the terms of the Schlegel's liberal attitude.

This liberal attitude is at the centre of the book. The Schlegels are by and large presented in honorific terms:

> In their own fashion they cared deeply about politics, though not as politicians would have us care; they desired that public life should mirror whatever is good in the life within. Temperance, tolerance, and sexual equality were intelligible cries to them; whereas they did not follow our Forward Policy in Tibet with the keen attention which it merits, and would at times dismiss the whole British Empire with a puzzled, if reverent, sigh. Not out of them are the shows of history erected; the world would be a grey bloodless place were it entirely composed of Miss Schlegels. But the world being what it is, perhaps they shine out in it like stars.

We have it explicitly, though, that they are limited. Yet their interests constitute the interests of the novel as a whole. Its intellectual dimensions are humanist; it is concerned with questions about man, about good and evil, and about what is civilized, and these issues enter into thought and conversation primarily because of the Schlegels. The book is concerned with ideas and abstractions that get into the action only because of the high sensitivity of these characters. We are indeed closer to them; we see the Wilcoxes through the Schlegels, and the elaborate paraphernalia of letters and telegrams with which the book begins enables Forster to filter our first picture of the Wilcoxes through their values. It also functions to show the apparatus by which private things are made into public things, the apparatus of a world where personal relations are not supreme, where death does simply mean death duties and marriage marriage settlements. It serves too to show the way in which Margaret becomes the ethical centre for the Schlegels, just as Mrs. Wilcox is detached from the other Wilcoxes and shown as their ethical centre and origin.

In the second chapter our attention is constantly turned in Margaret's direction—"Away she hurried, not beautiful, not supremely brilliant, but filled with something that took the place of both qualities—something best described as a profound vivacity, a continual and sincere response to all that she encountered in her path through life." A similar note is hit in a rather more comic passage, once again involving the intervention of the novelist, in which there is both approval and criticism of Margaret:

> To Margaret—I hope this will not set the reader against her—the station of King's Cross had always suggested Infinity. Its very situation—withdrawn a little behind the facile splendours of St. Pancras—implied a comment on the materialism of life. Those two great arches, colourless, indifferent, shouldering between them an unlovely clock, were fit portals for some eternal adventure, whose issue might be prosperous, but would certainly not

be expressed in the ordinary language of prosperity. If you think this ridiculous, remember that it is not Margaret who is telling you about it; and let
me hasten to add that they were in plenty of time for the train. . . .

So Margaret's romanticism is generally dissipated by the author in this
way in a genial common sense, a common sense that doesn't free us from
the importance of the discussion of infinity—this is a novel in which infinity matters, but also one in which it is rather embarrassing to talk
about it. Like *The Catcher in the Rye,* which seems to me entirely built
on the device that you have to create a comic, deprecating structure to
handle the big things in these anti-romantic days, *Howards End* has its
self-protection. The comic method of the book has broader purposes, but
this is certainly an aspect of it, an aspect that enables Forster to be wry
and yet to give a terminology for Margaret's liberalism. A taste for Infinity, a profound reverence, a continual and sincere response to all she
encountered—these notions take on force in the novel as they are given
not simply explicitly but dramatically, in action. That the Schlegels are
linked with Imagination, as opposed to the celebration of Bigness, that
they put the intellect first but answer to spontaneous emotion, that they
believe that individuals are nearer to the unseen than any organization,
that they are averse to journalism of feeling, "the gutter press of the emotions," we go on to discover, and in discovering this we are turned to
Margaret as opposed to Helen—with her "more irresponsible tread."
Margaret is not beautiful, a fact which leads to sobriety, she is not as
spontaneous and rash as Helen, and we are thus pulled toward sobriety
and intelligence. Helen romanticizes music; Margaret sees the object as
it really is. She wants to see things steadily as well as to see them whole.
Helen has an arch side to her; Margaret is straightforwardly sensible. And
as we pick up the tone of Margaret, we pick up much of the tone of the
book.

But the book does contain three contesting value-systems, one of which
—that associated with Bast—is below our level as readers; only that of
the Wilcoxes and the Schlegels is taken seriously, and we must always be
alert to the terms in which they interpenetrate and criticize each other.
Thus when Mrs. Wilcox comes to Margaret's disastrous luncheon party,
we see what she is criticizing and why she criticizes it. It is not just the
self-criticism that Margaret has been capable of up to now when she
looks at Bast and realizes that her cultivation is in part a simple matter
of economics; she must also see that it is in many ways *thin.* When Mrs.
Wilcox's delicate imaginings are withered by the clever talk at the party,
when Margaret is compelled to confess her "inexperience" to Mrs. Wilcox, when she has to say to her: "We live the lives of gibbering monkeys.
Mrs. Wilcox—really—we have something quiet and stable at the bottom.
We really have. All my friends have," we are in the presence of a forceful
criticism, one that is attached to Mrs. Wilcox's special capacities:

She was not intellectual, nor even alert, and it was odd that, all the same, she should give the idea of greatness. Margaret, zig-zagging with her friends over Thought and Art, was conscious of a personality that transcended their own and dwarfed their activities. There was no bitterness in Mrs. Wilcox; there was not even criticism; she was lovable, and no ungracious or uncharitable word had passed her lips. Yet she and daily life were out of focus: one or the other must show blurred. And at lunch she seemed more out of focus than usual, and nearer the line that divides daily life from a life that may be of greater importance.

Here we are reminded of two things. On the one hand it is of a more stable social order than that of the rather glib intellectual cosmopolitan life, seen as a product of a highly urbanized, rapidly changing society which creates ideas in an irresponsible context. The other reminder is of the infinity that lies beyond King's Cross, the panic and emptiness that Beethoven calls up twice and then dissipates in the fifth symphony. We are reminded of the "grotesque impact of the unseen upon the seen," that Margaret feels as she sees in London the commercial spirit of Christmas, and reflects that in public the unseen cannot be expressed adequately. "It is private life alone that holds out the mirror to infinity; personal intercourse, and that alone, that ever hints at a personality beyond our daily vision." All this reminds Margaret that her purpose is not to contrast the unseen and the seen, but to reconcile them. Margaret must fill out both the prose and the poetry in her own life, and this filling out is the principle of expansion of the novel.

To some degree, then, this reconciliation depends on Margaret's movement from the cosmopolitan to the honest-English vein, to her understanding of an essential kinship between the Mr. Wilcoxes and herself, based on the fact that art and culture are the products of leisure and wealth and a high degree of social stability, and to her feeling that England is shared both by those who have moulded her, civilized her and made her powerful and those who have seen her *sub specie aeternitatis*. To show this the book has to elaborate two modes, one of social documentation, the other the mode which enables a poetic communication about life. The intimations of the unseen, which help build up the symbolic apparatus of the book and also the sense that the prose is not all and that the passion is also the poetry, do in a sense constitute a literary problem for Forster, a problem that he comes near to not solving. On one level the book is a social comedy, an area of ground which does not give itself easily to metaphysics. The problem which Henry James solves by the use of a high degree of consciousness in his characters, symbolism, and the device of an omniscient narrator Forster solves in a not dissimilar way. But there are important differences. One is in the use of the narrator —"the commentator," as Forster calls himself at one point in the novel —who does appear, does describe, but not with the conscious finesse of James's commentators. Here he is so close to Margaret at times that it is hard to disentangle his and her thoughts, and indeed the phrases invented by the narrator pass almost unnoticed into the conversation of the characters. There are extended essayistic passages, like the eulogy of "unpreparedness" in Chapter XII, where the commentator intervenes to observe that life is a romance and its essence is romantic beauty, or the descriptive beginning and end to Chapter XIX which, enclosing it like a sandwich, enable Forster to look on Margaret from a distance, and evoke the general British landscape to which her aspirations are more and more to relate. Most of the time authorial observation is used to convey a general humanism which reinforces the Schlegels (reinforces them not only in their humanism and their sensitivity but also in their class position); at other times it serves to reinforce the comedy—as when we learn that Mr. Wilcox did not kiss Margaret "for the hour was half-past twelve, and the car was passing by the stables of Buckingham Palace"; but it does also provide a major means by which ideas and abstractions can be conveyed. We need to have the passage about the commercial spirit of Christmas filtered to us through Margaret's critical mind, but the passage at the beginning of Chapter XI about the empty churchyard in which Mrs. Wilcox lies has to be done by the author himself, done in order to reinforce the reader's sense of the unseen as a competitive force in the passage of social comedy—the Wilcoxes treating the death as a matter for a committee meeting—that follows. This use of the novelist as essayist enables Forster to triumph over the shortcomings of the fiction, with its highly disconnected plot, moving rapidly about in time, place and mood, and to produce the remarkable modulations from social comedy to romance and poetry which constitute the dominant mode of the book—even if these do sometimes spill over into uncertainties of treatment or an arch literariness.

The passage at the beginning of Chapter XI provides an apt example of how these modulations work. The aim of this chapter—it is the first chapter in which we see the Wilcoxes together as a family—is to make us judge by Schlegel standards in the absence of the Schlegels. This is the first time we have not seen the Wilcoxes through the Schlegels, and this change in point of view also occurs at a remarkable break in the time sequence. In the previous scene we have had Mrs. Wilcox alive and talking with Margaret; the chapter begins by breaking up the chronological account of events in order to get the maximum dramatic effect: "The funeral was over." It is a remarkable alteration in tone, and the new tone goes on slowly to reveal, through the strange and indirect figure of the countryman pollarding the elms, that Mrs. Wilcox's death is a ritual intimately related to the land, is the lopping off of a bough. Thus the poetic is directly related to an agrarian standard, a standard of the unified rhythms of country life, about which, in the novel, a whole cluster of associations—in particular the wych-elm with its pig's teeth—is constructed. The woodcutter is one of the figures for this; he follows the funeral with a night of joy; he is "mating"; he is a natural animal figure. In fact, of course, he functions at a very risky level of invention, for he has to carry in a short paragraph that whole "poetic" side of the story which exists beyond the social comedy we are most of the time concerned with. Lightly touched as the poetic is, it is the central standard of the book. Leonard Bast, for instance, is tested against it; he not only has a "cramped little mind," he is also one of the men who moving historically from country to town have lost the life of the body and have thinly tried to find the life of the spirit. The woodcutter is followed by "silence absolute," and the church is seen as a ship, "highly-prowed, steering with all its company towards infinity."

Then, in a rapid shift of tone, we move back to the social level of the action ("Up at Howards End they were attempting breakfast") and to a semi-comic scene in which Mrs. Wilcox's last wish is questioned by a Wilcox "committee":

> Considered item by item, the emotional context was minimized, and all went forward smoothly. The clock ticked, the coals blazed higher, and contended with the white radiance that poured in through the windows. Unnoticed, the sun occupied his sky, and the shadows of the tree stems, extraordinarily solid, fell like trenches of purple across the frosted lawn. It was a glorious winter morning. Evie's fox terrier, who had passed for white, was only a dirty grey dog now, so intense was the purity that surrounded him. He was discredited, but the blackbirds that he was chasing glowed with Arabian darkness, for all the conventional colouring of life had been altered. . . .
>
> To follow it is unnecessary. It is rather a moment when the commentator should step forward. Ought the Wilcoxes to have offered their home to Margaret? . . . The practical moralist may acquit them absolutely. He who strives to look deeper may acquit them—almost. For one hard fact remains. They did neglect a personal appeal.

Here the passage functions by winning the reader to an acceptance of the standard of the man who "strives to look deeper," who accepts a level of good, "undogged" emotion, an appreciation of the demands of the personal and the unseen. And these standards are linked with the poetic, with the church sailing toward infinity, with the sun and the glowing blackbird and the colouring of life. And we do this within a chapter that reinforces these standards with other poetic and moral overtones, predominantly agrarian in character. Behind the book indeed lies the evocation of a feudal order that Margaret reverts to when she changes houses —"The feudal ownership of land did bring dignity, whereas the modern ownership of moveables is reducing us again to a nomadic horde. We are reverting to the civilization of luggage, and historians of the future will note how the middle classes accreted possessions without taking root in the earth, and may find in this the secret of their imaginative poverty." The central image of this agrarian liberalism is, of course, Howards End itself, with its evocation of the warrior-yeoman spirit, its vaguely Hellenic associations, yet its essential Englishness, which makes it human. "House and tree transcended any simile of sex. . . . Yet they kept within limits of the human. Their message was not of eternity, but of hope on this side of the grave." The temporal hope which the house offers depends upon an imaginative richness drawn from the land—on "understanding" in the colloquial and intellectual sense of the term, on not blaming Helen for her violation of the code and also on "knowing the realities." The "peace of the country" reassures man that life goes on and has its essential routines and traditions which survive the individual life. The development of the novel involves a development of certain characters, and those who change—they are Helen, Bast, Mr. Wilcox and of course Margaret herself—do so around the house and the tree.

Near the end of the book the poetic aspect of the story grows denser, even as, in a succession of rapid events, the plot rushes forward. "Events succeeded in a logical, yet senseless, train. People lost their humanity, and took values as arbitrary as those in a pack of playing-cards." Action and change being the means by which the sensible order of life is violated, working, like London's "flux" against the truth of things, the reinstatement of truth involves a final stability. And this compels on Margaret the realization that Henry Wilcox is associated with inner darkness, that her marriage did come out of a situation when, as we are told, she was having trouble with her eyes. But action and flux produce also the failure of Henry's fortress; Margaret also realizes that it is *through* the Wilcoxes that she has come to Howards End and this new stability, and in consequence her regrets are cancelled and her way of life throughout is vindicated afresh. Her solution is, of course, makeshift and temporal; but now, in affirming this as the book closes, Forster is able to criticize himself. Howards End cannot solve the problem of the present, the problem of the civilization of luggage ("No better plan had occurred to her"), and Margaret does realize that all that has been associated in the book with the agrarian ideal are "survivals, and the melting-pot was being prepared for them. Logically, they had no right to be alive. One's hope was in the weakness of logic." In this way the picture with which the novel concludes is of a world in decline, and a single optimistic possibility is offered—that this decline is a phase, as Margaret suggests:

". . . This craze for motion has only set in during the last hundred years. It may be followed by a civilization that won't be a movement, because it will rest on the earth. All the signs are against it now, but I can't help hoping, and very early in the morning in the garden I feel that our house is the future as well as the past."

This resolution answers therefore not only at the level of the book's domestic action, at the level of life concerned with love and attraction and dinner-parties and train-journeys, but also at the level of that more spiritual and more violent world which is concerned with infinity, panic and emptiness and in which Leonard Bast's death is possible. It offers a temporal solution, but leaves open and unresolved the question of the spiritual problem, requiring only a recognition that it exists. The wide range of inference contained by the ending is managed by the use of symbols and poetic evocation, devices which free the author from close plotting. One of the main developments of the book is in fact a widening of the circle established at the opening, so that our sense of the possibilities of what might be connected, and of the problems that must be resolved, is steadily increased. It intimates that the cultural problem the novel is concerned with—the problem of the continuation of those who "will kindle the light within"—can in one sense be solved, in that *Howards End* may gain a rightful owner, in another sense it cannot, since there is no necessary perpetuation of Howards End. To a point, then, the book ends with the kind of rhythmic "opening out" that Forster speaks of in *Aspects of the Novel*:

> Music, though it does not employ human beings, though it is governed by intricate laws, nevertheless does offer in its final expression a type of beauty which fiction might achieve in its own way. Expansion. That is the idea the novelist must cling to. Not completion. Not rounding off but opening out.

The loose plotting, the use of accident and muddle, the presence of the "little phrases" (the motifs of "greyness," "panic and emptiness," "telegrams and anger") all contribute to this sense of an expanding, "poetic" structure. There is indeed a sense in which the metaphysical dimensions of the novel survive the book and give a sense of an important spiritual reality.

Yet at the end of the book Margaret does not so much come to terms with "infinity" as allow room for it; her spiritual as well as her social life are at a point of achievement which have their ambiguities. Margaret's "uncanny" sense of triumph is built in both areas on a kind of willed optimism. She has established an epistemology which enables her to act as the moral centre for those who surround her, for she has shown a greater endurance than they; the mantle of Mrs. Wilcox falls upon her. But we are surely not meant to understand that the intelligentsia—even the yeoman intelligentsia—are to inherit England. Even symbolically Helen's child is an ambiguous gesture toward the future. And the strongly poetic note of the last chapter has, therefore, its ironies, ironies consequent upon the whole manner of the book. Forster has realized throughout the action that his central character—and his own voice as commentator—can be criticized both from the point of view of the vast reaches of the infinite and by the impersonal process of history. Both are belittled by the future; both are ironically placed. Indeed the gestures to the poetic and religious serve to leave loopholes to which the book never has to answer; and were they to do so even grander ironies might well have ensued. As it is, they leave the book open to allow for a future which will have to go further than Margaret Schlegel or the novelist himself can; both must compromise or assert what must be a partial hope, a hope that "all the signs are against." And because the novel is a moral novel about acting in a social dimension, is a novel in which the communities that are contained in the society are fully established in their historical as well as their moral significance, the voice of irony is relevant throughout. The poetry never quite goes unplaced; the comedy and irony are there throughout to touch in a disturbance, a sense of pervasive anarchy, which is central to this book as it is to its successor, *A Passage to India.*

Rhythm in E.M. Forster's
A Passage to India

by E.K. Brown

I

A novelist may use many kinds of rhythm in one work. In this last discourse I propose to consider one work, to touch on the varied forms of the device, and to inquire briefly into the effect that comes from the combination of phrases, characters, and incidents, rhythmically arranged, with a profusion of expanding symbols, and with a complex evolution of themes. The one work is E.M. Forster's *A Passage to India*, and I may as well say now that I believe it to be a great novel. It is so unlike most great novels that for a long time I thought of it as remarkable rather than great. After many rereadings, always finding more in the work than I had before, I have changed my mind. One of the reasons why I set *A Passage to India* so high will, perhaps, appear in these pages: its greatness is intimately dependent on E.M. Forster's mastery of expanding symbols and thematic structure, and on that element in his spirit for which expanding symbols and thematic structure are appropriate language.

One of the first examples I gave of repetition with variation was from *Esther Waters*:[1] the word-for-word repetition late in the book of the first paragraph, followed by the repetition with significant variation of the second paragraph. In *A Passage to India* there is something very like this, but subtle as well as emphatic.

In the second chapter of Forster's novel characters begin to appear. There is Aziz, the Mohammedan physician, engaged in friendly argument with Mohammedan friends: "they were discussing as to whether or no it is possible to be friends with an Englishman." The conclusion is that in India, at least, friendship with the invader is impossible, unpermitted. Aziz is summoned to his chief, the Civil Surgeon, Dr. Callendar, and on the steps of Callendar's bungalow suffers a slight from two

[1] In earlier chapters of *Rhythm in the Novel* [ED.].

Anglo-Indian women. As they come out on the verandah he lifts his hat; instinctively they turn away. They jump into the carriage he has hired and are about to drive off without asking consent. Aziz says "You are most welcome, ladies"; they do not think of replying. The Civil Surgeon has left, and there is no message. Aziz takes his injured feelings to the mosque, and in the night's coolness he meditates upon the past of Islam. He recalls a Persian inscription he had once seen on the tomb of a Deccan king, especially these closing lines:

> But those who have secretly understood my heart—
> They will approach and visit the grave where I lie.

As he is repeating the words "the secret understanding of the heart" in the one place in Chandrapore where he was sure no European would intrude, an Englishwoman steps into the moonlight. Aziz rages at her. But Mrs. Moore has done the right thing, has removed her shoes—says the right thing, "God is here"—and in a minute they are friends. They talk of their children, of people round about, of India, of religion. "The flame that not even beauty can nourish" was springing up in Aziz, for this red-faced old woman; and when she remarks "I don't think I understand people very well. I only know whether I like or dislike them," Aziz declares: "Then you are an Oriental." He has learned that one can be friends with an Englishman, even with an Englishwoman, and in India. Two years later when the novel is about to close, Aziz repeats the declaration. Not to Mrs. Moore—she is dead—but to her son, the young boy Ralph.

Aziz is no longer in British India. He has resolved to have no more to do with the invader, and is physician to the rajah of a Hindu state. Into a seclusion even deeper than that of the mosque where he had met Mrs. Moore, once more the English penetrate. One of the intruders is Ralph, who is stung by bees. So great is Aziz' hatred of the English that he is sadistically happy to have an English boy in his power. He will treat him with the savagery the Civil Surgeon had used towards the young son of a Nawab. Ralph astonishes Aziz with a most unEnglish expression: "Your hands are unkind." The memory of Mrs. Moore floods in, expelling all hatred. Aziz bids Ralph a gentle good-bye, and Ralph responds with equal gentleness. Aziz asks "Can you always tell whether a stranger is your friend?" "Yes," Ralph replies simply. "Then you are an Oriental" —the words are drawn out of Aziz, and he is appalled. "He unclasped as he spoke, with a little shudder. Those words—he had said them to Mrs. Moore in the mosque in the beginning of the cycle, from which, after so much suffering, he had got free." Instead of the good-bye Aziz had planned, and the hurried escape from reinvolvement with the English, he talks with Ralph about Mrs. Moore and in friendship takes the boy out on the water, as in friendship he had taken Mrs. Moore to the Marabar Caves. What they say of Mrs. Moore, and what befalls them on the water I am not yet ready to consider. But the cycle is clearly beginning again. The effect that George Moore sought in *Esther Waters*, and achieved, was of a closing in of the life in his tale; the effect in *A Passage to India* is of an opening out of life. It is as if at the point where one circle was completed, another and larger circle immediately began.

Ralph Moore serves in another kind of rhythmic process. I used the two daughters in *Le Père Goriot* and the two in *A Lear of the Steppes* as examples of a pair of characters radically alike in nature and in function. Balzac's daughters have only surface differences; with Turgenev's there is also gradation, a significant difference in the degree to which they are mastered by the same ruling passion, and a surprise. The likeness between Ralph Moore and his mother, profound, intimate, mysterious, is a gradation and a surprise of Turgenev's sort. Ralph is a prolongation of his mother. He is a simpler person because he lacks the shell of practical sense and adaptability which hid her essential nature from almost everyone until "India brought her into the open." It may be said of Ralph that he is what his mother is so far as she eternally matters. The repetition of Mrs. Moore in the two children of her second marriage—for Ralph's sister Stella is of the same substance, although she remains a faint figure—hits the reader more strongly since the child of the first marriage, the only one of her children to appear in the early and middle parts of the book, derives nothing from his mother. Ronnie Heaslop, bureaucrat, conventionalist, empire-builder, snob, is a thorough Wilcox. He could have changed places with the younger Wilcox boy and no one would have noticed the shift. Especially to one who reads *A Passage to India* after reading *Howards End* the prolongation of Mrs. Moore in her youngest child is emotionally effective. It is a vehicle for the mystery in which the meaning of *A Passage to India* is so deeply engaged.

II

I mentioned the bee-stings which led to Ralph's encounter with Aziz. They will take us to one of the expanding symbols.

Early in the novel, on the evening when she had met Aziz at the mosque, Mrs. Moore is undressing in her son's bungalow. As she is about to hang up her cloak she notices that on the tip of the peg is a wasp, a quite unEnglish wasp, an "Indian Social Wasp."

Perhaps he mistook the peg for a branch—no Indian animal has any sense of an interior. Bats, rats, birds, insects will as soon nest inside a house as out; it is to them a normal growth of the eternal jungle, which alternately produces houses trees, houses trees. There he clung, asleep, while jackals in the plain bayed their desires and mingled with the percussion of drums.

"Pretty dear," said Mrs. Moore to the wasp. He did not wake, but her voice floated out, to swell the night's uneasiness.

There the chapter ends. If you read these lines in the context they take on certain precise meanings. Mrs. Moore had divided her evening between the English club (where no native was allowed) and the mosque (where no English folk came). None of the sundried Anglo-Indians would have called the wasp a pretty dear; all of them would have been irritated by the wasp's inability to discriminate a house from a tree, which is India's inability, India's disinclination, to make the sharp tidy distinctions by which the Western intelligence operates. At the club that evening the talk had turned to religion. The Civil Surgeon's wife had said that the kindest thing one could do for a native was to let him die. Mrs. Moore had inquired, with a "crooked smile," what if he went to heaven? A woman who had been a nurse in a native state was ready for this with a razor-sharp distinction: "I am all for Chaplains, but all against Missionaries." The little incident with which the evening closes epitomizes Mrs. Moore's behaviour at the club and at the mosque, her indifference to sharp distinctions, her instinctive affection and consideration. But this, and other precise meanings in her approach to the wasp, do not exhaust the force or account for the charm of the passage. The disturbing noises which accompany Mrs. Moore's gesture of affection and consideration— the minatory baying of the jackals and percussion of the drums offer an undertone of suggestion that, unexpectedly beautiful and adequate as Mrs. Moore's response to Aziz and to the wasp had been, there are ordeals ahead to which even Mrs. Moore may be insufficient.

Late in the novel, long after her death, the wasp returns, or rather it is now the idea of the wasp. The Brahman Godbole, at the climactic moment in the book, is attempting union with the divine. He does so in a ceremony that could satisfy no Western person. It is a ceremony abounding in jumble, amorphousness. Each of the noisy Corybantic worshippers is inviting the return of the strongest, purest attachments in his experience. "Thus Godbole, though she was not important to him, remembered an old woman he had met in Chandrapore days . . . she happened to occur among the throng of soliciting images, a tiny splinter, and he impelled her by his spiritual force to that place where completeness can be found." Having impelled Mrs. Moore triumphantly to her place, he tried again. "His senses grew thinner, he remembered a wasp seen he forgot where, perhaps on a stone. He loved the wasp equally, he impelled it likewise, he was imitating God." There his triumph flared out. He found he could do nothing with the stone, arbitrarily, superficially, cognitively associated with the wasp. " 'One old Englishwoman and one little, little wasp,' he thought, as he stepped out of the temple into the grey of a pouring wet morning. 'It does not seem much, still it is more than I am myself.' "

Just what is achieved by the recurrence of the wasp? To have shown Godbole triumphantly impelling Mrs. Moore would have established the effect that is most obviously needed: that of an affinity between Godbole

and the old Englishwoman who has not come so far as he along the mystical path. In the novel they have but one important interchange—an interchange of spiritual ideas—and apart from this they scarcely see each
other. They do not wish to, do not need to. Godbole's recollection of her
at a spiritual moment crucial for him establishes that one interchange is
enough. It tells us something that for E.M. Forster is most important
about human relationships. All this, and more perhaps, can be achieved
without the recurrence of the wasp.

The recurrence of the wasp does not point, as one of my students once
suggested, to Professor Godbole's having taken an unrecorded walk by
Mrs. Moore's window when she was undressing. The recurrence of the
wasp points to an identity in the objects to which the analogous characters were drawn. That each should have been powerfully attracted to
something so apparently trivial as a wasp suggests that they were not only
alike but mysteriously alike. Because of the wasp we appear to be in the
presence of something so elusive that we cannot understand it, that we
brood about it with a conviction that it contains some kernel of meaning we do not know how to extract. It can be said of the wasp as E.M.
Forster said of Vinteuil's music that it has a life of its own, that it is almost an actor in the novel but not quite.

Between its two big moments the wasp is not wholly neglected. Not all
the English in Forster's India adopt the prejudices of the official classes.
The nurse from the native state was opposed to missionaries; but the
missionaries in Chandrapore are more sensitive, more human, than the
mass of their countrymen. In a review printed four years before the novel
Forster wrote: "It is the missionary rather than the Government official
who is in touch with native opinion. The official need only learn how
people can be governed. The missionary, since he wants to alter them,
must learn what they are." The missionaries never came to the club
at Chandrapore, and on principle they used the third-class cars on the
trains. The call to salvation, they knew and taught and lived, was addressed to all mankind. But what, their Indian friends would ask, of
the animals? Were there mansions in heaven for the monkeys? The
elder missionary thought not, but the younger was liberal, and "saw
no reason why monkeys should not have their collateral share of bliss."
As the conversation descended below the mammalian the younger
missionary felt less at ease, and when the wasp was mentioned he was
prone to change the subject. The call of the Western intelligence for a
razor-sharp distinction became imperious. "We must exclude someone
from our gathering, or we shall be left with nothing." The use of the
wasp in this passage beautifully underlines by contrast the spiritual agreement between the Brahman and the contemplative Christian Mrs. Moore:
for them the divine call has no fixed exclusions—would not be divine if
it had.

And then there are the bees with which I began. They live in the

shrine of a Mohammedan saint, who had freed prisoners, and when the
police intervened and cut off his head, "ignored" this misadventure and
slew as many of them as were about. The shrine is not a mosque, but
there is a miniature mosque beside it. We are brought back to the encounter between Aziz and Mrs. Moore at the beginning of the novel. The
sudden rage of the bees against the intruders is like Aziz' sudden rage
against her; and it ends as quickly. The rage of the bees seems to suggest
that subhuman India is hostile to interracial friendships, a suggestion repeated with virtuosity throughout the book, and nowhere so forcibly as
in the final paragraph. Aziz and the Englishman he has liked most, Cyril
Fielding, are riding in the country. Aziz, in a sudden spurt of affection,
pulls his horse so close to Fielding's that he can half kiss him; and Fielding responds by holding Aziz affectionately.

> But the horses didn't want it—they swerved apart; the earth didn't want
> it, sending up rocks through which riders must pass single file; the temples,
> the tank, the jail, the palace, the birds, the carrion, the Guest House, that
> came into view as they issued from the gap and saw Mau beneath: they
> didn't want it, they said in their hundred voices, "No, not yet," and the
> sky said, "No, not there."

Clearly, the bees are divisive as the wasps are not. And yet the bees are
not merely divisive—they were the occasion for the personal relation between Aziz and Ralph Moore, just as the wasp was, not indeed the occasion, but the evidence of mystery in the personal relation between Godbole and Mrs. Moore.

The greatest of the expanding symbols in *A Passage to India* is the
echo. The most lasting among the effects of the visit that Mrs. Moore
and Adela Quested made to the Marabar Caves as the guests of Aziz was
the echo. Mrs. Moore disliked the echo when she was in the one cave she
entered; but after she had emerged and had had time to arrange her impressions she minded it much more. "The echo began in some indescrib-
able way to undermine her hold on life." It blurred all distinctions, and
even Mrs. Moore had enough of the West in her to become uneasy. To the
highest poetry and the coarsest obscenity the echo would have offered the
same reply—"ou-boum." Other Indian echoes, Forster pauses to insist,
are quite different; at Mandu long sentences will journey through the air
and return to their speaker intact. At the Marabar the utterance is reduced to the dullness of one flat response mercilessly reiterated. Mrs.
Moore found that the echo voided of all meaning the past, present, and
future of her life. The echo disturbed Adela Quested's steady balance.
Love and marriage were on her mind as she moved towards the second
cave, and she suffered the delusion that Aziz, who did not in fact care for
her in any way except as an honoured guest, attempted to rape her.

The reader has been lured into pondering about echoes before they
dominate the crucial scene at the caves. The Collector, the principal Eng-

lish official at Chandrapore, learning that Mrs. Moore and Miss Quested wish to meet "the Aryan Brother," gives what he calls a "Bridge Party" for the leading local people of both colours. In vain do the two visitors from England try to bridge a gap, crossing from the side of the garden chosen by the pinko-greys, as Fielding calls them, to the side where India seems to promise revelations to anyone bold enough to seek. Mrs. Moore and Miss Quested make special efforts with two Hindu women; but everything dies against "the echoing walls of their civility." At home the evening after the ineffectual party Mrs. Moore takes stock of what India has done for her in a few weeks. It has made her speak more often of God; but it has also moved the old spiritual landmarks, and God has seemed a less satisfactory formulation for the content of her belief. "Outside the arch [and the arch is also a powerful expanding symbol with which I have not space to deal] there seemed always an arch, beyond the remotest echo a silence."

As the narrative begins to move directly towards the Marabar Caves, sounds exercise a decisive effect on the two women who are to find the echoes in those caves so disturbing. The Brahman Godbole concludes a tea party at Fielding's by singing a song whose spiritual content is as bemusing as its form is at variance with Western conceptions of music. The Englishwomen are so affected by his song that in the days intervening between their hearing it and their starting for the caves they exist as if in cocoons. On the local train that takes them to the Marabar the dull repetitive sound of the wheels has an effect prefiguring the echo's on Mrs. Moore. "Pomper, pomper, pomper," say the wheels and rob Adela Quested's sentences and ideas of any distinctness. On another line not far away the crack mail train that linked Calcutta with Lahore shot along with a shriek that meant business. That shriek Adela could have understood, it was of her world; but with "pomper, pomper, pomper" she can do nothing. Unless one can do something, even do a great deal, with "pomper, pomper, pomper," one can do nothing with India. For the meanings of India are indistinct and repetitive. Until the Western visitor can make something of the indistinctness indefinitely repeated, he can neither comprehend any of the meanings of India nor begin to cope with them. India, says Forster, is not a promise, it is nothing so definite, it is only an appeal.

The indistinctness and repetitiveness, exasperating to a Western mind, are beautifully captured at the beginning of a notice that in 1919 Forster wrote for the *Athenaeum*. The book reviewed was *Hindu and Buddhist Monuments, Northern Circle,* published by the Mysore Archaeological Department.

"Ought we not to start? The elephants must be waiting."
"There is no necessity. Elephants sometimes wait four hours."
"But the temple is far."
"Oh no, there are thirty of them."

"Thirty temples! Are they far?"

"No, no, no, not at all—fifteen really, but much jungle; fifteen to come and fifteen to go."

"Fifteen of what?"

"Fifteen all."

After such preparations, and in such a spirit, the Temple used to be attacked; and came off victorious. Whether it was one, or fifteen or thirty, or thirty miles off, was never proved, because the elephant misunderstood, or plans changed, or tiffin was too delicious. Evening fell, and the pale blue dome of the sky was corniced with purple where it touched the trees. "It will now be too late for the Temple." So it keeps its secret in some stony gorge or field of tough grass, or, more triumphant still, in the land beyond either, where a mile and an elephant are identical and everything is nothing.

The Mysore Achaeological Department does not approach a monument in this instinctive fashion. It is as precise, as Western, as Aziz' plans for the expedition to the Marabar Caves. Aziz worked out a schedule that would honour the secretary of a national convention: transport, food, seating, even jokes, were minutely arranged. Lest he and his servants be late they spend the preceding night at the station. India is too much for them. Fielding and Godbole miss the train; and Mrs. Moore and Miss Quested hate the caves—Mrs. Moore will enter only one of them, Adela only two.

In the caves the indistinct meanings of India have agglomerated in a form of shocking intensity and explode at the visitors in the horrifying echo. Until she entered a cave Adela Quested had made nothing of these meanings. The most that can be said for her is that unlike the Anglo-Indians she has been aware of bafflement, conscious of a profound un-easiness. Mrs. Moore was not quite so pitifully unprepared: she was spiritually active, moving blindly towards a more adequate formulation of the divine. She too was shattered by the echoes. For the length of many chapters after the scene at the caves, the echo leaves a disturbing residue in the minds of both Englishwomen. What the residue was I shall inquire when looking at the thematic structure of the novel.

After Mrs. Moore's death and Adela's return to England, the echo begins to matter to Cyril Fielding. When, after the catastrophe, he entered a Marabar cave, the echo had no impact on him. In the hubbub of distorted rumour and opinion released in Chandrapore by Adela's charge against Aziz, Fielding kept his head, and was the only Englishman to do so. It was now his turn to exist within a cocoon—he was enclosed by his intuitive assurance that Aziz could not have done what he was charged with doing. No distorting, dispiriting echo could penetrate that cocoon. When Adela withdrew her charge the Anglo-Indian world at Chandra-pore collapsed. But when a new crop of officials arrived they were, Field-ing found, just like those who had been withdrawn. After he has met them at the club, Fielding muses: "Everything echoes now; there's no stopping the echo. The original sound may be harmless, but the echo is always evil." On this musing Forster comments: "This reflection about an echo lay at the verge of Fielding's mind. He could never develop it. It belonged to the universe that he had missed or rejected." Indistinct meanings were almost as alien to his fluid but yet Western mind as to the more rigid mind of Adela Quested. What he has, and she has not, is some grasp of the nature of personal relationships. He has shown again and again his appreciation of how attractive personalities falsify themselves and show at their worst when they suffer the impact of aggressive personalities that are antagonistic to them. At the close of his tea party he saw Aziz behaving in a repulsive way—"impertinent" to Ronnie Heaslop, "loud and jolly" to Godbole, "greasily confidential" to Adela Quested—and instead of revising his opinion of Aziz, he merely concluded that something had happened to upset the nervous Mohammedan. Ronnie Heaslop had happened. And what is true of individuals, Fielding's political shrewdness tells him, is more painfully true of national groups and social classes. "The original sound may be harmless, but the echo is always evil."

As the novel approaches a close, Forster introduces perhaps the most moving of all his uses of the echo. In the courtroom scene at the middle of the *Passage,* when Mrs. Moore's name is mentioned in testimony, the native crowd outside distorts it into "Esmiss Esmoor," and chants these mysterious syllables as if they were the name of a goddess, or the means to salvation. Indeed they are. For it was after the crowd had chanted the distortion that Adela was freed from her delusion, and changing her story, saved Aziz. When at the end Mrs. Moore's younger children fall in with Aziz, the Hindus at their worship are repeating: "Radhakrishna Radhakrishna Krishnaradha Radhakrishna"; and, suddenly in the interstices of the chant Aziz "heard, almost certainly, the syllables of salvation that had sounded during his trial at Chandrapore."

The echo, like the bee-wasp symbol, is manifold in meaning. An echo distorts Mrs. Moore's sense of the purport of life, but that distortion, we may shortly see, is not entirely ruinous. An echo distorts Adela's sense of what happened in the cave; but another echo restores her to the truth. Good and evil interweave in these expanding symbols, making them more mysterious; just as we shall see them interweave in the development of the themes.

III

A Passage to India is in three parts. Their titles—"Mosque," "Caves," "Temple"—warn of a meaning which goes behind story, people, even setting. Each part has a curious and beautiful prefatory chapter, and each of these chapters abounds in symbols, abstractions, suggestions. Their full weight of meaning is slow in revealing itself; indeed I am not sure that any reader of the novel will ever possess all that has been flung into these chapters.

It is obvious that they are in balance. They also interweave. The first chapter in the part called "Mosque" begins: "Except for the Marabar Caves," and ends: "These fists and fingers are the Marabar Hills, containing the extraordinary caves." There is a reference to temples tucked away in a detailed catalogue of the topography of Chandrapore. To mosques the only reference is in the title for this part of the novel, standing at the top of the opening page and then used as a running head. The first chapter of the part called "Caves" has no backward glance towards the mosque or any element of the Moslem faith; but it is packed with suggestive remarks that point forward to the temple and the Hindu faith; and these are sharply in contrast with the chief substance of the chapter, the account of an India far older than Moslem or Hindu, whose faith has left a mysterious residue in the primitive Marabar Caves. The first chapter of the part called "Temple" opens as the first chapter of "Mosque" opened, with a reference to the caves; and the Moslem element is gathered in by the importance to the action in the chapter of the chief Moslem person in the novel, Aziz. In the interweaving of elements in these prefatory chapters there is increasing complication but no petty mechanical balancing, no sterile exactness of repetition. Vitality is not sacrificed to pattern.

It is useful to look at the prefatory chapters as a group; seen in this way they offer an initiation into the kind of approach the three parts of the novel will best respond to. What has appeared in the chapters will be recognized, although not so readily, in the three big blocks that compose *A Passage to India.*

In the first of these blocks we are brought to a mosque; in the second to the caves; in the third to a temple. Each visit has consequences which linger through the rest of the novel. The novel thus becomes progressively more complex. In the first block not only is the Moslem element dominant—it far outweighs the caves and the temple; all that we get about caves and temple is preparatory. At the other extreme, in the third block, where the Hindu element is dominant, the persistence of the Moslem and of that more primitive and elusive element represented by the caves is multiform and of a kind to command a great part of the reader's attention and emotion.

In her visit to the mosque at Chandrapore Mrs. Moore enters with a happy and intuitive adequacy into an understanding of the Moslem element. She leaves the stifling club late in the evening and approaches the mosque alone. We have seen how easily she enters into a personal understanding of Aziz. The understanding so quickly and strangely established endures throughout the novel. She never doubts that Aziz is innocent of the charge Adela brings against him. In the next to last chapter Aziz tells Ralph Moore: "Yes, your mother was my best friend in all the world."

"He was silent," the passage continues, "puzzled by his own great grati-
tude. What did this eternal goodness of Mrs. Moore amount to? To
nothing, if brought to the test of thought. She had not borne witness in
his favour [Adela had done that], nor visited him in the prison [Fielding
had done that], yet she had stolen to the depths of his heart, and he always adored her." To return to the images in Helen Schlegel's interpretation of the Fifth Symphony, the goblins have no power whatever over
the relation between Mrs. Moore and Aziz. When he first saw her white
form in the darkness of the mosque, he had been repeating to himself in
Persian "the secret understanding of the heart." So far as the main meaning of the first block in the novel admits of formulation, there is the
formula.

Before the second part of the novel has begun, at Fielding's tea party
(an indirect outcome of the meeting at the mosque) the Marabar Caves
begin to threaten. Aziz has never seen them, nor has he any knowledge
of them beyond common report. But when the English visitors express a
wish to see more of India, and see more deeply, he proposes an expedition
to the caves. He asks the Brahman Godbole to describe them. Godbole
confines himself to brief negatives. The caves contain no sculpture, no
ornament of any kind; nor are they especially holy. To every effort Aziz
makes to discover why the caves are worth seeing, Godbole is impene-
trable. The comparatively simple mind of the Mohammedan, we are
told, "was encountering Ancient Night." It is an ominous and mysterious
overture. Godbole is invited to join the expedition, and agrees; but when
the time comes he prolongs his prayers, innocently misses the train, and
makes Fielding miss it too. The visitors from England approach the caves
under the guidance of Aziz, the blind led by the blind.

The caves are in an outpost of the high places of Dravidia, which were
land when the oceans covered the holy places of Hindustan, before there
was a Ganges, before there were Himalayas. Forster has moved them
some hundreds of miles, as he tells us in a note to the "Everyman" edition,
doubtless to bring them within reach of the Ganges where for many
reasons he prefers to situate the early and middle parts of his story. The
hills in which they lie were flesh of the sun's flesh, their contours never
softened by the flow of water, and some of the edges and masses they had
when they belonged to the sun they still preserve. The hills, like so many
of the aspects of India, strike Forster as violating the beauties of proportion and thus certain to confuse and depress a European. When Cyril
Fielding returns to Europe at the end of the second block of the novel
he lands at Venice after a stay in Egypt and a sight of Crete. "The buildings of Venice," he noted, "like the mountains of Crete and the fields of
Egypt, stood in the right place, whereas in poor India everything was
placed wrong. He had forgotten the beauty of form among idol temples
and lumpy hills." The Marabar Hills are lumpy; they rise "abruptly,
insanely, without the proportion that is kept by the wildest hills else-

where." Mrs. Moore and Miss Quested did not find them attractive or
interesting; they could not see why these hills should have a reputation
and draw people to look on them. They did not understand that to lack
form is not simply a negation: that the vacuum left is filled by something
else, elusive but perhaps of equal importance.

What Forster is doing in the description of the hills, and later of the
caves, is easy to formulate if one is content with general terms. He is
taking his characters beyond their depth; the minds of Mrs. Moore and
Miss Quested, Western, modern, complex, cannot operate on the level
of primitivism which the hills and the caves exemplify. Mrs. Moore is
not so much at a loss as Miss Quested, even momentarily, for she is less
Western, less modern, even less complex. Miss Quested's mind goes wild
and she makes the absurd charge against Aziz; Mrs. Moore's mind goes
dead—she is aware of its incompetence, aware that in the circumstances of
the caves and hills it cannot operate at all. The secret understanding of
the heart is no longer enough.

The echo in a Marabar cave is almost exactly like the utterance of the
goblins in the Fifth Symphony, a denial of human values, in this case by
way of a denial of all distinctions. "Pathos, piety, courage—they exist, but
are identical, and so is filth," the echo persuades Mrs. Moore. "Everything exists, nothing has value." Panic and emptiness were what the goblins infused into Helen Schlegel listening to Beethoven in the Queen's
Hall; and the echo infuses them into Mrs. Moore. Emptiness. The relations that have made hers a full life—her affection for her children, her
devotion to God—have suddenly snapped. She could not—and this happens in a moment—interest herself in the fortunes of her children, either
in those of the son at Chandrapore or in those of the youngest two in
England. The Christian God, whom she had worshipped with so much
fervour in her parish in the Northamptonshire countryside, and who was
once the source of her greatest happiness, ceased, also in a moment, to
have any meaning. Panic. "She was terrified over an area larger than
usual; the universe, never comprehensible to her intellect, offered no
repose to her soul."

For Mrs. Moore there is no re-establishment from what befell her on
the Marabar. Soon afterwards she leaves India. By her own estimate her
passage to that land has been a failure. As she crosses the country by
train to go aboard at Bombay she thinks "I have not seen the right
places." The voice of the Marabar Caves was not the voice of India, only
one of the voices; but it had prevented her hearing the others. The voice
of Asirgarh, for instance, a fortress among wooded hills passed at sunset.
She at once forgets Asirgarh; but ten minutes later Asirgarh reappears—
the train has made a semicircle. "What could she connect it with, except
its own name? Nothing; she knew no one who lived there. But it had
looked at her twice and seemed to say: 'I do not vanish.' " On the passage home, she dies, and her body is committed to the Indian Ocean. She

will never hear the voice of Asirgarh again; but Asirgarh will hear hers.

The goblins are powerful in this novel, but before the dark second part ends Forster begins to put them to rout. It is true that Mrs. Moore could not cope with what the caves had spoken to her. But, like Mrs. Wilcox, she is a redemptive character; unable to save herself, she did miraculous things for others. She did them by being the sort of person she was. She continued to do them after her ordeal at the Marabar. Whenever Adela Quested is in her company, and only then, Adela is relieved of the echo, and becomes not her usual self, but at times a better self than she has ever been. The mention of Mrs. Moore's name at the trial clears the confusion from Adela's brain, and in this way Aziz is saved. A little later the mention of her name to Aziz persuades him to be generous with Adela and give over an action for damages. And the beneficent influence of Mrs. Moore flowing out of the secret understanding of the heart will swell throughout the third part until it becomes next to the main determinant in the final scenes of the novel.

Even in the second part, the dark part of the novel, the goblins encounter another powerful enemy in the Brahman Godbole. He is asked by Fielding for his opinion of what occurred in the cave. The breadth of his conception brings a quietude that reassures the reader if it leaves Fielding exasperated. What happened, says Godbole, was an evil thing. But the precise nature of the evil is not of any real account: nothing is to be achieved through the law courts, by ascertaining whether Aziz attacked Adela Quested, or whether someone else, the guide or a wandering Pathan, attacked her, or whether she was attacked by her own poisoned imagination. What concerns Godbole is why she was attacked. Evil had the power to attack her because of the shortcomings of the universe, because, to take an example of the shortcomings—this is my example, not Godbole's —of the warped society in which Adela and Aziz are living. Perhaps if the cave had been in Wiltshire or in Greece, Aziz and Adela might have left it unscathed. "When evil occurs," says Godbole, "it expresses the whole of the universe." But if all have a responsibility for letting the goblins loose, the power of the goblins is no proper reason for despair. Evil is not unrelated to good: it is the absence of good, and thus has a subtle unbreakable bond with the good. The presence of evil does not imply that good has been vanquished, only that it has receded. Godbole is also concerned with what should be done; not at the trial of Aziz, which, like Mrs. Moore, he will not take seriously, but in the effort to make good return. It is right, Godbole thinks, indeed it is imperative, that we continue our plea to God that He "come," that good may return and evil recede before it. Even so intimate a friend of the author as Lowes Dickinson was impatient to know what did occur in the cave; Forster never offers even a hint, and we must thus conclude that like Godbole and Mrs. Moore he is concerned, and wants us to be concerned, not with what happened, but only with why it happened and with what could and should be done to assure and speed the recession of evil and the return of good.

The third part of the novel is Godbole's until it becomes also Mrs. Moore's. Godbole leads the mysterious ceremony of Hindu worship with which this last part opens. The temple where he dances and prays, smears his forehead with butter and tries to swallow the butter as it trickles down his face and the faces of his friends, is not in Chandrapore; it lies outside the strains of British India, in a small native state a few miles only from the fortress of Asirgarh. If the ceremony violates all Western feelings about proportion and religious decorum, we are brought to understand that the violation of proportion and religious decorum is the very circumstance that enables the ceremony to intensify the spiritual being of the worshippers. Godbole achieves union with the divine, he propels Mrs. Moore and the wasp into this union, he routs the goblins, because in his worship he makes no fixed exclusions, he does not exclude humour, he does not exclude ugliness. Everything but evil becomes the ally of good. So powerful is the effect of this worship that even the non-Hindus in the native state find their spiritual being intensified.

The next scene is theirs. Aziz takes Ralph Moore on the water to witness the last stage in the Hindu ceremony. Fielding and Stella Moore, his wife, are in another boat. The four non-Hindus are intent on the ceremony unrolling by the shore. A raft is launched bearing a clay god, who is to melt in the water. Suddenly the two boats are very close to the raft and to each other. From the Hindus lining the shore comes a howl, whether of wrath or of joy no one else can tell, but it is reassuring that Godbole is there. Stella leans first towards her husband, then with an instinctive recognition of affinity that is among the most delicate and moving touches in the novel, she leans towards Aziz. The strange and unexpected gesture leads the two boats to overturn in the shallow water, after colliding with the raft. The god and his earthen retinue are involved in the confusion and the clay melts into mud. Meanwhile with a volume and complexity that reminds one of Forster's description of the close of the Fifth Symphony, guns roar, elephants trumpet, and like a mallet beating on a dome comes one crack of thunder loud enough to drown all else. A part of the god's retinue, now turned to mud, is swept back to shore and Godbole happily smears it on his forehead. The goblins are routed. All are one. The spirit of the ceremony with which this third part began reappears, to affect all the personages. Even a letter from Adela Quested, and another from Ronnie Heaslop, which had confirmed Aziz in his suspicions, float in the water with the sacred clay. The passage to India is over, and it has not been a failure. One of the voices of India that Mrs. Moore had not heard has spoken with trenchant power, and strangely her own voice has spoken in unison with it.

But no, the passage is not quite over. In Helen Schlegel's elucidation of the Fifth Symphony it was said that the goblins were still there. "They

could return. He had said so bravely, and that is why one can trust Beethoven when he says other things." Forster too will say bravely that the
goblins could return. The last ride together of the two friends Aziz and
Fielding is a proof of the force and the fineness of the revived friendship;
but it also shows how precarious their personal understanding was, how
impotent they were to maintain it equably, how dependent it was on aid
drawn from above themselves, from the Brahman Godbole, from Mrs
Moore.

Three big blocks of sound—that was Forster's account of rhythm in
the Fifth Symphony. Three big blocks of sound—that is what *A Passage
to India* consists of. A first block in which evil creeps about weakly, and
the secret understanding of the heart is easily dominant. A second block,
very long, and very dark, in which evil streams forth from the caves and
lays waste almost everything about, but yet meets an opposition, inde-
cisive in some ways, but unyielding, in the contemplative insight of
Professor Godbole, and the intuitive fidelity of Mrs. Moore. A third
block in which evil is forced to recede, summarily, and spectacularly,
not by the secret understanding of the heart, but by the strength on
which the secret understanding of the heart depends, contemplative
insight, intuitive fidelity. Then the final reminder, that good has merely
obliged evil to recede as good receded before evil a little before.

Reduced to the barest terms, the structure of *A Passage to India* has the
"rhythmic rise-fall-rise" that Forster found in what has been for him,
early and late, the greatest of novels, *War and Peace*.

IV

It is time, and perhaps rather more than time, to ask how the varied
kinds of repetition with variation that abound in *A Passage to India* aid
that book in producing its effect. A question that is difficult, perhaps impossible, but it must be asked. It is so difficult because the effect of *A
Passage to India* is not a simple one, as the effect of *The Old Wives' Tale*
or *Vanity Fair* is simple. Forster's imaginative sympathies have outrun
his intellectual commitments, and when this happens to a novelist the
result is either a confusion or a fine complexity. Forster's intellectual
commitments are clearly set out in his pamphlet *What I Believe*. "My
law givers are Erasmus and Montaigne, not Moses and St. Paul." And
again: "Tolerance, good temper and sympathy—they are what matter
really." The person in *A Passage to India* who has the best combination
of tolerance, good temper, and sympathy, who would be most likely to
take Erasmus and Montaigne as law givers, is Cyril Fielding. But *A Passage to India* is not conceived according to Fielding's liberal, sceptical,
humanist values. It is conceived according to values much better apprehended by Mrs. Moore, who is irritable, of uncertain sympathies, in her
time of crisis acridly intolerant, and who quotes only one author—St.

Paul. It should not be too much of a disturbance in interpreting a novel to find the artist's imaginative sympathies outrunning his intellectual commitments—even so temperate an artist as Turgenev had it happen to him in rendering Bazarov in *Fathers and Sons*.

The main effect in *A Passage to India* is, I believe, of order in the universe, but order that can be merely glimpsed, never seized for sure. In the poem from which the title comes, Whitman ends by bidding us

> steer for the deep waters only,
> Reckless O soul, exploring, I with thee, and thou with me,
> For we are bound where mariner has not yet dared to go,
> And we will risk the ship, ourselves and all.
>
> O my brave soul!
> O farther farther sail!
> O daring joy, but safe! are they not all the seas of God?
> O farther, farther, farther sail.

It is because they are exploring in the seas of God that Mrs. Moore is not deluded in respecting the admonition of Asirgarh "I do not vanish"; that Godbole is not deluded when among the circling images he is led to propel Mrs. Moore and the wasp towards the divine. They move in mystery, but the mystery is not a muddle. It is an order.

To express what is both an order and a mystery, rhythmic processes, repetitions with intricate variations, are the most appropriate of idioms. Repetition is the strongest assurance an author can give of order; the extraordinary complexity of the variations is the reminder that the order is so involute that it must remain a mystery. *A Passage to India* is a prophetic novel, a singing in the halls of fiction: the infinite resourcefulness of Forster has given it a rhythmic form that enables us to respond to it as prophecy and song; to pass beyond character, story, and setting, and attend, delightedly, to the grouping and ungrouping of ideas and emotions; to feel that numinous element so constantly present in the experience of the great man whom in these discourses I have wished to honour.

Passage To More Than India

by Benita Parry

The aspiration of man to understand himself and his universe has resulted in various systems of belief and codes of behaviour—but also in alienation from his fellow-men within other cultures, and therefore in a more complex bewilderment about his social and spiritual identity. This is the paradox explored in *A Passage to India,* explored by examining the areas of relationship and dissonance between the ancient and enduring patterns of Indian civilization and the more "advanced" patterns of the West. Forster avoids the familiar contrast of the materialist West and the contemplative East, so often the subject of this type of international fiction. He does concern himself with questions about which society more effectively satisfies man's quest for certainty and revelation, but his answers are neither confident, nor entirely spiritual. The book has a deep social and historical sense; the clash of cultures is firmly placed, in the historical situation of a British Raj ruling a subject people at a particular point in time; cultural and political as well as spiritual matters are fully explored by the action; and if East and West are in any way to meet, then Forster considers a change in the external relations between them to be quite as necessary as a revolution in man's restricted spiritual and human responses.

"India's a muddle," says Fielding; and while Forster understands this bewilderment, his own perplexity is more complex than his character's.[1] By Western standards, India is indeed equivocal, intricate, and strange; nothing is identifiable, nothing quite fits, and seen with eyes that take their human norm from the Mediterranean and that conceive of proportion as the ideal of beauty, moderation as the standard of deportment,

[1] In his essay "Syed Ross Masood" (1937), reprinted in *Two Cheers for Democracy* (New York: Harcourt, Brace, and World, Inc., 1951), Forster observes that Syed Ross Masood (the Indian to whom *A Passage to India* is dedicated, and on whom Aziz is modelled) "showed me new horizons and a new civilization and helped me towards the understanding of a continent. Until I met him, India was a vague jumble of rajahs, sahibs, babus, and elephants, and I was not interested in such a jumble: who could be?" If Forster is compared with the tradition of Anglo-Indian fiction, and with a sizable proportion of the memoirs that were produced in the late nineteenth and early twentieth centuries, it is striking how far he gets beyond the amazed evocations of the dark, unknowable, menacing East and of its "colourful" atmosphere.

the excesses of India and Indians must seem grotesque. Reason and form are frustrated; yet India "could it be viewed from the moon" might acquire a "definite outline," and Forster's detached, and sympathetic, perceptions about this ambiguous country bring suggestions of shape to it. Even so, because his is a view from a distance, the obscurities of India remain even while the meanings of its various civilizations are brought into focus.

One particular area of difficulty is the implacable and malignant quality of nature in India, which hardly encourages the Western view that man is in harmony with the earth.[2] Here, man is subject to weather and landscape. The Hot Weather dictates how he shall regard himself and others; people entering the valley by the Marabar Hills seem to have attempted a "feeble invasion of it," just as a train in its vicinity is a "coffin from the scientific north which troubled the scenery four times a day". Significantly, the scenic beauty of India is seldom mentioned in the novel, though we know that Forster was very much aware of it; the hopeless and melancholy plains and a treacherous sun without splendour dominate. The depiction of man in nature's grip is sharpened by the use of natural imagery for social facts and tensions: the unease at the leave-taking after Fielding's tea-party is likened to irritation exuding "from the very soil. Could one have been so petty on a Scotch moor or an Italian alp?" In the opening pages, man is shown as imprisoned in a divided town precariously maintaining itself against the encroachments of nature; ultimately it is the earth and sky which intrude to separate Aziz and Fielding.

The Indian landscape is an essential force in the novel. It seems to confuse distinctions: an elephant looks like a hill, a train like an insect, a patch of field jumps as if it were being fried, a snake is a stick or perhaps a stick is a snake; if the boulders in the heat seem alive, why should a stone not feel? This abolition of barriers between animate and inanimate, and the listing of layers from man through animals to insects, plants and stones, and from birds to the sky and beyond, make meaningful the Hindu view of man as just another creature in the chain of creation, and suggest the possibility that equal value attaches to all things. How are men to accommodate to the indifference of nature, which mocks at their categories and derides their aspirations?[3] Hinduism imitates the

---

[2] James McConkey, in *The Novels of E.M. Forster* (Ithaca, N.Y.: Cornell University Press, 1957), regards man's alienation from the earth "and hence from ultimate reality" as a fundamental modern dilemma, and so finds Forster's India "the contemporary condition, the separation between all mankind and all earth." But Forster does not see India so abstractly, and recognises the way in which pre-industrial civilizations of the Indian type must have a special relationship with the earth.

[3] Cf. Rabindranath Tagore, *Glimpses of Bengal Selected from the Letters of Rabindranath Tagore: 1885 to 1895* (London: Macmillan and Co., Ltd., 1921). Tagore speaks of the Indian sense of nature belittling man and creating a distinctive passiveness before it.

appearance of the physical world in India, overriding barriers between man and the inarticulate world; and while this allows for subtle speculation on the nature of creation and the transcendental, it short-circuits a scientific understanding of the universe. Hinduism in this sense both matches and perpetuates an undynamic society. Because *A Passage to India* is informed by Forster's Western concern with rootlessness, and the need for harmony and stability, there is conjecture on the value of accommodation—perhaps unchanging India, its material growth stunted by the predominance of a malevolent nature, nurtures modes of thought and feeling which make for greater personal harmony, a more integrated social and spiritual life.

By shifting focus from the mud-like monotony of Chandrapore, where the soaring vegetation is terrifyingly stronger than man or his works, to hints of value in the very immobility and passivity, Forster gives tension to this possibility. Two world views are suggested in a significant passage where the boundaries of a well-ordered mind, Adela Quested's, are identified with the limitations of Western consciousness and priorities. Adela's thoughts about her future in India are accompanied by the rhythm of the train:

> . . . the train half asleep, going nowhere in particular and with no passenger of importance in any of its carriages, the branch-line train, lost on a low embankment between dull fields. Its message—for it had one—avoided her well-equipped mind. Far away behind her, with a shriek that meant business, rushed the Mail, connecting up important towns such as Calcutta and Lahore, where interesting events occur and personalities are developed. She understood that. Unfortunately, India has few important towns. India is the country, fields, fields, then hills, jungle, hills, and more fields. The branch line stops, the road is only practicable for cars to a point, the bullock-carts lumber down the side tracks, paths fray out into the cultivation, and disappear near a splash of red paint. How can the mind take hold of such a country? Generations of invaders have tried, but they remain in exile. The important towns they build are only retreats, their quarrels the malaise of men who cannot find their way home.   (p. 136) [4]

An India indifferent to the intentions of the technically advanced intruders, an India with a past remote from anything in recorded history, still evident in a red splash signifying perhaps a god, perhaps a sati, is measured against the "important," the "interesting," the world of "shriek" and "rush." The contrast satirises Western pretensions and bustle; but the scales do not easily reach equilibrium. The sense of the continuity, cohesion, and stability of village life at Mau is balanced by the glimpse of the mild-featured ryots "for whom anything outside their village passed in a dream"; perhaps they have harmonious relationships with each other and their environment, but does not their circumscribed

---

[4] All page-references are to the American edition of *A Passage to India* published by Harcourt Brace and Co. in 1924.

stagnation diminish them as human beings? [5] The sight of the god-like untouchable punkah-wallah, aloof from and unconscious of his surroundings, seated opposite the westernized assistant-magistrate, Mr. Das, who is "cultivated, self-conscious, and conscientious," jolts Adela Quested into reappraising her assumptions: "Her particular brand of opinions, and the suburban Jehovah who sanctified them—by what right did they claim so much importance in the world, and assume the title of civilization?" (p. 218) This juxtaposition of alternatives is shown without sentimentality: the "god's" blankness is a reduction of his humanity; thrown out by nature in defiance of society's categories, he had been nourished by the city's garbage and "would end on its rubbish heaps." Caste-ridden, poverty-stricken India is not screened from sight; these are the accompaniments of that India where men are not divorced from the earth and have not refashioned their surroundings.

The close relationship between the Indian mind and the Indian landscape throws the weight of the challenge onto the Westerners. Natural disasters, religious injunctions and invasions are accepted by the Hindus; passivity towards conditions imposed by nature or thrust upon them by men provides the strength to resist the punishments of both. So the invaders remain in exile, while the Hindus, here identified with India, are peculiarly victorious:

> The triumphant machine of civilization may suddenly hitch and be immobilized into a car of stone, and at such moments the destiny of the English seems to resemble their predecessors', who also entered the country with intent to refashion it, but were in the end worked into its pattern and covered with its dust.   (p. 211)

India's passivity, then, is not absolute; the apparent flabbiness of the Hindus contains their unique activity of passive resistance. Forster presents this, yet equally affirms man's insistence on activity and creation as a true assertion of his humanity; and the images of bowed acquiescence are balanced by those of liberation from the chains of circumstances. It is man's "itch for the seemly" which has transformed the shapeless universe, still potent in the Marabar Hills—which "rise abruptly, insanely, without the proportion that is kept by the wildest hills elsewhere." The emptiness and denial of meaning in the Caves—"Pathos, piety, courage —they exist, but are identical, and so is filth" (p. 149)—are counteracted by the works of man. The abased Indian section of Chandrapore which persists "like some low but indestructible form of life," or "the indestructible life of man and his changing faces, and the houses he has built for

---

[5] In "Art for Art's Sake" (1949), reprinted in *Two Cheers* . . . , Forster touches again on this problem, which has long interested him: "How can man get into harmony with his surroundings when he is constantly altering them? The future of our race is, in this direction, more unpleasant than we care to admit, and it has sometimes seemed to me that the best chance lies through apathy, uninventiveness, and inertia."

himself and God," which revive Mrs. Moore on her journey to Bombay, are victories against meaninglessness. The use of "indestructible" conveys the toughness and durability of man's triumphs and gives the physical world reality and importance, just as Mrs. Moore's thoughts of the Indian cities she had never seen, and of "the obscurer marvels that had sometimes shone through men's speech: the bilingual rock of Girnar, the statue of Shri Belgola, the ruins of Mandu and Hampi, temples of Khajraha, gardens of Shalimar" (p. 210) are a tribute to human imagination and creative genius.[6] Though the Indian masses appear at first to be without identity, to be inseparable from the natural scene—the inhabitants of Chandrapore seem to be moving mud, the villagers collected round the elephant's feet are the scurf of life—they gradually reveal their potential. During Aziz' trial the moving mud is stirred to anger; the sweepers strike, leaving the commodes of Chandrapore unattended; a new spirit is abroad which the Anglo-Indians, whose official boast it is that they know the "real Indians," cannot understand.

I

Hinduism takes its place at the core of the novel just as it lies at the heart of India. It succeeds and survives because it is relevant to the lives of the people.[7] In the state of Mau, where Western influence is waning, the cultivators, officials, tradesmen, courtiers, and nobles are united in common worship which for them expresses a total outlook and way of life, and which entails a complete, if temporary, spiritual involvement. Their religion is for them a living force, embracing as it does all spirit and all matter and intertwining the secular with the divine—God is apprehended in so many ways that there are gods who own cows and the betal leaf industry and are shareholders in the Asirgarh motor omnibus. Its "myriad of merging gods" (Forster in the essay "The Emperor Babur," 1921, reprinted in *Abinger Harvest*) reflects nature's energies and, unlike the symmetrical injunctions of Islam suitable "to pilgrimages and universities," it is a faith constant with feudalism and agriculture. Like India, which embraces a hundred Indias, Hinduism has grown through assimilating the customs and beliefs of the indigenous peoples and cushioning

---

[6] Critics like Glen O. Allen, McConkey, and Frederick C. Crews have perhaps overestimated the degree to which Forster stresses the insignificance of human endeavour; he also puts much stress on man's indestructibility and creativity.

[7] Even incidental comments draw on Hindu concepts. Thus, after Aziz' trial the victorious Indians "suffered from the usual disillusionment that attends warfare. The aims of battle and the fruits of conquest are never the same." This is a reference to Arjuna's encounter with Krishna in the *Bhagavad-Gita* (Forster comments on it in his essay "Hymn Before Action" (1912), reprinted in *Abinger Harvest*). Clearly, too, Forster grasped the depth of popular involvement with Hinduism before the great political upsurge of the later twenties; historians have pointed out that the Indian masses only moved decisively when Gandhi appealed to them through Hinduism.

the onslaught of invaders' ideas by partial absorption; and this syncre-tistic impulse of Indian religious faith is woven into the novel's fabric. In Mau, the Moslem Aziz finds that a Moslem saint is worshipped by Hindus after their fashion and that under their influence the Moslems of the area had grown idolatrous. He is at first scornful and, like Alamgir, longs to purify the place: "But soon he didn't mind, like Akbar." (p. 296) India has tamed the proselytizing zeal of Islam; it triumphs against all comers simply by being; and Hinduism, mirroring India, survives, grows, and influences by undogmatic integration. Mrs. Moore is transformed into "Esmiss Esmoor," a Hindu goddess, just as a century earlier Europeans who had settled in the country occasionally became local deities after death, "not a whole god, perhaps, but part of one, adding an epithet or gesture to what already existed, just as the gods contribute to the great gods, and they to the philosophic Brahm." (p. 257)

India is the nullity of the Caves, and the obscure marvels fashioned by men; the hopeless plains, and the cities of Kashmir and Delhi. Its infinite variety is echoed in the diversity of Hinduism: the incarnation of God as a monkey, God conceived as Krishna sporting with the milk-maids, ascetics who suppress the senses, saddhus who satiate them, the creed of harmlessness to all living things, violent sacrificial rites—all have their place. Hinduism's all-inclusiveness contains a profound apprehen-sion of a world in which good and evil, the ridiculous and the august, cruelty and pacifism coexist. In her moment of anti-vision Mrs. Moore, nurtured in concepts of exclusive truths ("God is Love"), understands the message of the Caves and of India to be: "Everything exists, nothing has value." Hinduism has nothing in common with this nihilism, and the novel moves away from it. Godbole distinguishes between good and evil and defines their nature, and his concepts are played back through the thoughts and reactions of the other characters. He tells Fielding: "All perform a good action, when one is performed, and when an evil action is performed, all perform it. . . . When evil occurs, it expresses the whole of the universe. Similarly when good occurs." (pp. 177, 178) Both Adela and Fielding, as they see evil loose, entering and infecting the lives of all around, as if it had an existence of its own, reach this awareness. No one character in the book is good or evil, and Mrs. Moore and Adela come to realise that they contain these opposites within them-selves, just as Hinduism embraces the contest. The eclecticism of Hindu-ism is all-important; because truth is not conceived as monolithic, varied beliefs are accepted as revealing different aspects of truth; thus contradic-tions do not exclude a fruitful coexistence. The Caves reconcile ideas both of pacifism and violence. Forster, in his *Paris Review* interview, has called the scene in the Caves a "good substitute for violence" (certainly its impact on Mrs. Moore and Adela *is* violent) but during the trial we learn that the Caves are Jain—the most pacific sect within Hinduism, to whose creed respect for all forms of life is cardinal. Hinduism can accommodate the mystic and the sceptic, the free-thinker and the believer, the ascetic and the hedonist, and perhaps this is its lesson to the world, just as perhaps "the hundred Indias which fuss and squabble so tiresomely are one, and the universe they mirror is one." (p. 263) Yet Forster, who in his essay "Mohammed Iqbal" (1949, reprinted in *Two Cheers For Democracy*) has expressed preference for pantheism rather than the orderliness of Islam, surely fears that the breadth and tolerance of Hinduism (which in *A Passage to India* he imaginatively reconstructs) inevitably carries within itself the seeds of muddle and chaos. This seems evident in his description of the Gokal Ashtami Festival; although the mess is divine and the confusion benign, the great blur lacks an emotional center. "God si Love"—the precise Christian definition is incorporated into the worship to indicate God's universality, but in the process has become muddled. Perhaps exclusion and exclusiveness is the price of accuracy in meaning; perhaps, as the timid missionaries nervously insist, "We must exclude someone from our gathering, or we shall be left with nothing." (p. 38)

Forster, aware of the "conventional conclusion" that India is the home of religion (in *Goldsworthy Lowes Dickinson,* Harcourt, Brace, & World, Inc., New York, 1934), and therefore that India constitutes a special test of man's capacity to respond to the infinite,[8] handles this theme with great complexity. Fielding comments that there is "something in religion that may not be true, but has not yet been sung. . . . Something that the Hindus have perhaps found," (p. 277) and this points to Forster's interest. In the Indian landscape Eternity ceases to be an abstraction and becomes reality, dwarfing man. The Marabar Hills and Caves contain visible remnants of the aeons preceding man's evolution; and this gives a perspective, largely obscured in the West, of the infinitesimal area within which man exists, and of the immensity of ages to come. In the landscape near the hills, "a new quality occurred, a spiritual silence which invaded more senses than the ear. Life went on as usual, but had no consequences, that is to say, sounds did not echo or thoughts develop. . . . Nothing was explained, and yet there was no romance." It is an atmosphere which necessarily impels men to psychic exploration. Lionel Trilling, in his book on Forster, makes the point that Forster has a tenderness for religion because "it expresses, though it does not solve, the human mystery." This mystery is identified with India; and this, together with the variety and many-textured quality of Hinduism, is expressed in Godbole. In part, he is a comic figure, the opaque word-spinner possessed of an inexplicable prescience, a sort of wise fool. But he is also an expression of

---

[8] This view was held by Whitman, whose poem "Passage to India" (1871) gave Forster his title. Hugh MacLean, in "The Structure of *A Passage to India*," *The University of Toronto Quarterly*, XXII (January 1953), 151-71, makes much of the connection between Forster and Whitman.

Hinduism, embodying passive resistance, harmonious contradictions. He is a series of characteristics rather than an individual, fulfilling Forster's observation that "there is scarcely anything in that tormented land which fills up the gulf between the illimitable and the inane." ("Pan," 1922, reprinted in *Abinger Harvest*.) His appearance suggests harmony, "as if he had reconciled the products of East and West, mental as well as physical, and could never be discomposed." (pp. 72-73) Yet from the West he has taken only the externals, the English language and socks with clocks. Aloof and tranquil, he embodies an India which tolerated the invaders but submitted only physically to them. The thoughts and motives of the enigmatic Deccani Brahman remain obscure, and the presentation of these is prefaced by "as if" and "perhaps." That Godbole is saturated with the traditions and concepts of the continent is made vivid by the reference to him as "Ancient Night," with its implication of a mind which has inherited and contains the memory of an India interminably old. Godbole's energies are directed towards developing the life of the spirit, and this philosophy makes him ill-equipped for practical tasks; he can neither catch a train nor establish the King Emperor George V High School at Mau. He epitomises an abstract stance: he who must eat apart from the outcastes and eliminate their touch by bathing, who lives within "the sects and clans" of Hinduism, responds warmly to Aziz' enlightened poem acclaiming internationalism: "Ah, that is bhakti; ah, my young friend, that is different and very good. Ah, India, who seems not to move, will go straight there while the other nations waste their time." (p. 293) Godbole accommodates both a speculative, flexible, and tolerant philosophy and acceptance of its earthly expression in a caste-divided social sytem; he accepts internationalism in his head just as Hinduism obliterates identities, eliminates suffering, and loves all things in the abstract. Hinduism contains within itself both the recognition and acceptance of divisions as well as the impulse to eliminate barriers and embrace all; the religious injunctions commit men to untouchability, and the holy festival includes in its ritual "the moment of the Despised and the Rejected." (p. 305)

Hinduism is the central factor in India; but the Moslems too have been integrated into a communal Oriental civilization in which all Indians share and from which the West is excluded. While Godbole and Aziz personify the divisions within India, they also represent its unity. Both want the pre-British past back; Aziz dreams of the vanished Moghul Empire, Godbole's heritage is the great days of the Mahrattas. Both are poets and can be transported from the confines of the immediate, and there is a striking similarity in the descriptions of these flights and their disruption. In the heated state of his religious ecstasy, Godbole strives to impel towards completeness the images which come unsolicited to his mind, but he fails with the stone: "logic and conscious effort had seduced, he came back to the strip of red carpet and discovered that he was dancing upon it." (p. 286) Similarly, across the surface of Aziz' mind, always responsive to the unseen, flit thoughts of Mecca, the Friend, his wife, "and then the whole semi-mystic, semi-sensuous overturn, so characteristic of his spiritual life, came to end like a landslip and rested in its due place, and he found himself riding in the jungle with his dear Cyril." (p. 320) While Forster persuades us to accept that Mrs. Moore and Ralph Moore are Orientals, he *shows* that Aziz, the Moslem, and Godbole, the Hindu, are. Godbole's invocations to the God Krishna, who neglects to Come, is akin to Aziz' recital of poetry which voices "our loneliness . . . , our isolation, our need for the Friend [the Persian expression for God] who never comes yet is not entirely disproved." (p. 106) There are recurring references to the difficulties of entente between Hindus and Moslems; yet it is clear that they share more with each other than with the West—the Moslem "restfulness of gesture—it is the Peace that passeth Understanding, after all, it is the social equivalent of Yoga. When the whirring of action ceases, it becomes visible, and reveals a civilization which the West can disturb but will never acquire." (pp. 251-52) Aziz' experiences at the hands of the Anglo-Indians drive him towards a conscious identification with his common civilization; he expresses his nationalism in an illogical, unstable and contradictory way which, because it is in character, is wholly convincing. He comes to have a genuine, if abstract, hatred for the English—"I am an Indian at last," he thinks, (p. 293) and to the British he says: "I do not want you, I do not want one of you in my private life, with my dying breath I say it." (p. 302) But this does not prevent him from responding again to Fielding and to Mrs. Moore's children. Though he continues to write poems with bulbuls and roses, lamenting the decay of Islam, he longs to compose a song of the future which would transcend creed and be acclaimed by the multitudes. He moves "towards the vague and bulky figure of a mother-land. He was without natural affection for the land of his birth, but the Marabar Hills drove him to it. Half closing his eyes, he attempted to love India." (p. 268) While retaining his bored cynicism at their religion, and while still finding it difficult to like them, Aziz determines to move closer to Hindus, and becomes aware that Hinduism is, in a fundamental sense, India. His explanations to Ralph Moore during the Krishna festival suggest the flux of his responses—in his use of "our" or "my" and "they" or "their" is revealed both the need and desire to identify himself with a mother-land, and his continuing sense of estrangement from Hindus:

> This is our monsoon, the best weather. . . . How I wish she [Mrs. Moore] could have seen them, our rains. Now is the time when all things are happy, young and old. They are happy out there with their savage noise, though we cannot follow them; the tanks are all full so they dance, and this is India. I wish you were not with officials, then I would show you my country.
>
> (p. 312)

Aziz of course continues to love Islam but he gains insight into its equivocal role in India:

> Of what help, in this latitude and hour, are the glories of Cordova and Samarcand? They have gone, and while we lament them the English occupy Delhi and exclude us from East Africa. Islam itself, though true, throws cross-lights over the path to freedom."   (p. 268)

II

In blind arrogance towards the Oriental civilizations stand the Anglo-Indians, their attitudes epitomizing the hostility which a self-contained group can display towards alien concepts and customs. Any real intercourse with India is to them unthinkable, and despite their cry of bringing "civilization," their purpose is not to share their ideas and techniques with Indians, but to administer a subject people. Official relationships take the place of human ones, social intimacy is taboo; those Indians who are dependent on the good will of the Raj must fawn and be patronized by the British officials and humiliated by their wives. In a land where excessive heat is part of the seasons' cycle, the British "circulate like an ice-stream," and talking of them brings a "wintry surface" to the conversation of the Moslems. The Anglo-Indian divorcement from the land and its peoples is one of the cliches of the Indian services; its members live amidst scenery they do not understand, in a country they see as poisonous and intending evil against them. Lacking in intellectual curiosity, their range of responses corsetted, they have little insight into their motives and are unaware of the gap between the pretentious myth they have evolved about themselves and the smallness of their stale and ungenerous views. Themselves caught in the net which Britain has thrown over India, they give vent to the frustrated bewilderment lying behind official boasts of their indispensability in emotional brutality towards Indians and nonconformists in their own ranks. The presence of erotic obsessions in their image of Indians is made explicit; furtive fantasies about the prowess and perversions which they believe are part of Indians' sexual habits lie in the undergrowth of their attitudes—consider the remarks of Major Callendar and McBryde, and the expression of Adela's hallucination,[9] at a point when she is bending towards accepting Anglo-India. Behind their calculated alienation from the land lies a fear that India will discompose

[9] Of course, we do not know quite what happened in the caves. Following a review of *A Passage to India*, a correspondent, E.A. Horne, offered in *The New Statesman* (August 16, 1924) an interesting version: because of his sexual vanity and physical obsession, Aziz, thrown off balance by Adela's question about the number of his wives, suffers the hallucination and communicates it to Adela. But Adela's fears fit in very well with those expressed by Anglo-Indian lady-novelists in the first two decades of the century.

their codes and values. India does destroy Mrs. Moore's tidy view of the world, and it unbalances Adela; she who refuses to believe in the Hot Weather is defeated by the Indian sun, and she comes to realise that she must return to an environment in which her mould of responses is relevant: "I am not astray in England. I fit in there—no, don't think I shall do harm in England," (p. 262) she tells Fielding.

The social and political elements of *A Passage to India* are important, though they have been somewhat overstressed in much of the early criticism. To read the book as a social document about the British in India, and the Indians in British India, does stunt an appraisal of its complexities of meaning; but the political insights should not be ignored,[10] for the pressures of imperialism are very much involved in the development of characters and relationships and in the shaping of the area and nature of contact between the civilizations represented. It is not only the dissimilarities of the cultures which inhibit understanding and interflow, but a particular insensitivity in the English, which generates unease, mistrust, and a sense of inferiority in the Indians. In the relationship so spontaneously and effortlessly established between Aziz and Mrs. Moore, more is stated than explored, and we do not here see an effective contact between the cultures. Far more satisfying in this respect is the friendship between Fielding and Aziz. The ebb and flow of their relationship is disturbed by differences of background and values and by the clash of standards on beauty, propriety, and emotional expression—"A pause in the wrong place, an intonation misunderstood, and a whole conversation went awry." (p. 274) But the primary barrier to their communication is that Fielding is one of the British in India and Aziz a member of a subject people.[11] Yet they do have an interlude of friendship before India intervenes to separate them, and both, having previously shied away from politics, now assume firmer positions within the divisions, Fielding with Anglo-India, Aziz with Indian nationalism. This divisive tendency in the book is very evident, and it creates difficulties for those critics who suggest that the novel is an affirmation of proportion, as the truth about the

---

[10] In *E.M. Forster: A Tribute* (New York: Harcourt, Brace, & World, Inc., 1964), edited by K. Natwar Singh, Forster is reported as saying of the political impact of the novel: "It had some political influence—it caused people to think of the link between India and Britain and to doubt if that link was altogether of a healthy nature. The influence was not intended; I was interested in the story of the characters. But I welcomed it." And Forster's understanding of the political forces playing upon his characters is deep—particularly in his understanding of the political role of the Moslems, sadly placed between a potentially powerful Hindu majority and the British Raj. However, for a dissenting view see Nirad C. Chaudhuri, "Passage to and from India," *Encounter*, II (June 1954), 19-24.

[11] Though it is true that there are much more fundamental differences than political ones between East and West, there are quite evidently political pressures distorting the relationship between Aziz and Fielding, as Arnold Kettle points out in his essay on the novel in his *An Introduction to the English Novel* (Volume 2). (London: Hutchinson University Library, 1953).

way life is or ought to be.[12] John Beer argues, more aptly, that the point of the novel lies "not in an assertion of normality but in an exploration of extremes. And this exploration is not simply social or political. Further issues are involved, which reflect Forster's basic preoccupation as a thinker, and his own experience in India." [13]

This is surely true. Fielding, who epitomizes normality and proportion (his discontent appears to be a temporary aberration), emerges as spiritually incomplete and ready to compromise with a milieu he had formerly despised. The letter to him from Heaslop indicates this retreat: "I'm relieved you feel able to come into line with the Oppressors of India to some extent." (p. 307) If proportion is, as Allen suggests, "the final secret," then how poor final secrets are, and perhaps this is the implication Forster intends. Despite Fielding's belief that the world "is a globe of men who are trying to reach one another and can best do so by the help of good will plus culture and intelligence," (p. 62) he prefers to "slink" through India and regrets having to take sides against the Anglo-Indians, whose very presence is a violation of his creed. The accusation against Aziz and its aftermath does lead him to take a stand and does involve him in doubts and dissatisfaction, but he returns to normality and ultimately his past heroism over Aziz seems "a momento, a trophy." The inconsistency and extravagances of Aziz, his need for friendship, affection, sensuality, and spiritual experiences, make him the most complete character in the novel. His volatile lack of proportion—"Is emotion a sack of potatoes, so much the pound, to be measured out? Am I a machine?"—is more attractive than Fielding's prim reprimand, "Your emotions never seem in proportion to their objects." (p. 254) Forster is aware, it seems, both of the serenity of moderation and of its incompleteness.

The same sense of incompleteness, of personal limitation seen both in national and in general human terms, is surely present in the treatment of the spiritual theme. Trilling tells us that it is not easy to know what to make of the dominant Hinduism in the third section of the novel; and answers to the problem have come to assume a central place in critical interpretations. Gertrude M. White follows Trilling in suggesting that the major theme is that of "fission and fusion; of separateness and desired union," but goes beyond his cautious recognition of Hinduism as "the vision in which the arbitrary human barriers sink before the extinction of all things," to an affirmation of it as "a prophetic vision, for what happens in 'Temple' is reconciliation on the human level." [14] Glen O.

[12] See for instance Glen O. Allen's argument, in "Structure, Symbol, and Theme in E.M. Forster's *A Passage to India*," *PMLA*, LXX, December 1955, 934-54.

[13] In *The Achievement of E.M. Forster* (London: Chatto & Windus, Ltd., 1962).

[14] Gertrude M. White, "*A Passage to India:* Analysis and Revaluation," *PMLA*, LXVIII, September 1953, 652, where she holds that Godbole stands for "the union in reality of all men, whether they will or no." And V.A. Shanane, in his *E.M. Forster: A Reassessment* (Delhi: Kitab Mahal, 1963), goes one stage further and claims Forster for

Allen and James M. McConkey have subjected the words describing the
atmosphere in the caves to semantic analysis, finding parallels between
the text and Hindu Scriptures.[15] While McConkey points out that Forster is not a mystic, and warns against overemphasising the importance
of Hinduism in the book, observing, like Trilling, that Forster does not
so much accept Hinduism as select those aspects which have the greatest
affinity to his own attitudes, he does give prominence to the metaphysical strain, finding in Godbole the true prophetic character and the char-
acter-equivalent of the Forsterian voice. Yet the tone of the transcendental allusions is tentative and undefined, moving between uncertainty and
whimsicality. Forster's hesitant suggestions should not be read as affirma-
tions, and the irony in his voice should be considered. A squirrel with a
mangy tail whose squeals "were in tune with the infinite, no doubt, but
not attractive except to other squirrels," (p. 114) undermines the portent
of absolutes. Godbole's significant and poignant invocation to Krishna
is reduced to bathos by its application to the inferior countryside—"In
vain did each item in it call out, 'Come, come.' There was not enough
god to go round." (pp. 87-88)

That which lies beyond man's vision and understanding is conveyed as
without attributes: the farther distance beyond the blue sky is "beyond
colour," beyond the remotest echo in the vistas which evade Mrs. Moore's
understanding is silence. "Beyond the sky must not there be something
that overarches all the skies, more impartial even than they? Beyond
which again. . . ." (p. 40) This suggests the vastness of what is still unknown, and perhaps unknowable, to man, rather than, as McConkey
maintains, the order and harmony of unifying reality. When hints of the
transcendental serve to indicate man's dissatisfaction with the limits of
his knowledge and understanding, and to affirm his need to push back
the boundaries of his perceptions by science, art, and philosophy, these
merge with related themes of human insistence on inventing meanings
in the universe. Man's capacity for curiosity and the boundless possibilities of his imagination must lead him to assume that there are always
further realms to be penetrated, that there are systems and laws governing
the universe and society which he has not yet discerned. It is the incompleteness in man's comprehension which makes it impossible for him to
accept death and drives him to seek some form of immortality; Aziz,
whose belief in the life to come is infirm, is solaced by the knowledge that

---

Brahman mysticism, seeing the "Temple" section as a final solution to the problem
presented.

[15] Glen O. Allen observes that there are, in the Hindu scriptures, references to At-
man and Brahman, the Self and the Not-Self, dwelling "in the cave"; he also sees the
similarity between Forster's "Boum" and the mystical symbol "Om," the pronunciation
of and meditation on which is part of the discipline of this seeking Brahman. McConkey acknowledges this argument and sees Forster as intending the emptiness of the
caves to represent the absolute Brahman . . . while the echo represents Mrs. Moore's
incomplete awareness of that absolute.

he will live on in his children, while Fielding, an atheist, aspires to leave a thought behind.

The portrayal of Fielding and Adela as persons confronted with the awareness of their own limitations is fully realised: "Were there worlds beyond which they could never touch, or did all that is possible enter their consciousness? They could not tell. . . . They had not the apparatus for judging." (p. 263) But does anyone possess the apparatus? Herein lies a central difficulty of the novel, one which has created much critical discussion and has led to enormous variations of reading, frequently tempting critics to see Forster as *almost* a Christian, *almost* a Catholic, *almost* a Hindu. For though Mrs. Moore does not attain the desired oneness with the universe, and Professor Godbole's spiritual aspirations to reach unity with God are frustrated, both of these failures are converted by sleight of hand to imply triumphs. The evil released by the Marabar is driven back by Godbole's cult of love, and Mrs. Moore re-emerges after her death as a benign influence, guiding Adela to retract her wrongful accusation and Aziz to forgive his persecution. And in the scene of meeting between Mrs. Moore's son Ralph and Aziz there are intimations of her mysterious continuation. Ernest Beaumont has called Mrs. Moore a "strange mystic" and has commented that her intercessory role is a disquieting aspect of her portrayal; she represents a "somewhat dubious supernatural." [16] To critics who do not see the strong visionary concern of the novel, this scene can be especially puzzling; to those who do, it still presents a problem. F.R. Leavis points out that in the first part of the book Mrs. Moore is an ordinary character, but she becomes after her death "a vague pervasive suggestion of mystery." His objection is that it is "all too easy. It amounts to little more than saying, 'There may be something in it,' but has the effect of taking itself for a good deal more." [17] Forster has always been interested in the question of human continuity; it is within the pattern of his figurative writing that he should be so now. What, I think, worries us is that Forster asks us to suspend disbelief in the operation of mysteries without quite trusting in them himself.

Because of such difficulties, because *A Passage to India* is so difficult and intricate a book, critics will continue to debate its meaning. But it does seem important to single out, as I have tried to, one important feature—that the book is an interpretation of India, traditionally a land of mysteries and muddles, and an interpretation of its impact on those who live in it and on the aliens who come to it. Forster—working in what is in fact a traditional genre, the Anglo-Indian novel—advances it as a form far beyond a simple interpretation. He shows the land as challeng-

[16] Ernest Beaumont, "Mr. E.M. Forster's Strange Mystics," *The Dublin Review*, 453 (Third Quarter 1951), 41-51.

[17] F.R. Leavis, "E.M. Forster" in *The Common Pursuit* (London: Chatto & Windus, Ltd., 1952), pp. 261-77.

ing to the stranger—a land threatening what is hollow in his beliefs and incomplete in his outlook—and makes the experience a severe moral test, a test in encountering transcendence. It is an international novel which, like many such novels, challenges the characters with larger views than they have known. And Forster's judgment seems to be that, if East and West cannot meet, this is evidence of the limitations of man. Yet it would seem that he does not regard them as immutable; his hope, the hope of the novel, is surely that the final "No, not yet" can be transcended.

Chronology of Important Dates

1879	Edward Morgan Forster born on January 1 in London. His father was an architect of Anglo-Irish extraction, his mother descended from the Thornton family and the "Clapham Sect."
1897	After being a day boy at Tonbridge School, entered King's College, Cambridge. He took a Second Class in the Classical Tripos, Part I, in 1900, and a Second Class in the History Tripos, Part II, in 1901.
1901-2	Visited Greece and lived in Italy.
1903	G.E. Moore's *Principia Ethica* published; *The Independent Review* (to which Forster was soon to be a contributor) founded by his Cambridge friends Nathaniel Wedd and Goldsworthy Lowes Dickinson and others; Forster's first published story, "Albergo Empedocle," published in *Temple Bar.*
1905	*Where Angels Fear to Tread.*
1907	*The Longest Journey.*
1908	*A Room with a View* (though his third published novel, it was probably conceived first, since he drafted a large part of it in 1903).
1910	*Howards End.*
1911	*The Celestial Omnibus* (Forster's first collection of stories, written from 1903 on). In this year he finished a play, *The Heart of Bosnia*, which almost was staged in 1914.
1912-13	Visited India with Dickinson and R.C. Trevelyan, and began work on *A Passage to India.*
1914-18	Spent much of the war in Alexandria as a Red Cross voluntary worker.
1920	For a year was literary editor of the London *Daily Herald* (a Labour paper).
1922	*Alexandria: A History and a Guide;* made a second visit to India.
1923	*Pharos and Pharillon* (literary and historical sketches).
1924	*A Passage to India.*
1927	*Aspects of the Novel.*
1928	*The Eternal Moment* (short stories).
1934	*Goldsworthy Lowes Dickinson* (biography).
1936	*Abinger Harvest* (essays).
1939	*What I Believe.*
1951	*Two Cheers for Democracy* (essays).
1953	*The Hill of Devi.*
1956	*Marianne Thornton.*

Notes on the Editor and Authors

MALCOLM BRADBURY. Critic and novelist. Lecturer in English, the University of East Anglia. Author of *Eating People Is Wrong* (1959) (novel), *Evelyn Waugh* (1964), *Stepping Westward* (1965) (novel), and other works.

I.A. RICHARDS. Critic and poet. Professor Emeritus of Education, Harvard University, formerly Fellow of Magdalene College, Cambridge. Author of *Principles of Literary Criticism* (1924), *Science and Poetry* (1925), *Practical Criticism* (1929), *Speculative Instruments* (1955), and other works.

PETER BURRA. English critic and journalist, author of studies of Van Gogh and Wordsworth.

F.R. LEAVIS. Formerly Reader in English, Cambridge University, and Fellow of Downing College. Presently Professor of English, the University of York. Author of *Revaluation* (1936), *The Great Tradition* (1948), *The Common Pursuit* (1953), etc. Founding Editor of *Scrutiny*.

AUSTIN WARREN. Professor of English, the University of Michigan. Author of *Alexander Pope as Critic and Humanist* (1929), *The Elderly Henry James* (1934), *Crashaw: A Study in Baroque Sensibility* (1938), *The Theory of Literature* (1949) (with René Wellek), and other works.

LIONEL TRILLING. Critic and novelist. Professor of English, Columbia University. Author of *Matthew Arnold* (1939), *The Middle of the Journey* (1947) (novel), *The Liberal Imagination* (1950), *The Opposing Self* (1955), and other works.

D.S. SAVAGE. English poet and critic. Author of *A Time to Mourn* (1943) (poems), *The Personal Principle* (1944), *The Withered Branch* (1950), and other works.

HYATT H. WAGGONER. Professor of American Literature, Brown University. Author of *Hawthorne: A Critical Study* (1955; rev. 1963), *William Faulkner: From Jefferson to the World* (1959).

FRANK KERMODE. Professor of English, the University of Bristol. Author of *Romantic Image* (1957), *Puzzles and Epiphanies* (1963), and other works.

FREDERICK C. CREWS. Associate Professor of English, the University of California, Berkeley. Author of *Tragedy of Manners: Moral Drama in the Later Works of Henry James* (1957), *The Pooh Perplex* (1963).

H.A. SMITH. Lecturer in English Language and Literature, the University of Birmingham.

JOHN HARVEY. Professor of English, the Queen's University of Belfast. Author of *The Art of George Eliot* (1961), and other works.

E.K. BROWN. Critic and editor. Formerly Professor of English at the Universities of Toronto, Manitoba, Cornell, and Chicago. Author of *Edith Wharton: Étude*

Critique (1935), *On Canadian Poetry* (1943), *Matthew Arnold: A Study in Conflict* (1948), *Willa Cather: A Critical Biography* (1935), and other works. Died 1951.

BENITA PARRY. Research Fellow, Department of History, the University of Birmingham.

Selected Bibliography

NOTE: For bibliographical details of writings by E.M. Forster, see B.J. Kirkpatrick, *E.M. Forster* (The Soho Bibliographies, XIX), London: Rupert Hart-Davies, 1965. For bibliographical details of writings about Forster, see the useful listing by Helmut E. Gerber, "An Annotated Check-List of Writings on E.M. Forster," *English Fiction in Transition: 1880-1920*, II (Spring 1959), 4-27.

The list that follows is of critical essays and books—not including those represented in this volume—that seem to me of special interest.

Allen, Glen O., "Structure, Symbol, and Theme in E.M. Forster's *A Passage to India*," *PMLA*, LXX (December 1955), 934-54.

Beaumont, Ernest, "Mr. Forster's Strange Mystics," *The Dublin Review*, 453 (Third Quarter, 1951), 41-51.

Beer, J.B., *The Achievement of E.M. Forster*. London: Chatto & Windus, Ltd., 1962.

Belgion, Montgomery, "The Diabolism of E.M. Forster," *The Criterion*, XIV (October 1934), 54-73.

Brower, Reuben A., *The Fields of Light: An Experiment in Critical Reading*. New York: Oxford University Press, 1951.

Brown, E.K., "E.M. Forster and the Contemplative Novel," *The University of Toronto Quarterly*, III (April 1934), 349-61.

Brown, E.K., "The Revival of E.M. Forster," *The Yale Review*, XXXIII (June 1944), 668-81.

Cecil, Lord David, *Poets and Story-Tellers: A Book of Critical Essays*. London: Constable; New York: Macmillan, 1949.

Churchill, Thomas, "Place and Personality in *Howards End*," *Critique*, VI (Spring-Summer 1962), 61-74.

Cox, C.B., *The Free Spirit: A Study of Liberal Humanism in the Novels of George Eliot, Henry James, E.M. Forster, Virginia Woolf, Angus Wilson*. London: Oxford University Press, 1963.

Furbank, P.N., and F.J.H. Haskell (interviewers), "E.M. Forster" in *Writers at Work*, ed. Malcolm Cowley. New York: Viking Press; London: Secker and Warburg, Ltd., 1958.

Gransden, K.W., *E.M. Forster*. Edinburgh: Oliver and Boyd; New York: Grove Press, 1962 (Writers and Critics Series).

Hall, James, *The Tragic Comedians: Seven Modern British Novelists*. Bloomington, Ind.: Indiana University Press, 1963.

Hickley, Dennis, "Ou-Boum and Verbum," *The Downside Review*, LXXII (Spring, 1954), 172-80.

Hoare, Dorothy M., *Some Studies in the Modern Novel*. London: Chatto & Windus, Ltd., 1938. Philadelphia: Dufour Editions, 1953.

Holt, Lee Elbert, "E.M. Forster and Samuel Butler," *PMLA*, LXI (September 1946), 804-19.

Hoy, Cyrus, "Forster's Metaphysical Novel," *PMLA*, LXXV (March 1960), 126-36.

Johnstone, J.K., *The Bloomsbury Group: A Study of E.M. Forster, Lytton Strachey, Virginia Woolf, and Their Circle*. London: Secker and Warburg, Ltd., 1954.

Kettle, Arnold, *An Introduction to the English Novel* (Volume 2). London: Hutchinson University Library, 1953.

Macaulay, Rose, *The Writings of E.M. Forster*. London: Chatto & Windus, Ltd.; New York: New York University Press; 1938.

McConkey, James, *The Novels of E.M. Forster*. Ithaca, N.Y.: Cornell University Press, 1957.

McDowell, Frederick P.W., " 'The Mild, Intellectual Light'; Idea and Theme in *Howards End*," *PMLA*, LXXIV (September 1959), 453-63.

Maclean, Hugh, "The Structure of *A Passage to India*," *The University of Toronto Quarterly*, XXII (January 1953), 157-71.

McLuhan, H.M., "Kipling and Forster," *Sewanee Review*, LII (Summer 1944), 332-42.

Natwar-Singh, K. (ed.), *E.M. Forster: A Tribute*. New York: Harcourt, Brace & World, Inc., 1964.

Oliver, H.J., *The Art of E.M. Forster*. Melbourne, Australia: Melbourne University Press, 1960.

Warner, Rex, *E.M. Forster*. London: Longmans, Green and Co., for the British Council and the National Book League, 1950 (revised 1954). (Writers and Their Work series: No. 7)

Werry, Richard R., "Rhythm in Forster's *A Passage to India*," in *Studies in Honor of John Wilcox*, ed. A.D. Wallace and W.O. Ross. Detroit, Michigan: Wayne State University Press, 1958.

White, Gertrude M., "*A Passage to India*: Analysis and Revaluation," *PMLA*, LXVIII (September 1953), 641-57.

Wilde, Alan, *Art and Order: A Study of E.M. Forster*. New York: New York University Press, 1964; London: Peter Owen, 1965.

Wilson, Angus, "A Conversation with E.M. Forster," *Encounter*, IX (November 1957), 52-57.

Woolf, Virginia, *The Death of the Moth, and Other Essays*. London: Hogarth Press; New York: Harcourt, Brace and Co., 1942.

Zabel, Morton D., *Craft and Character: Texts, Method, and Vocation in Modern Fiction*. New York: Viking Press; London: Gollancz, 1957 (under the title *Craft and Character in Modern Fiction*).

British Authors in the Twentieth Century Views Series

American Authors in the Twentieth Century Views Series